A Canadian Girl in South Africa

A Canadian Girl in South Africa

A Teacher's Experiences in the South African War, 1899–1902

E. MAUD GRAHAM

Edited and with an Introduction by

MICHAEL DAWSON, CATHERINE GIDNEY, AND

SUSANNE M. KLAUSEN

The University of Alberta Press

Published by

The University of Alberta Press
Ring House 2
Edmonton, Alberta, Canada T6G 2E1
www.uap.ualberta.ca

LIBRARY AND ARCHIVES CANADA CATALOGUING IN PUBLICATION

Graham, E. Maud, 1876–1949, author
A Canadian girl in South Africa : a teacher's experiences in the South African War, 1899–1902 / E. Maud Graham ; edited and with an introduction by Michael Dawson, Catherine Gidney, and Susanne M. Klausen.

Includes bibliographical references and index.
Issued in print and electronic formats.
ISBN 978-1-77212-046-2 (paperback).–
ISBN 978-1-77212-053-0 (epub).–
ISBN 978-1-77212-054-7 (kindle).–
ISBN 978-1-77212-055-4 (PDF)

1. Graham, E. Maud, 1876-1949. 2. Teachers—Canada—Biography. 3. Teachers—South Africa—Biography. 4. South African War, 1899-1902—Personal narratives, Canadian. 5. South African War, 1899-1902—Education and the war. 6. South African War, 1899-1902—Concentration camps—South Africa. 7. Education—South Africa—History. 8. Education—Great Britain—Colonies. I. Dawson, Michael, 1971–, editor II. Gidney, Catherine (Catherine Anne), 1969–, editor III. Klausen, Susanne M., 1965–, editor IV. Title.

DT1916.G73 2015 968.04'8 C2015-902406-4
C2015-902407-2

Index available in print and PDF editions.

First edition, first printing, 2015.
Printed and bound in Canada by Houghton Boston Printers, Saskatoon, Saskatchewan.
Copyediting and proofreading by Joanne Muzak.
Photos scanned by Dave Vasicek.
Maps by Wendy Johnson.
Indexing by Judy Dunlop.

The University of Alberta Press is committed to protecting our natural environment. As part of our efforts, this book is printed on Enviro Paper: it contains 100% post-consumer recycled fibres and is acid- and chlorine-free.

The University of Alberta Press gratefully acknowledges the support received for its publishing program from The Canada Council for the Arts. The University of Alberta Press also gratefully acknowledges the financial support of the Government of Canada through the Canada Book Fund (CBF) and the Government of Alberta through the Alberta Media Fund (AMF) for its publishing activities.

This book has been published with the help of a grant from the Canadian Federation for the Humanities and Social Sciences, through the Awards to Scholarly Publications Program, using funds provided by the Social Sciences and Humanities Research Council of Canada.

Canada | Canada Council for the Arts | Conseil des Arts du Canada
Alberta Government

Contents

Acknowledgements

WE WOULD LIKE TO THANK John and Delores Becker for supporting this project and for generously providing us with Maud Graham's South Africa photo album. We also very much appreciate Joan Chandler's assistance in locating photographs and helping us with some additional historical context. Helen Millar Becker carefully preserved many of Maud Graham's papers and photographs and wrote up her own recollections of Graham. This book is much richer for her work of historical preservation. Our thanks as well to Wyn Millar and R.D. Gidney, who provided useful commentary on the Introduction and to the anonymous assessors who provided valuable ideas and suggestions for the book.

A General Research Grant from St. Thomas University facilitated research in Toronto, Ottawa, and Owen Sound, Ontario. Funding from the St. Thomas University JOBS Programme and the Social Sciences and Humanities Research Council allowed us to hire Ashley Doiron and Molly Egerdie as research assistants. Both of these students made important contributions to this project.

Peter Midgley has provided enthusiastic support for this project from the very beginning. We would like to thank him, as well as the production staff at University of Alberta Press, who did a wonderful job—especially when it came to the tricky task of working with old photographs. We also very much appreciated Joanne Muzak's copy-editing skills.

Maud Graham's South Africa photo album, her scrapbook, as well as additional family papers will be donated to the Thomas Fisher Rare Book Library, University of Toronto.

Maud Graham, 1908.

[Joan Chandler private collection]

Introduction

LORD MINTO was looking for a few good women. Forty, to be precise. In the early months of 1902 Canada's governor general had before him an urgent request from Britain's colonial secretary, Joseph Chamberlain. To consolidate wartime gains and secure British control in South Africa, Chamberlain was keen to recruit female teachers[1] from Canada, Australia, and New Zealand to assist Britain in educating Boer[2] children living in Transvaal and Orange River Colony concentration camps.[3] He asked for forty of Canada's top teachers and provided Minto with details of the scheme. In doing so, he strongly encouraged Canadian officials to undertake personal interviews with potential candidates, declared that Roman Catholics should not be considered for these positions, and demanded that "no teacher is selected who is opposed to British rule in South Africa."[4] Federal officials went straight to work recruiting Canada's best and brightest young female teachers. Working closely with provincial authorities, they issued a call for volunteers and were overwhelmed by the response, for in just a few months over five hundred women put forward their names for consideration.[5]

Humanitarian and imperial rationales intertwined as the scheme was developed. Recalling her briefings en route to the camps, Isabel Perry, a teacher from Montreal, noted that "our mission was a very important one, equally as important as that of the soldiers, for it was to implant feelings of loyalty to the British flag in the hearts of the Dutch children and to endeavour to reconcile Dutch women to

British rule."[6] To this end, the recruitment campaign focused intently on finding the right women for the job. As he sifted through applications from Manitobans, for example, W.A. McIntyre, principal of the Normal School in Winnipeg, endorsed candidates who fit an ideal of Canadian and imperial womanhood. Susie Younghusband was a model prospect. She had ten years of teaching experience, "most of it with younger pupils," was "kind, patient," and "tender," and was "loved by pupils and respected by mothers." Just as important, McIntyre noted, she "possesses the missionary spirit." And since she was "accustomed to working under adverse conditions," she "would be a quiet but effective force for good in a new community" and "would do nothing foolish." Margaret MacDonald was another of McIntyre's favourites: She had a "very fine character," was "gentle" and "ladylike," and possessed "a proper missionary spirit." McIntyre was also keen to support Edith Murray, "a bright and capable teacher" who boasted "dash, vigor, and strong individuality."[7] Across Canada the search was on for female teachers who were nurturing but confident, experienced but energized, and, above all, dedicated to the task at hand: remaking South Africa in Britain's image.

Enter Maud Graham, an intelligent and resourceful young woman, who, in 1902, was serving as a governess in Quebec. Graham lacked the extensive teaching experience of some of the other candidates but boasted first-rate teacher-training qualifications. Given the prohibition on Catholics, her Methodist background also stood her in good stead. An active athlete in university, her physical fitness was another feather in her cap, for the authorities were keen to find women capable of working hard and living under rough conditions. In addition, her musical training meant that she would appeal to officials keen to adhere to the British government's observation that the "ability to teach singing is an essential qualification" for applicants.[8] Finally, and equally importantly, she was keen to do her part for the empire.

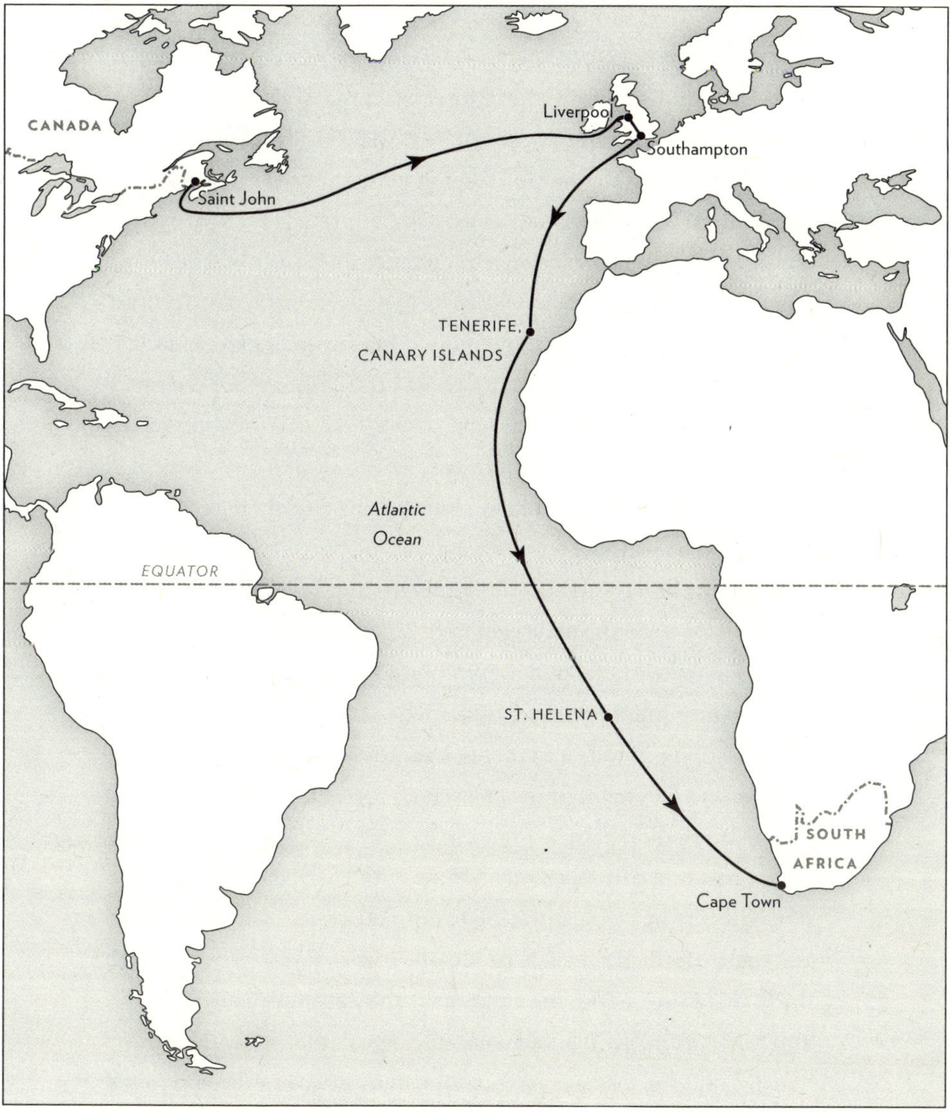

Maud Graham's route to South Africa, 1902.

But Maud Graham was also just genuinely excited by the prospect of travelling overseas. At the age of twenty-six she possessed maturity, self-confidence, and a keen interest in the world around her. As those unlucky enough to raise her ire could quickly learn, she also possessed a sharp tongue and did not suffer fools gladly. Chosen as one of seven teachers from Quebec, Graham set off for South Africa in April 1902—and recorded her experience for posterity. The result was A *Canadian Girl in South Africa*, originally published in Toronto by William Briggs in 1905, a memoir of her two-year experience as a teacher in South Africa, first in a concentration camp for Boer refugees of the South African War (1899–1902) and afterwards in schools for Boer children in two small towns. In addition to documenting her own activities as a teacher in South Africa, Graham offered extensive observations on race relations, postwar reconstruction, and farming and economic development. She saved her most biting critiques for what she perceived to be woeful, and potentially tragic, failures in educational policy perpetrated by "men of mediocre talent...and sometimes more than mediocre stupidity" (Chapter XIII). Just how Maud Graham held her tongue during the formal interview requirement of the selection process is unclear. But we are glad that she did.

In providing a first-person account of the final days of that epic war, daily life in a concentration camp, settler–African relations, and more, Graham's book is invaluable for scholars concerned with the South African War, the creation of the South African state, imperial racism, gender and colonialism, colonial education, travel writing, and the formation of and tension between British colonial and imperial identities. Moreover, the book, and the scheme that it documents, offers a window onto a key moment in the history of the "British World." The South African War, and Britain's call for military, and then pedagogical, support, occurred amidst an awkward and contested refashioning of its relationship with its white settler societies. As John Eddy and Deryck Schreuder explain, "keeping the British Empire of settlement together became an increasingly urgent matter from the Anglo-Boer War...onwards," and Joseph Chamberlain was perhaps the central figure in a campaign to "call on the colonies of white settlement for greater co-operation in carrying the burdens of empire."[9] This would prove no easy task; as essayist and traveller Richard Jebb noted in 1905, the populations of Canada, Australia, and New Zealand were each developing a variation of what he termed "colonial nationalism"—an outlook that increasingly prioritized local autonomy and self-interest while retaining and respecting their political and cultural connections to Britain.[10] As Jebb detailed at length in his study, the South African War profoundly shaped their shifting conceptions of the proper relationship with the mother country and divided public opinion in all three societies.[11] The conflict that in Chamberlain's mind necessitated the enlistment of Canadian teachers for the imperial cause thus brought into sharp relief the divergent interests of Britain and its white settler societies.

Yet Graham's story, which featured British, Canadian, Australian, and New Zealand women travelling abroad to assist in the reconstruction of South African society, is also an important reminder of the transnational nature of the British World at the beginning of the twentieth century—and of the cultural bonds that continued to unite these settlements.[12] Recent studies on a wide range of topics including music, education, and the law have underscored the persistent influence of British culture beyond the boundaries of the United Kingdom.[13] English Canadians were not alone in struggling to articulate a patriotism that balanced local interests and a cultural allegiance to Great Britain. Nor were their actions on this front confined to Canada's borders. Their lives and identities were shaped, directly in the case of Maud Graham, by experiences and developments on the other side of the world.

Like Canadian adventurer William Stairs, who travelled to Equatoria in 1887 to assist Henry Stanley in rescuing Emin Pasha from his Muslim captors and to Katanga in 1891 to flex his muscles on behalf of Belgium's King Leopold, Maud Graham was a colonial contributor to imperial endeavours. But while Stairs's pursuits were facilitated by well-recognized mechanisms of imperial power—training at Kingston, Ontario's Royal Military College, a stint with the Royal Engineers in England, and then key roles on the two state-sponsored formal expeditions replete with graphic violence—Graham's adventure, befitting a woman at the turn of the century, unfolded amidst the more prosaic setting of a make-shift classroom and group sing-a-longs.[14] It was, nonetheless, a staunchly imperial undertaking—one explicitly designed to maintain and enhance Britain's hegemony in Southern Africa amidst growing fears of a looming reckoning for the British Empire.

Moreover, it shared with many imperial, neocolonial, and contemporary development schemes an exaggerated confidence in its ability to "save" imperiled children from a despondent present and bleak future. A growing literature critically assessing the unintended consequences of Global South development schemes insists on the need to recognize the cultural assumptions that inform policy development and the actions of on-the-ground workers and volunteers.[15] It underscores the difficulties involved in actually delivering tangible goods and services to the targeted population.[16] And, for sub-Saharan Africa, in particular, it documents a repeated tendency to view the continent as "sufficiently exotic, and far enough away" that it can be approached "with a kind of untroubled certainty."[17] The scheme to anglicize and "uplift" Boer children in 1902 lacked such reflective observations. As with so many British imperial endeavours, it was shaped by a combination of altruistic ideals (assisting displaced civilians to become more civilized) and Machiavellian goals (reasserting British control in an important economic and military location). In Graham's words, the benefits that she and others brought to Boer children meant that "such people were never so well off in their lives as when in camp" (Chapter V). As Ann Stoler notes in her study of the Dutch Indies, children's welfare was an important symbolic marker of colonial success (or failure). "Children were seen to be particularly susceptible to degraded environments," she explains, "and it is no accident that colonial policy makers looked to upbringing and education, to schools and homes...and thus to the quotidian social ecology of children's lives."[18]

That the plan to send teachers to South Africa appealed so strongly to women across Canada and elsewhere is also significant. As Barbara Heron observes, the majority of workers in today's development industry are middle-class white women.[19] The roots of this phenomenon, she argues, were planted in the late nineteenth century. Constraints on middle-class women's place in the public sphere combined with an idealization of them as nurturing and selfless "white mother-teacher[s]" to encourage thousands of women to embrace the possibilities of social reform and missionary work.[20] While the nature of overseas development initiatives has changed significantly over time, Heron notes some important "colonial continuities" informing contemporary female development workers' motivations, including a sense of obligation and entitlement.[21] Maud Graham and the other thirty-nine white, middle-class female Canadian teachers who embraced the opportunity to travel to South Africa in 1902 are an important part of this story.

In the pages that follow, we begin by providing a brief overview of the war itself, including both its causes and impact. In doing so, we highlight the value of Graham's story for understanding life in the concentration camps, their contested political legacy, and the ramifications of British educational policy in South Africa during the postwar reconstruction period. We then provide a detailed biography of Maud Graham that explores the cultural influences that shaped her assessment of her overseas adventure. Finally, we introduce readers to the book itself by focusing on Graham's national (and imperial) identity, her observations as an overseas traveller, her experience as a teacher in South Africa, the manner in which her observations were refracted through common racial categories of the time, and the liminal position she occupied as a New Woman at the turn of the century.

The South African War was fought between the British Empire and the two Boer republics, the South African Republic (also known as the Transvaal) (SAR; est. 1852) and the Orange Free State (OFS; est. 1854), though its effects were also profound for indigenous African inhabitants in the region. The conflict was the culmination of decades of intensifying hostility between the two white groups. The British formally secured the Cape Colony, originally settled by the Dutch Vereenigde Oost-Indische Compagnie (United East India Company), in 1814, and from the start relations were tense with the established Boer settlers. The British infuriated the Boer population by abolishing slavery throughout the empire (in 1834) and fostering British settlement and culture in the colony. Consequently, starting in the 1830s, thousands of Boers left the Cape and travelled north by ox-wagon in search of land, freedom from governmental authority, and the ability to continue practicing white dominance without British interference. Ultimately, after many clashes with African kingdoms and a relentless process of encroaching on their lands, the *Voortrekkers* (pioneers) established the two republics.

At first the British had no interest in conquering the Boer states but the discovery of valuable mineral deposits on their territories (diamonds in OFS in 1867 and gold in SAR in 1886) changed everything. For economic and strategic reasons, the British wanted control of the entire region, and their efforts to obtain it inevitably provoked hostilities between the two settler populations. In 1877 Britain annexed the SAR and renamed it the British Colony of the Transvaal; three years later, Boers in the colony (aided by the OFS) revolted against British rule in what has become known as the First Anglo-Boer War (also called the First Transvaal War of Independence) that lasted from November 1880 to March 1881.

The discovery of gold in the SAR five years later rekindled British land lust and spurred plans for another annexation. The two Boer republics, feeling increasingly provoked and under threat

The Boer republics and British colonies during the South African War.

of invasion, joined forces and attacked the British first in hopes of gaining the upper hand in a war they considered unavoidable.[22] They invaded the Cape Colony in October 1899, thereby starting the South African War (known at the time as the Second Anglo-Boer War). The Boer attack had the effect of mobilizing Britain's military and unifying colonial support for the British, and nearly five hundred thousand British troops were ultimately sent to the region. In Canada, despite vociferous French Canadian hostility towards the British Empire, Prime Minister Wilfrid Laurier's cabinet approved enlisting, equipping, and transporting a Canadian contingent of volunteers a few days after the outbreak of hostilities. Over seven thousand Canadian soldiers served in the war.[23]

British imperial strategists assumed the war would be easy to win and quickly over. After all, they wondered, how long could it take for the world's most powerful military to defeat the republics' rag-tag commandos comprised mainly of farmers? Indeed, in the beginning, events unfolded as expected: by September 1900, Britain had annexed the two republics, immediately renamed the Transvaal and Orange River Colony, and victory seemed at hand. But the Boers proved surprisingly tenacious, daring, and wily; rather than engaging British troops directly in a traditional style of warfare, they employed guerrilla tactics, learned during decades of war with indigenous Africans, that were extremely difficult to counteract. In response, in March 1901, Lord Horatio Kitchener (1850–1916), charged with devising a strategy for dealing with the commandos, set out to destroy all sources of food, shelter, and information that were sustaining the Boer soldiers with a vicious scorched earth campaign: British soldiers destroyed Boer farms, seized or killed their livestock and poisoned water wells.[24] Boers made homeless by the campaign either fled for refuge or were forcibly relocated to civilian camps.

Originally, the British had established camps to bestow political recognition to "protected burghers," republican citizens who had surrendered voluntarily, and to ensure their protection from retaliation by Boer forces (who nicknamed them the "hands-uppers"). Starting in September 1900, protected burghers and their families moved to "protection camps" where soon afterwards they were joined by victims of the scorched earth policy. Ultimately, the British removed over one hundred thousand Boers, mainly women and children, from their homes and "concentrated" them into camps established along railway lines on British-controlled territory. By the end of the war, there were about fifty camps for white civilians and sixty-four for the tens of thousands of black civilians who were also displaced during the campaign.[25]

However, the British were ill prepared to manage the camps. Some camp authorities proved thoroughly incompetent. But others were simply overwhelmed because they were not given advance notice about military police incursions onto Boer land and thus could not properly prepare for the arrival of new refugees. Instead, victims of forced removals arrived at camps without prior warning, often putting administrators who were already facing a shortage of resources into an impossible position. Food, clothing, fuel, and medical care were consistently in short supply, the tents that provided shelter quickly became overcrowded, and the combination caused waves of deadly epidemics—measles, enteritis, and typhoid—as well as widespread outbreaks of diarrhea and pneumonia.[26]

British mismanagement, rather than deliberate cruelty, had lethal consequences: by the end of the war, approximately 28,000 Boers had died (about 10 per cent of the total Boer population), of which a shocking 22,000 were children. In the separate camps for Africans, whose accommodation and food supply were worse than in the Boer camps, at least 15,000 people perished.[27] In contrast, of the half million soldiers from across the empire who fought for the British, 21,000 died (the majority from disease).[28] Ultimately, the war deeply unsettled the British public, not least because of the reportage of British humanitarian Emily Hobhouse (1860–1926), whose scathing accounts of what she saw in the camps caused a sensation.[29] In fact, the South African War played an important role in the Conservative government's comprehensive defeat in 1906.[30] In Canada a vocal minority also expressed its opposition to the war.[31] Perhaps as a means of steeling Canada's teachers against anti-British criticism, the federal government placed an order for forty-five copies of Arthur Conan Doyle's *The War in South Africa*, which included a spirited defence of the camps, a week before their scheduled departure.[32]

When the war finally ended, the British immediately sought political reconciliation with the Boers, and a major step taken towards its attainment was the policy of reconstruction for the ravaged ex-Boer republics where towns and farms had been devastated if not destroyed. Sir Alfred Milner (1854–1925), British high commissioner for Southern Africa from 1897 to 1905, obtained the necessary funds by levying a tax on the annual net produce of the Transvaal gold mines. The reason for pursuing a rapprochement was purely pragmatic and had nothing to do with a sense of guilt about the devastating effects of the war. The British were fearful of a possible "Native rebellion" across the region because Africans, who had mostly taken the British side during the war, expected to finally obtain the political and economic rights denied them under Boer rule.[33] However, the British never had any intention of ending racial discrimination, in part because of the overriding need to control the supply and flow of African labour for the lucrative mines, and also because doing so would outrage the Boers and make political reconciliation impossible. Instead, the solution Britain decided upon was to unite the four colonies into a cohesive colonial state loyal to Britain and able to effectively police Africans' movements. Ultimately, in 1910, the Cape, Natal, Transvaal, and Orange River colonies combined to form the dominion of South Africa.[34]

In the four decades following their defeat, embittered Boers intent on constructing a new Afrikaner nationalist identity and winning control of the state produced what has since become the dominant narrative of the war, one of British brutality and Boer suffering. During the 1930s, for example, the story that British camp managers had mixed ground glass in the sugar supply started to circulate and gain credibility; though false, some descendants of the Boers believe it to this day.[35] By the Second World War, the history of the camps had been thoroughly politicized and the representation of victimized Boer women and children firmly harnessed to Afrikaner nationalism. However, the centenary of the South African War spurred historians with new research interests to take a fresh look at events and reconsider previous canonical conclusions.[36] As a result, recent scholarship employing new theoretical and political approaches has thrown into doubt crucial aspects of the Afrikaner nationalist version of the war. Historians implementing gender analysis,[37] utilizing the Dutch and Afrikaans primary sources produced by the "losers,"[38] situating the war in the larger context of British imperialism,[39] and placing Africans at the centre of analysis have displaced the almost exclusive focus on Boer victimization that lay at the heart of the previous, dominant narrative of the war.

As sociologist Liz Stanley has reminded us, every official commemoration of a tragic event is accompanied by acts of forgetting.[40] In the case of the British concentration camps, the presence of Africans in the supposedly white camps has been almost entirely forgotten. Africans not only participated in the war as soldiers, they also acted as servants to wealthy Boer camp inhabitants, aides to camp staff, and forced labour that largely sustained all of the camps.[41] Their involvement has finally started to come into sharper focus not least because of the changing political context in which the war was being re-examined—namely, the demise of apartheid that had distorted and marginalized black South African experience and contributions to history.

Scholars such as Stanley and Helen Dampier have also called for writing "everyday" experiences back into the history of the camps. In contrast to the dominant image of concentration camps that has gripped the public imagination in the aftermath of Nazism—one of slave labour and genocide—the camps in which Boers were interned were intended first and foremost to undermine Boer commandos, not to exterminate the civilian population, a crucial fact neglected in favour of "a nationalist version of events that represented the camps as places where the British carried out brutal mistreatment and even murder of Boer women and children."[42] Highlighting "the everyday" reveals many aspects of camp life that have been overlooked, including daily soup kitchens for white children and the elderly; regular church services; sports days; catechism classes for children; and the establishment of hospitals, shops where additional food could be purchased by inhabitants, and schools. Though the nationalist narrative of the war has been saturated with endlessly reproduced "iconic" images of rail-thin, dying, Boer children, Stanley describes how, in the course of conducting research, the vast majority of the thousands of photographs she examined concern prosaic elements of everyday life.[43]

Such observations are not intended to minimize the trauma and the tragedy of camps, places that were without question overcrowded, unpleasant, and frightening for most inhabitants and deadly to many. Instead, they are intended to help create discursive space for other, previously neglected, dimensions of camp experience such as that of the children "who were not ill or who survived and became well, helped their mothers, played with each other, went to school, enjoyed sports days and celebrations and amused themselves."[44] Indeed, many children appear to have enjoyed going to school: one woman recalled after the war that she cried when it was time to go home at the end of the day.[45] A Canadian teacher who travelled with Graham to South Africa in 1902, Florence Randal, recalls how the children enjoyed learning so much that they "actually disliked holidays in the camp schools."[46] As historian Sarah Duff writes, "by emphasising white children's victimhood, we lose sight of the broader picture of childhood in the camps during the South African War."[47] By describing activities she witnessed as a school teacher, such as food consumption and children playing games, Graham's memoir helps deepen our understanding of daily life in the notorious British camps.

And yet we must not lose sight of the fact that schooling for *kampkinders* (camp children) formed part of an explicit political project. Even as the war was still raging, Milner decided that the long-term success of the British in the region required fostering loyalty to the empire, and this in turn necessitated anglicizing the soon-to-be defeated Boers.[48] Key to achieving this goal was teaching Boer children English, both as a means to curb anti-British sentiment and assimilate the Boers into British-dominated colonial life. As historians have shown in relation to colonized Africans, education was fundamental to colonial rule.[49] Colonial education consisted of a power-knowledge discourse aimed at enabling colonial subjects to imagine themselves as belonging to a particular cultural polity.[50] The British had high hopes that education would have the same effect on the conquered Boers.

Beginning in 1901, Milner converted four Boer high schools in Pretoria into English schools, quickly nicknamed "Milner Schools."[51] He also oversaw the establishment of schools for Boer children in the concentration camps. (Education for African children was never considered.) His secretary of education for the two new British colonies, Edmund Beale Sargant (1855–1938), had an idea to win over "the young generation of Dutch Africanders to English ways of thought and speech and to English ideas of truthfulness and loyalty."[52] According to historian Eliza Riedi, Sargant had travelled to numerous colonies to study the role educational systems played in forging imperial unity, and the concentration camps offered an opportunity to put his theories into practice. Riedi writes, "Soon after arriving at Cape Town he visited a Boer prisoner-of-war camp where the prisoners had set up a school. Inspired, in late January 1901 he established a school at the nearest concentration camp, Norval's Pont, and acted as headmaster for a fortnight. The experiment proving successful, Sargant decided to extend it over the

Graham's text does not include images of the school at Norval's Pont Camp, where she first worked. This photograph shows kampkinders *at the nearby Bloemfontein Camp School in 1901.* [*The Photographical Collection of the Anglo-Boer War Museum, Bloemfontein, South Africa, scan 00811*]

1907

Bloemfontein Camp School, 1901. [*The Photographical Collection of the Anglo-Boer War Museum, Bloemfontein, South Africa, scan 00802*]

whole camp system."[53] Milner, who had a low opinion of Boers and their culture, approved, believing that education would end their "retrogression" and make them "outward-looking" and open to "progress" and "modern civilization." "Next to the composition of the population," he said, "the thing that matters most is its education. Everything that makes South African children look outside South Africa and realize the world makes for peace."[54] Because teaching the English language was paramount to this objective, the main aim of the schools was to make children proficient in English and therefore, with the exception of religious education, Sargant wanted a total immersion program. Classes were conducted in English, regardless of children's level of fluency in the language, and teaching the language dominated the curriculum, although some math, history, and geography were also taught, with the latter two subjects also imparting a British imperial worldview.[55]

Initially, local teachers with the necessary proficiency in English were employed but the rapid expansion of the student population rendered this approach unsustainable: by May 1902, the last month of the war, there were more than 17,000 students in the Transvaal camps and over 12,000 in the Orange River Colony camps.[56] Sargant told Milner in mid-June 1901 that "the opportunity during the next year of getting [the Boer children] to speak English is golden" and urged him to bring out patriotic young female teachers from England and the colonies; he "particularly admired the Canadian education system."[57] Milner agreed, for he was determined to bring Boer children "under influences which will promote future harmony of races."[58] (Milner was referring to harmony between the British and Boer "races" only.[59]) In late 1901, the British Colonial Office began recruiting teachers from Britain and its colonies, among them Maud Graham, who arrived at war's end to teach in the camp schools.[60] Graham was one of three hundred teachers from Britain, Canada, Australia, and New Zealand sent to the region that would soon become South Africa. As Riedi argues, this scheme presumed that young, white, professional, patriotic women were bringing "British civilization" to newly defeated enemies of the empire.[61] Though the Colonial Office worried about the cost of recruiting teachers from the Dominions, Joseph Chamberlain (1857–1913), the secretary of state for the colonies, insisted it be done, saying, "it would please the Colonies."[62]

Teachers were required to commit to their posts for a year for an annual salary of £100. The authorities also offered the prospect of permanent employment to those wishing to stay on after the expiration of their one-year contract.[63] Applications flooded in, with over 3,000 from Britain alone and over 800 from Canada, New Zealand, and Australia. Applicants were white women, predominantly of lower-middle-class and middle-class backgrounds.[64] Joseph Chamberlain's forceful suggestion that Catholic applicants not be considered for these positions was widely circulated amongst Canadian officials, thereby ensuring that the teachers from Canada were overwhelmingly Protestant.[65] Ultimately, 40 of the 300 teachers were recruited from Canada and sent to the Transvaal and Orange River Colony. After the Boers surrendered in May 1902, the refugees returned home and the camps were closed by September, after which the teachers were sent out in pairs to schools on Boer farms and in villages and small towns. Still perceived as important to the anglicization project, after completing their one-year contracts, the teachers were offered an increase in pay, free medical assistance, and free passage home as incentives to continue working, and many did, including Graham.[66]

In addition to anglicizing Boer children, the camp schools assisted the British government in defending its involvement in the South African War against critics such as Lloyd George (1863–1945), leader of the opposition Liberal Party. Anti-war sentiment had spread as a result of news coverage of the scorched earth policy and the lethal incarceration of Boer women and children, so the schools proved useful as propaganda. Defenders of the war emphasized the "humanitarian" nature of the camps, which were portrayed as safe refuges from war, starvation, and (by tapping into racist notions of African sexuality) the rape of white women by black men.[67] As MP Alfred Lyttelton (1857–1913), the government's chairman of the committee planning postwar reconstruction, explained in Parliament in response to criticism by Lloyd George, the camp schools

> will go far...in the future to cement the relations between the Dutch and English populations...and certainly, primary education has never been initiated under more romantic circumstances....Children were brought in from the farms and placed under the care of the people of the camps...and there they have been taught by the very best teachers which this country could supply, especially women teachers...the most excellent teachers, out of the thousands who volunteered, have been sent to those camps to teach the children.[68]

Chamberlain also cited the schools when responding in Parliament to criticism of the camps. After vigorously defending the need for, and management of, the camps, in March 1902 he lamented that his critics "have not said a word of praise for the gratuitous work of education which the Government have undertaken."[69]

Ultimately, however, Milner's policy of anglicizing Boer children was a double-edged sword for it stoked emergent Afrikaner nationalism. Indeed, a major aspect of Boer opposition to what came to be known as "Milnerism" was the compulsory use of English as the medium for educating Afrikaans-speaking children. This opposition quickly intensified into an anti-British nationalist movement that would have a profound impact on South Africa's political development.[70]

In April 1902 the (Toronto) *Globe* proudly reported that "The forty young ladies who are going to South Africa from Canada to instruct the young Boers in the English language and train them up in the ways of civilization are handsome, athletic specimens of Canadian womanhood....If the young Boer farmers are at all susceptible to feminine influences one can easily foresee what will be the result of the arrival of such a bevy of handsome Canadian girls."[71] Maud Graham, a young woman from Ontario, was one of these "girls." She was initially stationed at Norval's Pont, located in the Cape Colony on the south side of the Orange River that separated it from the Orange River Colony. The camp was established in 1900 to relieve the overcrowded Bloemfontein camp. It housed a population of about 3,500 people, most of whom were extremely impoverished Boers, and was a relatively well-managed and resourced camp.[72] Once the camps were dismantled, Graham would remain in this region to teach in the towns of Fauresmith and Kroonstad. As the pages of her text make clear, the self-proclaimed "Canadian Girl in South Africa" was a forceful and direct young woman who did not shy away from sharing her opinions. A sense of her formative years in Canada is thus helpful in understanding the cultural influences that shaped the assessments and evaluations she offers in her memoir.

Graham was born in 1876 in Owen Sound, Ontario, an industrial and port town on Georgian Bay, Lake Huron. She grew up an only child in a middle-class household of Irish Protestant descent. Her mother, Lydia Meir, came from a merchant family. In 1856 Lydia's father, John Houghton Meir, bought several tracts of land in and around Owen Sound and by the 1870s had become a prosperous merchant. In 1879, for example, he purchased a four-bedroom family home and employed at least a general cook, a chore woman for washing and scrubbing, a maid, a "man-of-all-work," and a "hired boy." In the 1880s the original business was destroyed by fire and

Norval's Pont Camp.

John Houghton Meir pursued a new endeavour with his son, George, opening the Montreal Tea Store. Maud's father, Samuel Graham (1840–1907), owned S. Graham and Co., Shoes and Boots. In the 1860s Samuel's father had moved from Brockville, in Eastern Ontario, to take up tracts of land near Chatsworth, a township located approximately fifteen kilometres south of Owen Sound. Samuel opened the store just after his marriage in 1868 to Lydia, and the family lived above the store. By 1882, the year Maud turned six, the family had prospered enough to purchase their own house.[73]

Both the Meirs and the Grahams attended the local First Methodist church. The families were deeply involved in temperance activities in an attempt to reform Owen Sound's reputation as a "hard drinking town"—a status reinforced by the existence of no less than six breweries by 1902.[74] Maud's mother, Lydia, and aunts Mary Ann and Martha, helped establish the Woman's Christian Temperance Union (WCTU) branch in Owen Sound.[75] After her marriage to an American Methodist minister, Martha (now Mrs. J.A. Allen) became a leading

WCTU worker in the United States.[76] Their involvement with the WCTU linked them to a broader Anglo-American culture and provided a means for public involvement in their communities at a time when they lacked full citizenship rights.[77] Maud grew up with a daily visual reminder of this activism as her mother had hung a large photograph of Frances Willard, a leading American temperance advocate, in the home. Her father, Samuel, held leadership positions within the church and local community as superintendent of the Sunday school and president of the local Young Men's Christian Association.[78] Graham's family was thus deeply committed to temperance and the ideals of religious service.

Maud Graham was also raised in a context that to some extent openly acknowledged the legacies and realities of slavery. Both the Graham and Meir families opposed slavery. Family lore indicates that Maud's maternal grandfather, John Meir Senior, settled in Canada rather than the United States because of his strong abolitionist beliefs.[79] In the mid-nineteenth century, Owen Sound became one of the end points of the underground railroad, an escape route for slaves fleeing the United States, and had a small black community of about 200 that lived in poor conditions separate from the white population. Maud's father, Samuel Graham, was actively involved in a local 1888 commemoration of the emancipation of British West Indian slaves.[80] He also served as assistant superintendent of the local British Methodist Episcopal Church sabbath school, which served the African-Canadian population.[81]

Given their family history and their strong involvement in temperance, a movement allied with abolitionism, Graham's immediate family, then, likely held abolitionist beliefs. Of course, this certainly did not preclude them from abiding by and reinforcing common class- and race-based categories. If Maud was taught that both blacks and whites were God's creations, her attitude was not one of equality. She encountered members of the black community primarily as servants, washer-women, gardeners, and cooks, and in her unpublished reminiscences she patronizingly notes with fondness, "many of these old ex-slaves were really fine characters."[82] She generally uses the term "negro," still a fairly common term when she wrote in 1931, but employs the term "nigger" when referring to an unrespectable black man who had deserted his wife.[83]

Graham was a highly educated woman. In 1892, at age sixteen, she graduated from Owen Sound Collegiate Institute.[84] In that year she began a four-year degree at the University of Toronto. This was a period when co-education was a hotly contested issue. Women only gained entry to the University of Toronto in 1884 and opponents of women's higher education questioned the propriety of co-education for both its emasculating impact on men and masculinizing effects on women.[85] While female students belonged to separate student societies and were segregated in their own common room and reading room, they had also begun to form "a sizeable group in the lecture halls and corridors" and participated with men in some campus politics.[86] Graham engaged in a variety of extracurricular activities; for example, she was recording secretary of the university's Women's Literary Society and business manager of its magazine. She became president of the Women's Athletic Club at the University of Toronto and organized the basketball team. She also participated in a number of tennis tournaments. She was an accompanist for the Ladies' Glee Club as well as for Glee Club soloists who sang as part of the annual concert of the University Glee Club held at Massey Hall. And, as a delegate for University College, University of Toronto, Graham attended the inaugural meeting of the Council of Women in the 1890s.[87] In 1896 Graham received her BA in modern history. She received a fellowship in history at Bryn Mawr, a prestigious American women's college, for the school year 1896–97.[88] She then returned to Canada to attend Ontario Normal College in Hamilton and qualified to teach at the high school or collegiate institute level in Ontario. Afterwards she took a position as a private governess in Quebec.[89] By the time she departed for South Africa, she had thus secured a record of scholarly, administrative, and extracurricular achievement amidst a highly conservative but liberalizing co-educational culture. The seeds of the blunt assessments of the political and educational administrators in South Africa that she offers in her book may well have been sown during this period of her life.

In 1902, at age twenty-six, Graham set off to teach in South Africa, where she remained for two years. While there, Graham wrote a number of articles for the Montreal *Daily Witness* that became the basis for her book, *A Canadian Girl in South Africa*, published in 1905. Graham was not the only teacher acting as a correspondent. Florence Randal, a journalist at the Ottawa *Journal* prior to accepting a post as a camp teacher, provided regular columns to that newspaper during her year abroad. In these activities Graham and Randal participated in a growing trend of Anglo-Canadian women's public writings for newspapers, magazines, and in book format.[90] Upon her return to Canada, Graham continued her support of imperial activities through participation in the local chapter of the Imperial Order Daughters of the Empire (IODE), a female imperialist organization established during the South African war aimed at strengthening Canada's links to the British Empire.[91] Indeed, she became first "current Events Director" and then president of the Earl Grey Chapter of the IODE in Owen Sound.[92] She also taught at a high school in Harriston, Ontario and in 1907 became principal of the Girls' High School in Quebec City. Graham does not seem to have continued her writing beyond the publication of *A Canadian Girl*, producing only one article in subsequent years.[93]

In 1908 Graham married Frederick Gourlay Millar (1876–1972) of Wiarton, Ontario, a small village not far from Owen Sound. Like Graham, Millar attended the University of Toronto, graduating in 1898 with a degree in political science and English. The next year he graduated from the Ontario Normal School. He then undertook several years of post-graduate work at the University of Marburg, in Hesse, Germany, in history and languages. Millar spent four years teaching at Hamilton Collegiate Institute and became classical master at the Boys' High School, Quebec City. Several years after their marriage, Graham and Millar moved to Brantford, Ontario where Millar became an assistant in the commercial department at Brantford Collegiate Institute. From 1924 to 1944 he worked in Hamilton, becoming, in 1928, principal of Hamilton's first High School of Commerce.[94] Graham and Millar had three children (1910, 1914, 1916). In 1924 Graham became caregiver to both her aunt and mother until their deaths in 1930 and 1934, respectively. Maud Graham died in 1949.

In many ways, Graham constituted the ideal of the New Woman—highly educated, newly independent, open to the latest in modern ideas, yet supported by middle-class professional business or farm families looking for respectable opportunities for their daughters. She was clearly strong-willed, ambitious, and ready to embrace the new opportunities opening up to women of her class at the turn of the century.[95] She also carried over into her own life her family's involvement in social and moral reform. She remained a member of the National Council of Women, becoming president of the Ontario Provincial Council of Women from 1937 to 1942, and in 1946 prepared a brief on behalf of the Council to the Royal Commission on Education. She became president of the Brantford Home and School Council and was involved with the Hamilton Society for the Prevention of Cruelty to Animals. During the Second World War, she undertook regional work on the Wartime Prices and Trades Board and participated in Red Cross Society activities.[96]

It is difficult from biographical details to determine the nature of her personality. Conversations with Graham's grandchildren, who would have been very young when she was alive, suggest she was formidable, if not a little terrifying. Her daughter remembered her as a loving mother and affectionate wife who was the disciplinarian of the family. She was a strong supporter of women's education and held great admiration for prominent female experts, activists, and politicians. She was progressive for the time, believing it important that her daughter be educated in the "facts of life" and supporting family planning and contraception, perceiving large families to be injurious to women's and children's health. Yet, from her daughter's perspective as a trained social worker, Graham seemed unaware of the deep racial prejudice in South Africa and, equally, during the Great Depression exhibited little empathy when it came to the causes of people's personal poverty.[97]

Graham's book suggests that she was highly opinionated. Other archival fragments reinforce this view. In 1896–97, when Graham attended Bryn Mawr, she wrote an article comparing the female students there to those at the University of Toronto for the latter's newspaper, *The Varsity*, in which she stated that "the Toronto girl is vastly more attractive and well-bred." She considered the conversation offered by the Bryn Mawr woman "to be as entertaining as that of a gawky ten-year-old school girl," and suggested that they "suffer from those common defects of the American girl, a loud shrill voice, and a bad complexion, the latter being made worse by the amazing quantity of tea, coffee and 'fudge,' consumed at all hours of the days and night, for each girl has her own five o'clock tea-table in her study."[98]

An incident prior to Graham's departure for South Africa confirms this feistiness. When Graham applied to become a camp teacher, she was working as a private governess for a family in Quebec City. After she learned that her application had been successful, she returned home to Owen Sound, likely to visit her parents and set her affairs in order before heading off. Because Graham had applied from Quebec, the government deemed she should only be reimbursed for expenses from that point of departure. Graham vigorously protested that decision and the government eventually capitulated.[99]

Graham's formidable manner is equally recounted by a young Northrop Frye, who would later become a renowned literary scholar but at the time was known to the family simply as her son Graham's friend from university. Visiting the family in the summer of 1933, Frye, in cutting tones, described a family ruled by Maud as matriarch:

> It is curious to watch the rhythms of this family. Mrs. Millar snaps out everything she says like a drill sergeant and is disconcertingly impatient—her whole manner would be something like mine after teaching a week at an idiot school. She talks as fast as I do, but, her voice being higher by its regulation octave, gets away with it better, informing me in no uncertain terms that I have picked up a mumbling Jewish jargon at the university and have forgotten my mother tongue. Well, the whole family in reaction have adopted a pose of almost exaggerated deliberation and slowness both of speech and motion. The ensemble is something like a model T Ford—a spitting engine galvanizing a languid pile of tin into action. There's nothing ill-natured about it, of course, and it's quite amusing.[100]

While Frye's comments are those of a precocious young man, he offers a rare glimpse of Graham's postwar domestic life. Graham's feistiness, independence, and ambition seem to parallel that of Florence Randal. Like Graham, Randal married in 1908, but her daughter, renowned poet Dorothy Livesay, remembers her parents' marriage as unhappy and recalls her mother's inefficiency as a housekeeper and distance as a parent.[101] While generalizations on the basis of these two women should be tentative at best, their position at the turn of the century as educated career women in their mid-twenties may indicate the kinds of qualities possessed by the women teachers who volunteered for such an adventure. Yet, like some of the veterans of the war who returned before them, they may also have found it difficult to settle into the expectations of marriage and family life. Indeed, neither fully gave up their career—Randal continuing her writing and Graham returning to high school supply teaching at several points in the 1920s.[102]

Graham's memoir details her trip to South Africa and the two years she spent living there. She departed Canada from Saint John, New Brunswick on April 19, 1902 and arrived June 1 to the announcement of peace. The book is informally divided into two sections. The first section, Chapters I to IX, describes the trip to South Africa, camp life, and her experiences teaching during the early reconstruction period. En route to South Africa the Canadian teachers stopped in London for several weeks where they were fêted and met a number of important British political and social figures, including the Balfours, Lord and Lady Roberts, Earl Grey, Lady Cecil, Joseph Chamberlain, the Baden-Powells, and Michael Sadler of the Education Department. Attention from such prominent people is another indication of the importance attached to this imperial endeavor. Once in South Africa, Graham describes her travels from Cape Town, through the interior sandy plateau of the Karoo, and on to Norval's Pont where she settled in to teach. The second section, Chapters X to XIV, focuses on Graham's explanations and opinions pertaining to five themes she thought important for understanding the social, political, and economic context of South Africa after the war: the reliance on African labour; the repatriation of displaced Boers and government compensation to them for the destruction of their homes and land; government relief works for landless Boers; the rising up of anti-British *predikants* (church ministers) and the creation of church schools; and the challenges facing (white) farmers. In the process, she addresses the bonds of, and divisions within, the British Empire, the tense relationship between the British and Boers, and the central role of African labour in the economic life of southern Africa as well as, indirectly, the subservience of Africans in white social life. A brief concluding chapter documents her return to Canada.

At the time of its publication, A *Canadian Girl* received favourable reviews in newspapers and magazines.[103] One contemporary reviewer went so far as to suggest that "The mission of Miss Graham and her companions to the war-stricken colonies was an incident unique of its kind and well deserving of the place in Canadian history which the present little volume should secure for it."[104] In fact, the book did not become a "classic" of Canadian non-fiction writing. Despite receiving some favourable publicity, it seems to have created little stir.[105] Yet, at the time, the material in the book became one source that helped to shape Canadians' outlook on the South African War and its aftermath. Many of the chapters, for example, were initially published as first-hand newspaper accounts of happenings in the new British colonies at the end of the war. After publication, extracts from the book appeared in magazines and newspapers.[106] And at least some reviewers thought the book a useful source for understanding the conditions in South Africa at the time. Graham's book is especially important given the need for a greater understanding of daily life in the camps, as discussed above, and in the recently defeated Boer states more generally. Indeed, after publication, a review in the *Manitoba Free Press* emphasized the usefulness of the book as "the clearest impression it had yet seen of *the even tenor of every-day life* in England's newest colony."[107]

Graham's memoir is useful for additional reasons: it provides an entry point into discussions about imperialism, emergent English-Canadian nationalism, New Women, schooling, issues of racism, and whiteness (the construction and maintenance of a white racial identity). First, it conveys the dominant Anglo views of the righteousness of the imperial mission and, in contrast to the critique developed by Hobhouse and others, of the camps' utility. Like many English Canadians of British descent at the time, Graham adhered to a belief in the civilizing nature of the empire, and refers to Britain as the "Home Country" (Chapter I). By the 1890s many English-Canadians supported British imperialism, seeing it as "a potent political, economic, social and spiritual force."[108] By the time she arrived at Norval's Pont, many of the more severe conditions documented by Hobhouse and others had been ameliorated. It is perhaps not

Vegetable Rations, Refugee Camp, Norval's Pont.

surprising, then, that Graham's view of the camps is much more benign. Indeed, her personal photograph album reveals an emphasis on the positive aspects of camp life. In an album that otherwise contains only brief captions, she wrote under one photograph of a mass of children in front of a building, "At 11 A.M. every one of the 1,300 school children was served with a mugful of rich hot soup, during the winter months." Under another, featuring rows of vegetables, she noted, "Three times a week all refugees had a generous vegetable ration."[109]

Graham's account thus fits within the suffrage tradition of Millicent Garrett Fawcett and other British imperialists, rather than that of the anti-war suffragists such as Hobhouse. In England, the National Union of Women's Suffrage Societies became divided with significant numbers holding the latter position. Fawcett, on the other hand, strongly supported the war and attributed the high infant mortality rates in the camps not to living conditions but rather to the ignorance of Boer women regarding basic hygiene.[110] En route to South Africa, it is through meetings in London with Fawcett's daughter and other female imperialists such as Agnes Baden-Powell, that the Canadian contingent received their first personal accounts of camp life, including the news that they "could hire Boer girls and Kafirs to do our housework" (Chapter II). Graham's narrative thus has the effect of countering the impression of the dreadful conditions of camp life and reinforcing Fawcett's assessment.

Graham's support for Britain was always balanced with a strong sense of herself as a "Canadian Girl." While the British rationale for the war emphasized both the defense and extension of the empire, for Canadians the lead up to the war raised questions about Canada's relationship to Britain and its place within the empire. Canadians' backing of the war was never assured. While support for the war proved particularly strong within urban English Canada and among those of British descent, others, including agrarian and labour radicals, Christian socialists, anglophones of Irish and German descent, as well as a number of French-Canadian leaders, voiced significant dissent prior to the war.[111] Even among those supporting the war, an insipient nationalism was evident. Indeed, the first contingent fought as a Canadian unit under the Maple Leaf insignia and was led by a Canadian, proudly representing, according to Robert Page, "their nation's first military effort on the world stage."[112]

Graham's sense of Canadian identity can be seen throughout the text. She readily identifies with Canadians that she meets along the way (Chapters VI and VIII). Relating the story of one soldier who appears on her travels, she explains, "we felt our pride in our country swelling as he stood there, six feet of well-developed young Canada, with fair hair and blue eyes gleaming out of his brown skin" (Chapter VIII).[113] Yet, in response to a Boer acquaintance's attack on the English as "white devils," she indignantly reminds the woman that she too is "British" (Chapter VIII). Throughout the text, then, Graham understands herself to be both British and Canadian.[114] This did not mean unquestioned support for either group, however. She and her colleagues are critical of some of the English teachers on board the ship from Southampton to South Africa because of their "immoral" behaviour of sitting on soldiers' knees (Chapter III). Moreover, while she supports British colonial policy, she is critical of the ability of local officials in South Africa—criticism that is sharpest in the chapter on "Education and Church Schools." Nor is she supportive of some of the questionable behaviour of Canadian soldiers (Chapter VIII). Yet it is clear that she supports the British endeavor in South Africa and that her time there reinforced her allegiance to the empire. She ends her account by referring to the memorials to fallen soldiers being erected across Canada in the wake of the war, including in her hometown of Owen Sound, as "silent but potent links binding us to our sister colony across the sea" (Chapter XV).

Graham's motives for volunteering, like those of many of the young men at the time from her town and country, included the desire to do her part for the empire.[115] Yet loyalty to the empire was but one reason for volunteering. The opportunity to teach in South Africa offered adventure too. Indeed, this is illustrated in the opening lines of the text, where Graham concurs with an old university acquaintance who, upon hearing of some of her experiences, exclaimed, "I wish I were a girl...You girls have the best of everything nowadays" (Chapter I). Graham's daughter recorded that her mother applied for the position because she saw it as an opportunity "to see the world," and in places the memoir pulses with a sense of excitement and eager anticipation of what lay ahead.[116] When describing the sea voyage from Southampton to Cape Town, for example, she recounts with pride and amusement how "with practice...we became quite skilful at dressing with our cabin boxes shooting in and out under our feet like trombones" (Chapter III). Her fellow teacher, Florence Randal wrote that she and the other Canadian teachers had "envied" the English and Scottish teachers who preceded them to South Africa by a few months and had wartime experiences to recount, such as being shot at while travelling by train.[117] For some, the trip also offered a means to further one's career. Randal recorded in her diary the possibilities that going to South Africa would provide in advancing her journalistic career, noting, "I would love the trip and the writing of it."[118] The Canadian teachers thus conform to the pattern historian Shula Marks has identified for nurses who volunteered from across the empire for the South African War, whose motives combined imperial loyalty, a wish for adventure, interest in travel, desire for career development, financial need, and a longing to emigrate.[119]

For many of the women engaged as teachers, the trip to South Africa would have been the opportunity of a lifetime. It offered a sea voyage; a stop in London where they rubbed shoulders with leading imperialists, famous performers, and members of the aristocracy, and, following established patterns, toured renowned sites such as the Royal Mews at Buckingham Palace, St. Paul's Cathedral, and Covent Garden (where they saw King Edward and Queen Alexandra);[120] rail travel; and travel across southern Africa by train and horse- and cattle-drawn cart. After arriving in Liverpool, Graham and her fellow teachers travelled by train to London in a reserved corridor coach, a recent innovation that facilitated passenger movement throughout the train car, of which she wrote, "That corridor coach was exciting. We visited from one compartment to another, and decided unanimously that such a car was ideal. Presently lunch was served in the dining-car, the way to which made us feel like a band of exploring Westerners" (Chapter II). By arriving at the end of the war, they witnessed the process of de-mobilization, received visits from soldiers as well as invitations to picnics, parties, and concerts, and found opportunities to engage in various athletic activities. For some, this socializing led to romantic evenings on the veldt and marriage proposals—indeed six of the twenty women that accompanied Graham married in South Africa (Chapter I).[121]

Graham socializing with other teachers and British soldiers at Norval's Pont in 1902. Left: Maud Graham and Miss Arbuckle.

At times Graham's rhetoric echoes that of the stereotypical "tourist." She gushes at the prospect of meeting members of the British aristocracy in London (Chapter II). She makes snide comments about her "fellow-passengers" en route to Cape Town (Chapter III). More unsettling is her assessment of the poor in Santa Cruz on Teneriffe in the Canary Islands. Here she offers not a vivid and complex portrait but a caricature of the town's beggars before triumphantly celebrating the teachers' ability to secure "bargains" at the local shops (Chapter III). On other occasions, however, she willingly reassesses her initial assumptions—about effective modes of transportation (Chapter IV) or the cultural amenities available in Johannesburg (Chapter VI). And when she stops off in another Canary Islands locale, Las Palmas, during the voyage home she interrupts her description of the local inhabitants to briefly highlight what she identifies as the difficult plight of the indigenous women (Chapter XV). Somewhere in between these extremes is her celebratory but seemingly reflexive observation that any "Canadian who has not galloped over our great prairie lands will find it hard to understand the 'monarch of all I survey' sort of feeling one experiences on the veldt" (Chapter XIV).[122]

Graham treats her time in South Africa as an adventure, often enduring rough conditions with little complaint. Instead, she emphasizes the games and various forms of entertainment the teachers created on their voyage to the camps, and offers descriptions of facets of daily life while teaching that she finds interesting. She also makes repeated reference to the Cape's natural beauty. Hence, Graham describes her first impression of Norval's Pont as she and her fellow teachers were travelling by cart and horse: "As we rounded the huge, steep kopje [hill] separating the military from the refugee camp, we exclaimed with delight at the picture before us. To the left were enormous kopjes; at their base was the Orange River, winding along between green banks; to the right, and sloping up the opposite hillsides was the camp, with its long lines of tents glistening white in the morning sun" (Chapter V). She also makes light of the military tents in which they slept and of the storm that blew down their tent on their first night at Norval's Pont, soaking their belongings. Later, in Fauresmith, she and a fellow teacher, Miss Arbuckle, kept house on their own rather than boarding with a local family. With scarce resources she downplays their efforts to secure fuel and leavened bread (Chapters V and VIII).

As Cecilia Morgan explains in her study of English-Canadian transatlantic tourism, women "comprised a significant group among anglophone Canadian travel writers" between 1870 and 1930.[123] In many ways, Graham can be counted among this group. After all, her observations on a wide range of topics including modern transportation, window-shopping opportunities, local populations, landscapes, and the historical significance of the sites she visits fit nicely within the pattern of turn-of-the-century English-Canadian female travellers' accounts. Moreover, like other Canadian transatlantic travellers' experiences of the period, Graham's overseas excursion reinforced some of her pre-existing notions about her destinations while challenging others. But there are important differences as well. First, as Morgan notes, there has been very little work undertaken to explore the motivations and experiences of Canadian travellers venturing beyond Britain and Europe in the late nineteenth and early twentieth centuries.[124] Graham's recollections provide a glimpse of such escapades. Second, while Canada's transatlantic tourists of the period showed a keen interest in political developments, such as suffrage campaigns, and embraced opportunities to expand their knowledge and cultural horizons, they did so primarily as leisure travellers. Graham, of course, travelled first to Britain and then to South Africa as a salaried employee with daily responsibilities in the classroom and beyond. Her observations on daily life and, in particular, contemporary political controversies were profoundly shaped by this subject position.

Yet Graham's experience was certainly not bereft of leisure. For example, physical culture and sport play a significant role in Graham's narrative. This is perhaps not surprising given that she was selected to teach in South Africa "by reason of her educational ability, her fine physique, and training in athletics."[125] Graham clearly embraced participation in organized sport—one more of the new freedoms offered to young women in the late nineteenth century. As president of the Women's Athletic Club at the University of Toronto, she would have been familiar with the facilities available to women at that institution. Her year at Bryn Mawr exposed her to more well-developed facilities and a formal physical culture program, including medical examinations and corrective exercises, increasingly common at the time at American women's educational institutions. Indeed,

Field hockey. From left to right: Mr. Purcell, Miss Webb, Capt. Smith, Mr. Carroll, Mr. Vandry, Miss Rose.

it led her to publicly admonish her alma mater for its lack of facilities and to advocate for a gymnasium.[126] She also embraced the opportunity at Normal School to take courses in physical training and drill.

Graham's narrative is, in fact, replete with references to physical activity, from participation in calisthenics on board the ship, to engaging in sports in camp, horseback riding, organizing the playground at the school in Fauresmith, and introducing children to games such as basketball, still a relatively recent invention at that time. Graham's photograph album contains a number of pictures of mixed-gender field hockey games as well as matches on the South African Constabulary tennis court during the period she lived in Fauresmith.[127] In Kroonstad, Graham and other teachers organized a community field hockey program as a means to overcome some of the social and political divisions between the Dutch and English (Chapters III and XII).[128] The teachers, then, used athletics as a means of building community. Yet their enthusiasm for athletics also reflects the way in which many of these women embraced the broadening social roles for women at home.

If travelling to South Africa offered adventure, so too did teaching in the camp and town schools. Camp schools, like the teachers' living conditions more generally, were very basic. Graham initially had 130 students at the Primer II level. School began at 9 A.M. and ended at 1:30 P.M. with a recess from 10:30 A.M. to 11 A.M. The school day started with twenty minutes of religious instruction in Dutch followed by a routine comprised of a hymn, a check for cleanliness, passing out of slates, pencils, and books, copying of figures and letters from the blackboard, singing (to teach English and release energy), recess, a lesson in reading, basic math, spelling, memorization of a new verse, and a simple story (Chapter V). The British government provided each teacher with £3 of teaching supplies. Teachers were free to choose from the Board of Education's extensive holdings but the books on offer, including *100 Gems of English Scenery*, *Pictorial Britain and Ireland*, *A Natural History Picture Book for Children*, and *England's History as Pictured by Famous Painters* are indicative of the kind of lessons the British government was keen to support. "Pictures will be found specially useful by the teachers in the camps," British officials explained, but warned that "in their selection great care should be taken to avoid unsuitable subjects."[129]

Graham and Miss Arbuckle left Norval's Pont for the town of Fauresmith in September 1902 where they worked until July 1903 and where Graham's class, consisting of four levels, from beginners to Primer II, reached eighty-five students. The school had been destroyed during the war so she had to make do with two portable blackboards and twenty broken slates, relying on scraps of chalk brought in by the children (Chapter VIII). In July 1903, deciding to stay after her contract expired, Graham moved to Kroonstad where she remained for another year. Her descriptions of teaching at the

Fauresmith teachers. From left to right: Mrs. V.D. Post, C. Gertrude Arbuckle, Mr. Morris, Miss Meintjes, Miss Blair, Maud Graham.

various schools include many observations about aspects of children's daily lives; for example, during the lunch break in Norval's Pont, "the favourite games at recess were marbles for the boys, and skipping with a long rope for the girls" and elsewhere she describes the kinds of games that children played on holidays (Chapters V and VII).

It is clear, particularly in the chapter on "Education and Church Schools," that Graham supported the idea of having one public school system for all white children. After the war, the Dutch Reformed Church began opening schools in order to preserve the use of the Dutch language and to protect its cultural and religious influence. Graham perceived this initiative to be dangerously divisive. Despite her own criticism of the Education Department for failing to employ effective Dutch teachers because they were suspected of pro-Boer sympathies—which resulted in a shortage of teachers able to instruct in Dutch—she gives short shrift to complaints that the British government was attempting to eradicate Dutch in the schools. While Graham supports the three hours a week of lessons in high Dutch, her assumption that English is the language of the educated is clear.

Graham's text illuminates the pervasive racism of the time—a racism that can be seen on two levels, in relation to Africans as well as to Boers. In her text, Africans remain largely invisible. At one point, Graham comments that "although the country is so large, the population is small and constantly moving about, and one is soon impressed with the 'knowability' of everyone, as Kipling says of India" (Chapter VIII). The "population" in her eyes is white. The invisibility of black Africans was due, in part, to the fact that most Africans interned during the war lived in separate camps, as noted above, making it easier for Graham, as well as those who opposed the camps, to ignore their plight. Thus, when they appear in details of camp life it is generally as cooks, laundresses, or maids. These African women became an important part of the teachers' lives, not only contributing to the daily functioning of the household but also to the positive atmosphere. Yet the sense of racial and class difference is redolent throughout the narrative. For example, Graham consistently uses the derogatory term "Kafir," an Arabic word for infidel that was used by Boer and Brit alike.[130] She describes Maria, their cook in Fauresmith, as "our Kafir" a woman who was "neat and smiling" and soon found to be "very teachable" (Chapter VIII). Equally, she uses the term "coolie" to refer to non-white workers (Chapters III, V, and VI). Attempting to relate the sense of humour of her African cooks, Graham un-self-consciously compares them to "mischievous children" (Chapter VIII). She also has a habit of employing the names "South Africa" and "Africa" interchangeably as though the two were the same thing—a typical example of how little Westerners knew (and often continue to know) about the incredible complexity and diversity of the continent's peoples, cultures, and environments.

The issue of race, and racism, also arises in regard to Boer–Brit relations. The British imperialists perceived themselves to be racially superior to the Boers. Sir Bartle Frere (1815–1884), British high commissioner for Southern Africa from 1877 to 1880, wrote to Queen Victoria that the Boers "were a 'most interesting and very primitive people' who could be made 'as loyal subjects to Your Majesty as the French Canadians.'"[131] Though ultimately wrong on both counts, Frere's sense of racial superiority is clear. Canadian and other imperialists perceived the war as one between British progress and Boer backwardness. Reports on the rationale for sending Canadian women to South Africa reflected that perception. A newspaper article in the *Globe* in April 1902 noted that the teachers' purpose was "to instruct the young Boers in the English language and train them up in the ways of civilization." The article continued, "The Canadian soldier boys won the admiration and respect of brother Boer by their prowess upon the field of battle. It now becomes the duty of Canadian maidens to bring the blessings of education and refinement into the homes of the Dutch."[132]

Graham's reports also affirm this general picture of the Boers, as she describes them as "too ignorant" to understand the need to stay in quarantine if they had a contagious disease and unaware of modern rules of hygiene (Chapter v). She claims that "the poorer Dutch women hadn't the faintest idea of cooking anything properly," thus contributing to their children's poor health and the need for the camp to provide hot soup. And she notes that "the dirty ones were also ignorant ones, unable to speak any English, their children being quite unschooled." This poorer class of Boers, she argues, "benefited by the camps. They had free schools, free medical attendance, wholesome food, and were obliged to be decently clean" (Chapter v). To Graham, imperial rule would act as a civilizing and uplifting force.[133]

Graham's racism is also refracted through the lens of class, positing the laziness of the peasant Boers who are unschooled against "the educated classes" of Dutch in the camps for whom she has sympathy and from whom she often received hospitality after leaving Norval's Pont (Chapters V and VIII). In her chapter on the landless Dutch, she reaffirms this class and racial hierarchy, commenting that these *bywoners* (squatters) as they were known, "seemed but little higher than the Kafirs in the scale of civilization." Following common eugenic beliefs of the time, Graham perceived their poverty and their suspiciously dark skin tones as visible evidence of mental inferiority. Noting the children, she explains that "All were dark-skinned, in some cases showing obvious traces of a dash of Kafir blood. Such children were dull and phlegmatic." Near the end of her memoir she states, "undoubtedly the triumph of the Afrikaner cause would have been a long step backward in the history of South African civilization" (Chapter XII).

Though the British perceived the Boers to be racially inferior, they were nevertheless white and of European ancestry. South Africa was to be treated, like Canada, New Zealand, or Australia, as a white settler society with whites given the political rights of their compatriots elsewhere. The fact that the war had pitted whites against whites raised racial anxieties. Piers Brendon notes that despite Lord Kitchener's requests during the South African War for military aid from Indian soldiers serving under British commanders, "the London government feared that if brown soldiers defeated whites in the 'Dark Continent' they might be emboldened to attempt another uprising in the subcontinent."[134] At the same time, in Britain the war raised concerns about the quality of Anglo manhood. The poor physical condition and high rejection rates of many recruits, Britain's inability to quickly defeat the Boers, the ineptness of some of its commanding officers, and the perceived moral lapse accompanying the creation of the camps, all fuelled broader fears about the degeneracy of the British race.[135] For Canadians, on the other hand, military success “encouraged their citizen soldiers and their admirers back home to view themselves as a new, healthier, hardier breed, born of their Nordic environment.”[136]

Although Graham exhibited the attitudes common among women of her ethnic and class background, she was, at times, notably curious about the places and people she encountered and open to having her assumptions about Boers and South Africa in general challenged and overturned.[137] En route to Norval's Pont she and other teachers stopped at De Aar Junction to have lunch and, with time to spare before moving on, they visited a small Boer school located at the railway. She writes, it “was very up-to-date, and somewhat jarred our preconceived ideas of South African schools” (Chapter IV). Elsewhere she explains that she learned “to judge nothing by Canadian standards” (Chapter V). She describes how, after a fun trip to Johannesburg, she and her fellow teachers “felt vastly ashamed of our preconceived ideas of Johannesburg, which we had imagined to be a rough mining town with few of the comforts and none of the luxuries of civilization” (Chapter VI). Moreover, soon after moving to Fauresmith, she and Miss Arbuckle caused “a perfect sensation” by organizing a tea for the upper-class members of the community: a formal tea was an “unheard-of function” and she acknowledges “we should have found out the customs of the place” before organizing the event (Chapter VIII). Notably, she does not extend this humble approach to her assumptions about Africans. She does condemn Boer racism towards Africans, stating that “the Dutch...have reason to fear the Kafirs, for in the old days they oppressed them. Many a Dutchman has told me unblushingly that the Kafirs had no souls and were only fit to be slaves” (Chapter X). Yet she also remains steadfast in her belief that British policy towards Africans—which had long included violently subjugating African kingdoms in the region—is more enlightened than the crude racism of the Boers. She approves of the British policy of racial segregation as well as the hated, humiliating pass system, which forced African men to carry passes that stipulated where they could work and live, and resulted in fines or imprisonment for those caught without them.[138]

Graham, like many of her fellow teachers, was in her mid-twenties, and had embarked upon a career prior to her arrival in South Africa. She reveled in her independence. Her attitude and behaviour reflect the tensions inherent in experiencing life as a New Woman in the early twentieth century. Her teaching positions in South Africa afforded her exciting opportunities for independent reflection and personal growth. Indeed, in the opening lines of the book, she expresses an almost giddy amazement at the fact that she and her fellow female teachers have been permitted to embark upon such a bold undertaking. And yet her exasperation with official decision making belies the fact that, as a woman, her ability to effect institutional change was tightly proscribed. Structural elements thus combined and intersected with Graham's own individual life experiences and personality to produce a memoir that boldly questions some widely shared contemporary assumptions about South Africa, British imperialism, and race relations, while reinforcing others.

CONCLUSION

Graham sailed for home in July 1904, by which time, she writes, "scarcely a trace of the war remained" (Chapter XV). Much has been written over the past one hundred years about the war's impact, but Graham's text provides insight into areas needing further research. Her eyewitness account of living and working in Norval's Pont can assist historians in the ongoing attempt to develop a more nuanced picture of life in the concentration camps. In addition, despite the broadening of military history to include aspects of social history, the history of Canadian women's involvement in the camps is limited. Equally, Graham forms part of a transnational women's history, of which we still know little from a Canadian perspective. While the teaching in the camps is often tacked on as an interesting or curious side note to the war itself, the camp schools in fact marked the beginning of the reconstruction of South African educational policy, a proposed keystone for the maintenance of British control in South Africa—an objective in which Canadian women played a significant role. Moreover, the memoir can serve as a useful tool for understanding the history of British colonial education policy in Africa and elsewhere in the empire—a body of research that to date has focused mainly on the political overtones and social effects of colonial education on non-white subjects.[139] Comparing and contrasting British colonial education policy for Boer *kampkinders* and Africans will provide a better understanding of the importance of whiteness in the formulation of colonial policy more generally.

Graham's reminiscences of her two years in South Africa provide historians with a valuable, first-person account of the period during which the infamous concentration camps were closed, the reconstruction process began, and tensions between British and Boer communities were reshaped in light of the war's end. Her observations, refracted through lenses shaped by dominant settler colonial discourses of race, gender, and class ideals, provide a valuable resource for historians of the South African War concentration camps as well as women's historians who are keen to understand the tensions inherent in the changing place of women in Canada and elsewhere in the British Empire at the turn of the twentieth century. They also provide revealing insights into the dominant imperial gaze of the time. Graham's racial identity, class position, and gender ideals all shaped her (sometimes highly problematic) evaluation of what she saw and chose to highlight. She was a middle-class Canadian woman staunchly supportive of British imperialism but frustrated by, and critical of, many of the male imperial authorities she encountered. At times, Graham's book offers conventional views about the nature and role of the British Empire as well as British opinion on the South African War. It is thus useful as a means of illustrating popular views held at the time by the British. But as a New Woman she was never shy about expressing her opinions, offering pointed suggestions pertaining to postwar reconstruction, and apportioning blame. No longer fully impeded by extremely restrictive traditional notions of femininity, Graham was able to take advantage of the new educational opportunities available to women at the turn of the century and participate in newly formed organizations aimed at advancing the cause of women. Her text provides an opportunity for scholars to gain insight into women's place at the turn of the century, the relationship between gender and imperialism, and the potential difference gender makes when the victors, the vanquished, the colonizers, and colonized meet in the very particular and complicated "contact zone" that developed out of this British government initiative.[140]

In reprinting Graham's account we have retained its original presentation as much as possible. We have kept the original spelling, grammar, and punctuation—including inconsistencies—throughout the text. For example, Graham employs a mixture of American and British spelling conventions. When necessary we have provided brief annotations to clarify the meaning of a misspelled word or the identity of a person whose name is misspelled. However, we have not adhered to the pagination of the original edition. The original publication contained thirty-nine images as well as the portraits of thirty-eight of the forty Canadian teachers. We have only been able to reproduce twenty-one of these.[141] They appear in the text in close proximity to their location in the original publication. Any information added to the captions appears in roman.

The maps and images that appear in this Introduction were not part of the original publication. Unless otherwise noted, the images are from Graham's personal photo album. This edition of Graham's account also includes extensive annotations. In addition to defining terms with which readers may be unfamiliar, the annotations focus primarily on providing historical context for Graham's observations.

Finally, we have provided a detailed subject and thematic Index to assist scholars interested in a particular aspect of Graham's experience. No index was included in the original publication.

NOTES

1. The decision to recruit women for this task undoubtedly reflected the feminization of the teaching profession. Janet Guildford notes that in England "women formed 75 per cent of the work force by 1914" and that they "formed the majority of the public school teaching force in Quebec and Ontario by 1871." By 1880, "women made up two-thirds of the public school work force" in Nova Scotia. The rapid expansion of the schooling, governments' desires to keep salaries low, a lack of alternative occupations, and the belief that women possessed a "natural aptitude" for teaching young children were all important factors in this development. See Janet Guildford, "'Separate Spheres': The Feminization of Public School Teaching in Nova Scotia, 1838–1900," *Acadiensis* 22, no. 1 (1992): 44–46.
2. "Boer" means "farmer" in Dutch. By the late nineteenth century, the term referred to Afrikaans-speaking descendants of the original Dutch settlers that arrived in the region in the seventeenth century. In the twentieth century, in conjunction with the rise of Afrikaner nationalism, the term "Afrikaner" increasingly displaced "Boer." For an overview of the history of the Boers and the settlement of the Cape and the regions north and eastwards, see *The Cambridge History of South Africa*, eds. Carolyn Hamilton, Bernard K. Mbenga, and Robert Ross (Cambridge: Cambridge University Press, 2010); George McCall Theal, *History of the Boers in South Africa, or, The Wanderings and Wars of the Emigrant Farmers: From Their Leaving the Cape Colony to the Acknowledgement of Their Independence by Great Britain* (London: S. Sonnenschein, Lowrey, 1887); Adam Giliomee, *The Afrikaners: Biography of a People*, rev. ed. (Charlottesville: University of Virginia Press; Cape Town, South Africa: Tafelberg, 2009); Peter Limb, Norman Etherington, and Peter Midgley, eds., *Grappling with the Beast: Indigenous Southern African Responses to Colonialism, 1840–1930* (Boston: Brill, 2010). On the rise of Afrikaner nationalism, see Dan O'Meara, *Volkskapitalisme: Class, Capital, and Ideology in the Development of Afrikaner Nationalism, 1934–1948*; and T. Dunbar Moodie, *The Rise of Afrikanerdom: Power, Apartheid, and the Afrikaner Civil Religion* (Berkeley: University of California Press, 1975).
3. As part of the war effort, the British removed over one hundred thousand Boers, mainly women and children, from their homes and "concentrated" them into civilian camps.
4. Chamberlain was concerned that Catholics would "likely be too far out of touch" with the Protestant Boers "in the matter of religious conviction." Library and Archives Canada, RG 6, A-1, Secretary of State Correspondence [hereafter SOSC], vol. 103, file 345, Joseph Chamberlain to Lord Minto, 18 January 1902.
5. SOSC, vol. 103, file 345, R.W. Scott, Secretary of State to Governor General in Council, 5 May 1902.

6. SOSC, vol. 138, file 1114, Isabel Perry, Montreal to Governor General Earl Grey, 17 March 1909.

7. SOSC, vol. 105, file 711, W.A. McIntyre, Principal, Provincial Normal School, Winnipeg, to Joseph Pope, Under-Secretary of State, Ottawa, 7 March 1902. Murray and Younghusband were selected as Manitoba's two representatives.

8. On the authorities' requirements for physical fitness and musical talent, see SOSC, vol. 103, file 345, Memorandum Respecting the Engagement of Teachers for the Refugee Camps in South Africa, n.d., c. November 1901.

9. John Eddy and Deryk Schreuder, Introduction to *The Rise of Colonial Nationalism*, eds. J. Eddy and D. Schreuder (Sydney: Allen & Unwin, 1988), 19–20.

10. Richard Jebb, *Studies in Colonial Nationalism* (London: Edward Arnold, 1905); Eddy and Schreuder, Introduction to *The Rise of Colonial Nationalism*, 7.

11. Jebb, *Studies in Colonial Nationalism*, Chapter 6.

12. For a study of the twenty women from New Zealand who taught in the camps, see Ellen Ellis, *Teachers for South Africa: New Zealand Women at the South African War Concentration Camps* (Paekakariki: Hanorah Books, 2010).

13. See, for example, Philip Buckner and R. Douglas Francis, eds., *Rediscovering the British World* (Calgary: University of Calgary Press, 2005); Philip Buckner and R. Douglas Francis, eds., *Canada and the British World: Culture, Migration, and Identity* (Vancouver: UBC Press, 2006); and Kate Darian Smith, Patricia Grimshaw, and Stuart Macintyre, eds., *Britishness Abroad: Transnational Movements and Imperial Cultures* (Melbourne: Melbourne University Press, 2007).

14. On Stairs, see Ian McKay and Jamie Swift, *Warrior Nation: Rebranding Canada in an Age of Anxiety* (Toronto: Between the Lines, 2012), Chapter 2.

15. Alisha Nicole Apale and Valerie Stem, eds., *Generation NGO* (Toronto: Between the Lines, 2011).

16. L. Gordon Flake and Scott Snyder, eds., *Paved With Good Intentions: The NGO Experience in North Korea* (Westport, CT: Praeger, 2003).

17. Larry Krotz, *The Uncertain Business of Doing Good: Outsiders in Africa* (East Lansing: Michigan State University Press, 2009), 3.

18. Ann Laura Stoler, *Carnal Knowledge and Imperial Power: Race and the Intimate in Colonial Rule* (Berkeley: University of California Press, 2002), 120.

19. Barbara Heron, *Desire for Development: Whiteness, Gender, and the Helping Imperative* (Waterloo, ON: Wilfrid Laurier University Press, 2007), 15.

20. Heron, *Desire for Development*, 32. On Canadian female missionaries of the period, see Ruth Compton Brouwer, *New Women for God: Canadian Presbyterian Women and Indian Missions, 1876–1914* (Toronto: University of Toronto Press, 1990).

21. Heron, *Desire for Development*, Chapter 2. On the awkward transition from religious to secular imperatives in Canadian overseas development pursuits, see Ruth Compton Brouwer, "When Missions Became Development: Ironies of 'NGOization' in Mainstream Canadian Churches in the 1960s," *Canadian Historical Review* 91, no. 4 (2010): 661–93.

22. For more on British–Boer–African relations in the region in the nineteenth century, see Hermann Giliomee and Andre du Toit, *Afrikaner Political Thought: Documents and Analysis* (Berkeley: University of California Press, 1983); Norman Etherington, *Preachers, Peasants, and Politics in Southeast Africa, 1835–1880* (London: Royal Historical Society, and Boyle and Brewer, 1978).
23. At least twelve Canadian nurses also served; on Canada's involvement in the South African War, see Robert Page, *The Boer War and Canadian Imperialism*, Canadian Historical Association Booklet no. 44 (Ottawa: Canadian Historical Association, 1987), and "Canada and the Imperial Idea in the Boer War Years," *Journal of Canadian Studies* 5, no. 1 (1970): 33–49; Carman Miller, *Painting the Map Red: Canada and the South African War, 1899–1902* (Montreal and Kingston: Canadian War Museum and McGill-Queen's University Press, 1993); Carman Miller, *Canada's Little War* (Toronto: Lorimer, 2003), as well as "Canada & The South African War, 1899–1902," Canadian War Museum, accessed October 18, 2011, http://www.warmuseum.ca/cwm/exhibitions/boer/boerwarhistory_e.shtml.
24. Overviews of the war include, Denis Judd and Keith Surridge, *The Boer War* (New York: Palgrave Macmillan, 2003); Bill Nasson, *The South African War*, 1899–1902 (London: Arnold, 1999); Peter Warwick, ed., *The South African War. The Anglo-Boer War 1899–1902* (London: Longman, 1980); and Thomas Pakenham, *The Boer War* (London: Weidenfeld and Nicolson, 1979). See also Piers Brendon, *The Decline and Fall of the British Empire, 1781–1997* (London: Vintage Books, 2008), Chapter 8. A highly regarded first-person account of the war is Denys Reitz, *Commando: A Boer Journal of the Boer War* (London: Faber, 1933).
25. Albert Grundlingh, "Why Concentration Camps?" in *The War at Home: Women and Families in the Anglo-Boer War*, eds. Bill Nasson and Albert Grundlingh (Cape Town: Tafelberg, 2013), 25. An excellent resource on the history of the concentration camps is The British Concentration Camps of the South African War 1900–1902, a database funded by the Wellcome Trust, available at http://www2.lib.uct.ac.za/mss/bccd/. See also S.B. Spies, *Methods of Barbarism? Roberts and Kitchener and Civilians in the Boer Republics January 1900–May 1902* (Cape Town: Human & Rousseau, 1977).
26. Elizabeth van Heyningen, "Women and Disease: The Clash of Medical Cultures in the Concentration Camps of the South African War," in *Writing a Wider War: Rethinking Gender, Race, and Identity in the South African War, 1899–1902*, eds. Greg Cuthbertson, Albert Grundlingh, and Mary-Lynn Suttie (Athens: Ohio University Press, 2002), 186–212; Daniel Low-Beer, Matthew Smallman-Raynor, and Andrew Cliff, "Disease and Death in the South African War: Changing Disease Patterns from Soldiers to Refugees," *Social History of Medicine* 17, no. 2 (2004): 223–45; Bruce Fetter and Stowell Kessler, "Scars from a Childhood Disease: Measles in the Concentration Camps During the Boer War," *Social Science History* 20 (1996): 563–611.
27. "The Second Anglo-Boer War, 9 October 1899–31 May 1902," *South African History Online*, accessed October 26, 2014, http://www.sahistory.org.za/war. It is very likely that the mortality rates of both Boers and Africans have been underestimated.

28. William Beinart, *Twentieth-Century South Africa* (Oxford: Oxford University Press, 2001), 66.

29. Hobhouse's efforts to improve camp management and criticism of the scorched earth policy and camp system led to questions being asked by the Liberal Opposition in the House of Commons. In 1902 she wrote *The Brunt of the War and Where it Fell* (London: Methuen and Company, 1902) based on her experiences in the camps and interviews with female inhabitants. See also Emily Hobhouse, *Emily Hobhouse: A Memoir*, comp. A. Ruth Fry (London: Jonathan Cape, 1929); Rykie van Reenen, ed., *Emily Hobhouse: Boer War Letters* (Cape Town: Human & Rousseau, 1984); Jennifer Hobhouse Balme, ed., *To Love One's Enemies: The Work and Life of Emily Hobhouse Compiled from Letters and Writings, Newspaper Cuttings and Official Documents* (Cobble Hill, BC: Hobhouse Trust, 1994); and Brian Roberts, *Those Bloody Women: Three Heroines of the Boer War* (London: J. Murray, 1991). Studies of Hobhouse's writings and their influence include, Liz Stanley, "'A Strange Thing is Memory': Emily Hobhouse, Memory Work, Moral Life and the 'Concentration System,'" *South African Historical Journal* 52 (2005): 60–81, and John Fisher, *That Miss Hobhouse* (London: Secker & Warburg, 1971).

30. E.H.H. Green, *The Crisis in Conservatism: The Politics, Economics, and Ideology of the Conservative Party, 1880–1914* (London: Taylor & Francis e-Library, 2005), 17–19.

31. See Amy Shaw, "Dissent in Canada against the Anglo-Boer War, 1899-1902," in *Worth Fighting For: Canada's Tradition of War Resistance from 1812 to the War on Terror*, eds. Lara Campbell, Michael Dawson, and Catherine Gidney (Toronto: Between the Lines, 2015).

32. Arthur Conan Doyle, *The Great Boer War: A Two Year's Record, 1899–1902* (London: Smith, Elder & Co, 1901). Reference to the book is found in SOSC, file 345, Joseph Pope, Under-Secretary of State, Ottawa telegram to George. N. Morang & Co., Toronto, 8 April 1902.

33. Sol Plaatje, *The Boer War Diary of Sol T. Plaatje; An African at Mafeking*, ed. John L. Comaroff (Johannesburg: Macmillan, 1973).

34. For a historical overview of these and other pivotal events in modern South African history, see Beinart, *Twentieth-Century South Africa*.

35. Elizabeth van Heyningen, "The Concentration Camps of the South African (Anglo-Boer) War, 1900–1902," *History Compass* 7, no. 1 (2009): 26. For a recent uncritical study of the war that reinforces camp mythology, see Owen Coetzer, *Fire in the Sky: The Destruction of the Orange Free State 1899–1902* (Weltevreden Park: Covos-Day, 2000), which was written during the South African War centenary.

36. Recent studies include Elsabe Brink and Sue Krige, "Remapping and Remembering the South African War in Johannesburg and Pretoria," *South African Historical Journal* 41 (1999): 404–21; Jenny de Reuck, "Social Suffering and the Politics of Pain: Observations on the Concentration Camps in the Anglo-Boer War, 1899–1902," *English in Africa* 26, no. 2 (1999): 69–88; Albert Grundlingh, "The National Women's Monument: The Making and Mutation of Meaning in Afrikaner Memory of the South African War," in *Writing a Wider War: Rethinking Gender, Race, and Identity in the South African War, 1899–1902*,

eds. Greg Cuthbertson, Albert Grundlingh, and Mary-Lynn Suttie (Athens: Ohio University Press), 18–36; Albert Grundlingh, "Reframing Remembrance: The Politics of the Centenary Commemoration of the South African War of 1899–1902," *Journal of Southern African Studies* 30, no. 2 (June 2004): 359–75; Albert Grundlingh, "The War in Twentieth-Century Afrikaner Consciousness," in *The Impact of the South African War*, eds. David Omissi and Andrew Thompson (Basingstoke, UK: Palgrave Publishers, 2002), 23–37; Louis Grundlingh, "Another Side to Warfare: Caring for White Destitutes during the Anglo-Boer War, (October 1899–May1900)," *New Contree* 45 (1999): 137–63; Donal Lowry, ed., *The South African War Reappraised* (Manchester: Manchester University Press, 1985); Bill Nasson, "The South African War/Anglo-Boer War, 1899–1902 and Political Memory in South Africa," in *The Politics of War Memory and Commemoration*, eds. T.G. Ashplant, Graham Dawson, and Michael Roper (London: Routledge, 2001), 111–27; W.R. Nasson, "Tot Siens to All That? South Africa's Great War, 1899–1902," *South African Historical Journal* 32 (1995); Ian Phimister, "Unscrambling the Scramble for Southern Africa: The Jameson Raid and the South African War Revisited," *South African Historical Journal* 28, no. 1 (1993): 202–30; Andrew Porter, "The Origins of the South African War," *South African Historical Journal* 35 (1996): 155–61; Andrew Porter, "The South African War and the Historians," *African Affairs* 99 (2000): 633–48; Liz Stanley, *Mourning Becomes... Post/Memory and Commemoration of the Concentration Camps of the South African War 1899–1902* (Manchester: Manchester University Press, 2006); Elizabeth van Heyningen, "'Fools Rush In': Writing a History of the Concentration Camps of the South African War," *Historia* 55, no. 2 (2010): 12–33; Leslie Witz, Gary Minkley, and Ciraj Rassool, "No End of a (History) Lesson: Preparations for the Anglo-Boer War Centenary Commemoration," *South African Historical Journal* 41 (1999): 370–87.

37. Elizabeth van Heyningen, *The Concentration Camps of the Anglo-Boer War: A Social History* (Johannesburg and Cape Town: Jacana Media, 2013). See the following essays in *Writing a Wider War*: Helen Bradford, "Gentlemen and Boers: Afrikaner Nationalism, Gender, and Colonial Warfare in the South African War," 37–66; Shula Marks, "British Nursing and the South African War," 159–185; and Elizabeth van Heyningen, "Women and Disease: The Clash of Medical Cultures in the Concentration Camps of the South African War," 186–212. See also Elizabeth van Heyningnen, "Women and Gender in the South African War, 1899–1902," in *Women in South African History*, ed. Nomboniso Gasa (Cape Town: Human Sciences Research Council, 2007), 91–125; and Nasson and Grundlingh, *The War at Home*.

38. Albert Grundlingh, "War, Wordsmiths and the 'Volk': Afrikaans Historical Writing on the Anglo-Boer War of 1899–1902 and the War in Afrikaner Nationalist Consciousness, 1902–1990," in *Mfecane to Boer War: Versions of South African History*, eds. E. Lehmann and E. Reckwitz (Essen: Die Blaue Eule, 1992), 45–47; Ena Jansen and Wilfred Jonckheere, eds., *Boer en Brit: Afrikaanse en Nederlandse tekste uit en Om die Anglo-Boereoolog* (Pretoria: Protea Boekhuis, 2001); Elria Wessels, "Die Rol van die Vrou Buite die Konsentrasiecamp Tydens en na die Orrlog," *Joernaal vir Eietydse Geskiedenis/Journal of Contemporary History* 27, no. 2 (2002): 22–30.

39. Andrew Porter, "The South African War and Imperial Britain: A Question of Significance," in *Writing a Wider War*, 287–302; Paula Krebs, *Gender, Race, and the Writing of Empire: Public Discourse and the Boer War* (Cambridge: Cambridge University Press, 2004); Paul Laity, "The British Peace Movement and the War," in *The Impact of the South African War*, 138–56.
40. Stanley, *Mourning Becomes.*
41. For a comprehensive overview of the camps for Africans, see Stowell V. Kessler, "The Black Concentration Camps of the South African War, 1899–1902" (PHD diss., University of Cape Town, 2003). See also Felix Malunga, "The Anglo-Boer South African War: Sekhukhune II Goes on the Offensive in the Eastern Transvaal, 1899–1902," *Joernaal vir Eietydse Geskiedenis/Journal of Contemporary History* 25, no. 2 (2000): 57–78; J.S. Mohlamme, "Blacks in the Ex-Boer Republics of the Transvaal and Orange Free State in the Aftermath of the South African War of 1899–1902," *Joernaal vir Eietydse Geskiedenis/ Journal of Contemporary History* 25, no. 2 (2000): 270–83; J.S. Mohlamme, "African Refugee Camps in the Boer Republics," in *Scorched Earth*, ed. Fransjohan Pretorius (Cape Town: Human & Rousseau, 2001), 110–21; B.E. Mongalo and K.J. du Pisani, "Victims of a White Man's War: Blacks in Concentration Camps during the South African War (1899–1902)," *Historia* 44, no. 1 (1999): 148–82; Bill Nasson, *Abraham Esau's War: A Black South African War in the Cape, 1899–1902* (Cape Town: David Philip, 1991); Bill Nasson, *The South African War, 1899–1902* (London: Arnold, 1999); Bill Nasson, *Uyadela wen'osulapho: Black Participation in the Anglo-Boer War* (Randburg, South Africa: Navan, 1999); Liz Stanley, "Black Labour and the Concentration Camp System of the South African War," *Journal for Contemporary History* 28 (2003): 190–213; Peter Warwick, *Black People and the South African War, 1899–1902* (Cambridge: Cambridge University Press, 1983). Also see the following essays in *Writing a Wider War*: Manelisi Genge, "The Role of the EmaSwati in the South African War," 136–58; Bernard Mgenga, "The Role of the Bakgatla of the Pilanesberg in the South Africa War," 85–114; and John Lambert, "'Loyalty Its Own Reward': The South African War Experience of Natal's 'Loyal' Africans," 115–35.
42. Helen Dampier, "'Everyday Life' in Boer Women's Testimonies of the Concentration Camps of the South African War, 1899–1902," in *Crime and Empire 1840–1940: Criminal Justice in Local and Global Context*, eds. Graeme Dunstall and Barry Godfrey (Cullompton, UK: Willan Publishing, 2005), 202.
43. In one important collection of 1,400 photographs of concentration camps, there are four that depict skeletal children, and of the other two major collections that contain approximately 3,000 camp photographs, there are none. Stanley, *Mourning Becomes*, 39, 42.
44. Ibid., 163.
45. *Kampkinders, 1900-1902: 'n Gedenkboek*, compiled by M.C.E. van School in collaboration with C.G. Coetzee (Bloemfontein: Oorlogsmuseum van die Boererepublieke, 1982), 24, cited in Sarah Duff, "'Capture the Children': Writing Children into the South African War, 1899–1902," *Journal of the History of Childhood and Youth* 7 (2014): 374.
46. Florence Randal, "A Year in a Boer School," *The Canadian Magazine* 20, no. 5 (1901): 416.
47. Duff, "'Capture the Children,'" 367.

48. Shula Marks and Stanley Trapido, "Lord Milner and the South African State," *History Workshop Journal*, 8 (Autumn 1979): 50–80.
49. Terence Ranger, "African Attempts to Control Education in East and Central Africa 1900–1939," *Past and Present* 32, no. 1 (1965): 57–85.
50. Ana Isabel Madeira, "Portuguese, French and British Discourses on Colonial Education: Church-State Relations, School Expansion and Missionary Competition in Africa, 1890–1930," *Paedagogica Historica* 41, no. 1/2 (2005): 31.
51. These schools include present-day Pretoria High School for Girls, Pretoria Boys High School, Hamilton Primary School, and St. Mary's Diocesan School for Girls. For more on the "Milner schools," see William Worsfold, *Lord Milner's Work in South Africa from its Commencement in 1897 to the Peace of Vereeniging in 1902* (New York: Dutton, 1906) and *Standard Encyclopaedia of Southern Africa*, eds. D.J. Potgieter et al. (Cape Town: Nasionale Opvoedkundige Uitgewery, 1970), vol. 10, 237.

52. Eliza Riedi, "Teaching Empire: British and Dominions Women Teachers in the South African War Concentration Camps," *English Historical Review* 120, no. 489 (2005): 1320.
53. Ibid. British educators seemed to be particularly impressed by the New Brunswick education system. At the end of the war, Eldon Mullin, a former principal of the provincial Normal School, became the head of the Normal School at Pretoria and then deputy director of education for the Transvaal and Orange River colonies. See "The Late Dr. Eldon Mullin," *The Educational Review* 16, no. 10 (1903): 218. Our thanks to Wyn Millar and R.D. Gidney for passing on material from that journal. See also Katherine F.C. MacNaughton, *The Development of the Theory and Practice of Education in New Brunswick, 1784–1900*, University of New Brunswick Historical Studies, no. 1 (Fredericton: University of New Brunswick, 1947), 263.
54. Quoted in Riedi, "Teaching Empire," 1322.
55. Ibid., 1339.
56. Paul Zietsman, "The Concentration Camp Schools: Beacons of Light in the Darkness," in *Scorched Earth*, ed. Fransjohan Pretorius (Cape Town: Human & Rousseau, 2001), 87–89.
57. Riedi, "Teaching Empire," 1327.
58. Quoted in ibid., 1322.
59. After the war, the dominant form of race hostility was between the two white ethnic groups, British and Boers, and not between settlers and Africans. The concept of "race" did not become firmly synonymous with colour until the 1930s. For discussion of the meaning and politics of race in the early twentieth century, see Saul Dubow, "Afrikaner Nationalism, Apartheid and the Conceptualisation of 'Race,'" *Journal of African History* 33, no. 2 (1992): 209–37.
60. The Boers surrendered on May 31, 1902. Graham departed Canada on April 19, 1902 and arrived in Cape Town on June 1.
61. Riedi, "Teaching Empire," 1324.
62. Ibid., 1327.

63. SOSC, vol. 105, file 632, Selection of Lady Teachers from the Province of Ontario for South Africa, R.W. Scott, Secretary of State, Ottawa, to Lieut. Governor, Ontario, 26 February 1902.
64. Riedi, "Teaching Empire," 1329–30.
65. See, for example, SOSC, vol. 105, file 693, Under-Secretary of State, Selection of Lady Teachers in the Province of New Brunswick for South Africa, Scott to Lieut. Governor of New Brunswick, 26 February 1902.
66. Riedi, "Teaching Empire," 1343. Of the nineteen women teachers that accompanied Graham to South Africa, all continued on for at least a year. Some stayed considerably longer. For example, Miss Emma Ellis of Truro, NS, stayed on in South Africa for at least a decade. See *The Educational Review* (Dec. 1909): 165.
67. Riedi, "Teaching Empire," 1318.
68. Ibid., 1318.
69. "Concentration Camps. Mr. Chamberlain Defends the Policy Regarding Them," *Globe*, March 22, 1902.
70. This nationalist movement culminated in a National Party election victory in 1948 and the introduction of the white supremacist policy of *apartheid*.
71. "Their Qualifications," *Globe*, April 2, 1902, 1, quoted in Jessica Schagerl, "Global Imaginaries: Reading the International Interventions, Interactions and Imaginings of Women in English Canada, 1899–1919" (PHD diss., University of Western Ontario, London, ON, 2006), 137.
72. For a description of life in Norval's Pont, including its administration, the outbreak of disease, and doctors' response, see "Norval's Pont," The British Concentration Camps of the South African War, 1900–1902, accessed September 28, 2013, http://www2.lib.uct.ac.za/mss/bccd/Histories/Norvals_pont/.
73. Unpublished reminiscences by E. Maud Graham, dated 1931, but with last chapter dated 1947 (hereafter cited as MGUR) (copy in possession of the editors). Helen Mary Millar Becker, Recollections of Marianne Meir and Meir family, January 2005 (typescript copy in possession of the editors).
74. Andrew Armitage, *Owen Sound: Steamboat Days* (Erin, ON: Boston Mills Press, 1981), 47–48.
75. "A Farewell to Mrs. S. Graham and Miss Meir," newspaper article [newspaper and date not listed] in Maud Graham's Scrapbook [hereafter cited as MGS] (original in possession of the editors).
76. She was first elected president of the New York State WCTU, later elected in 1895 as superintendent of the Department of Medical Temperance, and by 1909 Superintendent for the Department of Medical Temperance for the World's and National Woman's Christian Temperance Union. "Mrs. J.A. Allen Died," [newspaper not listed], June 25, 1926, in MGS.
77. Sharon Anne Cook, *"Through Sunshine and Shadow": The Woman's Christian Temperance Union, Evangelism, and Reform in Ontario, 1874–1930* (Montreal and Kingston: McGill-Queen's University Press, 1995), 13.
78. "Samuel Graham Dead," newspaper article, c. 1907 in MGS.

79. "Death of Mr. John Meir, Senior," *Owen Sound Sun*, February 11, 1892.

80. Glenelg, *Broken Shackles: Old Man Henson From Slavery to Freedom*, ed. Peter Meyler (Toronto: Natural Heritage Books, 2001), 45, originally published 1889.

81. "B.M.E. Excursion," newspaper clipping in MGS.

82. MGUR, 27.

83. MGUR, 27–28.

84. This was one of a handful of such institutes in Ontario that offered advanced classical work and that had a reputation for successfully preparing its students for university entrance examinations. See R.D. Gidney and W.P.J. Millar, *Inventing Secondary Education: The Rise of the High School in Nineteenth-Century Ontario* (Montreal and Kingston: McGill-Queen's University Press, 1990), Chapters 9 and 10. On Owen Sound Collegiate Institute, in particular, note the illustrations and Maud Graham's school record.

85. Sara Z. Burke, "New Women and Old Romans: Co-education at the University of Toronto, 1884–95," *Canadian Historical Review* 80, 2 (1999): 223–25.

86. Ibid., 229.

87. See the following newspaper clippings in MGS: "Varsity Verities," [newspaper not listed], c. 1894; "Judicious Appointments," [no newspaper name or date]; "Going to South Africa," *Owen Sound Sun*, April 8, 1902; "Lawn Tennis" [no newspaper name or date]; No title, *Globe*, December 14, 1895.

88. "Personal Notes: Bryn Mawr College," *Annals of the American Academy of Political and Social Science* 8 (July 1896), 366.

89. Diana Brydon and Jessica Schagerl, "Empire Girls and Global Girls: A Dialogue on Spaces of Community in the Twentieth Century," in *Moveable Margins: The Shifting Spaces of Canadian Literature*, ed. Chelva Kanaganayakam (Toronto: Tsar Publications, 2005), 3; Helen Becker, "Memoir of Maud" (unpublished manuscript in possession of the editors), 9–10.

90. For this trend, see Carole Gerson, *Canadian Women in Print, 1750–1918* (Waterloo, ON: Wilfrid Laurier University Press, 2010). On Randal, see Sandra Gwyn, *The Private Capital: Ambition and Love in the Age of Macdonald and Laurier* (Toronto: McClelland and Stewart, 1984), 371–88.

91. See Katie Pickles, *Female Imperialism and National Identity: Imperial Order Daughters of the Empire* (Manchester: Manchester University Press, 2002).

92. Schagerl, "Global Imaginaries," 2.

93. "Christmas in Quebec," *The Farmer's Advocate*, December 9, 1909, in MGS.

94. "Many Enroll at New School of Commerce," September 8, 1928 [newspaper not listed], in MGS.

95. Such characteristics were also common among the New Zealand women recruited to teach in South Africa. Ellen Ellis writes, "They were representatives of a new social and economic group: single working women, independently pursuing higher qualifications and professional advancement." *Teachers for South Africa*, 170.

96. "Mrs. F.G. Millar Dies in Toronto," *Globe and Mail*, January 2, 1950; Becker, "Memoir of Maud," 60.

97. Becker, "Memoir of Maud," 49, 51, 61–62.

98. E. Maud Graham, "Bryn Mawr Girls and Toronto," clipping from *The Varsity*, n.d., Mary A. Meir Scrapbook, Owen Sound Public Library, quoted in Schagerl, "Global Imaginaries," 138–39.

99. Ian Hundey, *Nine Habits for Success in Teaching History* (Toronto: Emond Montgomery Publications, 2007), 106.

100. Quoted in Robert D. Denham, ed. *The Correspondence of Northrop Frye and Helen Kemp, 1932–1939*, vol. 1 (Toronto: University of Toronto Press, 1996), 98.

101. Gwyn, *The Private Capital*, 387.

102. Becker, "Memoir of Maud," 32, 52.

103. The book was reviewed in a variety of newspapers: the *Globe*, the *Review of Reviews*, *Manitoba Free Press*, *Methodist Magazine and Review*, *Glasgow Herald*. For some of this information, see Schagerl, "Global Imaginaries," 140.

104. "A Canadian Girl in South Africa," Toronto *Globe* review reprinted in *Owen Sound Sun*, January 5, 1906, in MGS. More recently, Graham's book has been used as a primary source by several historians and literary scholars writing on aspects of the South African War, the social gospel, and Canadian women's relationship to empire. See, for example, Riedi, "Teaching Empire"; Pierre Berton, *Marching as to War: Canada's Turbulent Years, 1899–1953* (Toronto: Doubleday, 2001), 68; Craig Wilcox, *Australia's Boer War: The War in South Africa, 1899–1902* (South Melbourne, Victoria: Oxford University Press, 2002); Richard Allen, *The View from Murney Tower: Salem Bland, the Late Victorian Controversies, and the Search for a New Christianity* (Toronto: University of Toronto Press, 2008), 524; Brydon and Schagerl, "Empire Girls and Global Girls"; Schagerl, "Global Imaginaries." The book is recognized as part of the culture of Canadian women's non-fiction writing and has been used as a source in more popular historical articles. Anne Innis Dagg, *The Feminine Gaze: A Canadian Compendium of Non-Fiction Women Authors and Their Books, 1836–1945* (Waterloo, ON: Wilfrid Laurier University Press, 2001), 116; William H. New, ed., *Encyclopedia of Literature in Canada* (Toronto: University of Toronto Press, 2002), 10. Graham's life and work have also been used by one specialist in education for a book aimed at demonstrating history methods to elementary and high school history teachers. See Hundey, *Nine Habits for Success in Teaching History*, 105–07.

105. Schagerl, "Global Imaginaries," 140.

106. See, for example, the Toronto *Globe*, December 23, 1905, 19. The *Methodist Magazine and Review* published a fifteen-page synopsis in March 1906. See Schagerl, "Global Imaginaries," 140.

107. Quoted in Schagerl, "Global Imaginaries," 140. Emphasis added by Schagerl.

108. Page, *The Boer War and Canadian Imperialism*, 4

109. Graham, South Africa photo album, in editors' possession.

110. Barbara Caine, *English Feminism, 1780–1980* (Oxford: Oxford University Press, 1997), 168–69. See also Elizabeth van Heyningen, "Medical History and Afrikaner Society in the Boer Republics at the end of the Nineteenth Century," *Kleio* 37 (2005): 5–25.

111. Miller, *Canada's Little War*, 16–19. Once the war was declared, English-Canadian support for the volunteers was widespread. Ibid., 30.

112. Page, *The Boer War and Canadian Imperialism*, 14. See also Carman Miller, "Loyalty, Patriotism and Resistance: Canada's Response to the Anglo-Boer War, 1899–1902," *South African Historical Journal* 41, no. 1 (1999): 317–18.

113. By "brown" Graham means tanned. This description is remarkably similar to the way in which anti-modern expressions of Canadian masculinity were projected onto the mythological and iconic Canadian Mountie. See Michael Dawson, "'That Nice Red Coat Goes to My Head Like Champagne': Gender, Antimodernism and the Mountie Image: 1880–1960," *Journal of Canadian Studies* 32, no. 3 (1997): 119–39. On depictions of Canadian manhood during the Great War, see Jonathan Vance, *Death So Noble: Memory Meaning and the First World War* (Vancouver: UBC Press, 1997), Chapter 5.

114. Graham thus fit a broader trend; Canadian historians have generally concluded that while Canadian nationalism and British imperialism were easily reconciled in the minds of English Canadians during the late nineteenth century, these two strands of identity began to unwind in the aftermath of the Great War. See Carl Berger, *The Sense of Power: Studies in the Ideas of Canadian Imperialism, 1867–1914* (Toronto: University of Toronto Press, 1970) and Mary Vipond, "Nationalism and Nativism: The Natives Sons of Canada in the 1920s." *Canadian Review of Studies in Nationalism* 9, no. 1 (1982): 81–95.

115. Three young men from Owen Sound who died in the Boer War (W.H. Ingram, 26; Chas. N. Evans, 28; T. Bertrand Day, 24), all of whom attended Owen Sound Collegiate Institute, were commemorated on a plaque unveiled at the school in 1902. "Unveiling of the Memorial Tablet," October 31, 1902, in MGS.

116. Becker, "Memoir of Maud," 12. For Florence Randal's positive account of the "Imperialistic aims" of anglicizing Boer children, whom she called "lovable" despite their "lack of truthfulness and sense of honour," see "A Year in a Boer School," 411–17.

117. Randal, "A Year in a Boer School," 412.

118. Gwyn, *The Private Capital*, 373. Seven of the twenty women in Graham's group were still teaching in South Africa in 1905 when the book was published. See Graham, Chapter I in this volume.

119. Shula Marks, "British Nursing and the South African War" in *Writing a Wider War*, 159–85. For similar findings regarding other teachers from Britain and the Dominions, see Riedi, "Teaching Empire," 1331–34. The New Zealand teachers, too, were lured to South Africa "by a sense of duty, but also adventure." Sandra Coney, Foreword to *Teachers for South Africa*, by Ellis, 7.

120. On the established itineraries for Canadian travellers to London, see Cecilia Morgan, *"A Happy Holiday": English Canadians and Transatlantic Tourism, 1870–1930* (Toronto: University of Toronto Press, 2008), Chapter 5.

121. Graham became engaged to an English soldier who, after returning home, broke off the engagement. See Becker, "Memoir of Maud," 14.

122. On this travel writing trope, see Mary Louise Pratt, *Imperial Eyes: Studies in Travel Writing and Transculturation* (London: Routledge, 1992), 201–08.

123. Morgan, *"A Happy Holiday,"* 26.

124. Ibid., 9. For an intriguing glimpse of Canadian female travellers in India, Southeast Asia, and Barbados, see Gail Campbell, "New Brunswick Women Travellers and the British Connection, 1845–1905," in *Canada and the British World*, eds., Buckner and Francis, 83–86.

125. Grey Roots Museum and Archives, Mary A. Meir Scrapbook, "A Bright Canadian Girl," *The Farmer's Advocate*, c. 1906.

126. Grey Roots Museum and Archives, Mary A. Meir Scrapbook, "Bryn Mawr Girls and Toronto," newspaper clipping (likely *The Varsity*), c. 1897.

127. Graham, South Africa photo album, in editors' possession.

128. On the imperial and pedagogic uses of sport see, for example, J.A. Mangan, *The Games Ethic and Imperialism: Aspects of the Diffusion of an Ideal* (New York: Viking, 1986) and Brian Stoddart, "Sport, Cultural Imperialism and Colonial Response in the British Empire" in *Sport, Culture and History: Region, Nation and Globe*, ed. Brian Stoddart (London: Routledge, 2008), 114–40. For an interpretation that cogently assesses late nineteenth- and early twentieth-century internationalist impulses in sport, see Barbara J. Keys, *Globalizing Sport: National Rivalry and International Community in the 1930s* (Cambridge, MA: Harvard University Press, 2006).

129. SOSC, vol. 103, file 345, Memorandum Respecting the Engagement of Teachers for the Refugee Camps in South Africa, n.d., c. November 1901.

130. Brendon, *The Decline and Fall of the British Empire*, 180.

131. W.B. Worsford, *Sir Bartle Frere* (1923), 225, quoted in Brendon, *The Decline and Fall of the British Empire*, 182.

132. Grey Roots Museum and Archives, Mary A. Meir Scrapbook, "Teachers for the Boers," *Globe*, 2 April 1902, 1.

133. On the prevalence of this type of thinking in Canada at the time, see Miller, *Painting the Map Red*, 17.

134. Brendon, *The Decline and Fall of the British Empire*, 227–28.

135. Ibid., 226–27.

136. Miller, "Loyalty, Patriotism and Resistance," 321.

137. On the possibilities of travel experiences encouraging reflective assessments and genuine intercultural exchange, see, for example, Pratt, *Imperial Eyes*; Jeremy Black, "France and the Grand Tour in the Early Eighteenth Century," *Francia* 11 (1983): 407–16; and Dennis Merrill, *Negotiating Paradise: U.S. Tourism and Empire in Twentieth-Century Latin America* (Chapel Hill: University of North Carolina Press, 2009).

138. For more on the complex history of pass laws, see the online encyclopedia *South African History Online*, s.v., "Pass Laws in South Africa 1800–1994," accessed October 19, 2011, http://www.sahistory.org.za/south-africa-1806-1899/pass-laws-south-africa-1800-1994.

139. See, for example, the work of Clive Whitehead: "The Education of Women and Girls: An Aspect of British Colonial Policy," *Journal of Educational Administration and History* 16, no. 2 (1984), 24–34; "The Historiography of British Imperial Education Policy, Part II: African and the Rest of the Colonial Empire," *History of Education* 34, no. 4 (2005),

441–54; and "The Concept of British Education Policy in the Colonies, 1850–1960," *Journal of Educational Administration and History* 39 (2007): 161–73.

140. For an early and important exploration of the influence of gender on the traveller's gaze, see Susan L. Blake, "A Woman's Trek: What Difference Does Gender Make?" *Women's Studies International Forum* 13, no. 4 (1990): 347–55. On "contact zones," see Pratt, *Imperial Eyes*.

141. The remainder of the images were either of poor quality, too small to reproduce effectively, or unavailable.

A Canadian Girl in South Africa

BY E. MAUD GRAHAM

Overleaf: Cover and title page image from the original edition of A *Canadian Girl in South Africa*. In her album, Graham wrote, “What, ho, she bumps!”

Dedication

TO THE MANY South African and Canadian friends who have urged me to publish these notes, but especially to the following eight ladies of Fauresmith and Kroonstad, whose birthplaces number almost as many parts of the Empire, and whose latchstrings were always hung out to me during my twenty-five months in the Orange River Colony, this book is dedicated:

Mrs. Jacobus Meintjes
" Peter Truby
" Philip Voortman
" John Polson
" E. Hely-Hutchison Burke
" Frank Pope
" Benjamin Noakes
" Homan James

A Note of Thanks

I WISH TO THANK Mr. Joseph Pope, Under-Secretary of State; Mr. F. Colson, of the Department of the Secretary of State; and the Bloemfontein *Post*, for help received.

E. MAUD GRAHAM.

Owen Sound, November 1st, 1905.

Contents

Illustrations

* *Indicates that these photos are not reproduced in this edition.*

Frontispiece from the original edition of *A Canadian Girl in South Africa*. Norval's Pont Refugee Camp Teachers, With Gen. De Wet in Centre, June 21st, 1902. English, Scottish, Dutch and Canadian female teachers. The back row features, starting sixth from left, Canadians "McDonald, Graham, Arbuckle and McKenzie." The front row features, starting fourth from left, Mr. Erasmus, Dutch Headmaster in Camp; Mr. Gunn, Director of Education, Orange River Colony; Gen. Christiaan De Wet; Mr. Malerby, Dutch Minister in the Camp.

CHAPTER I

The Call to South Africa

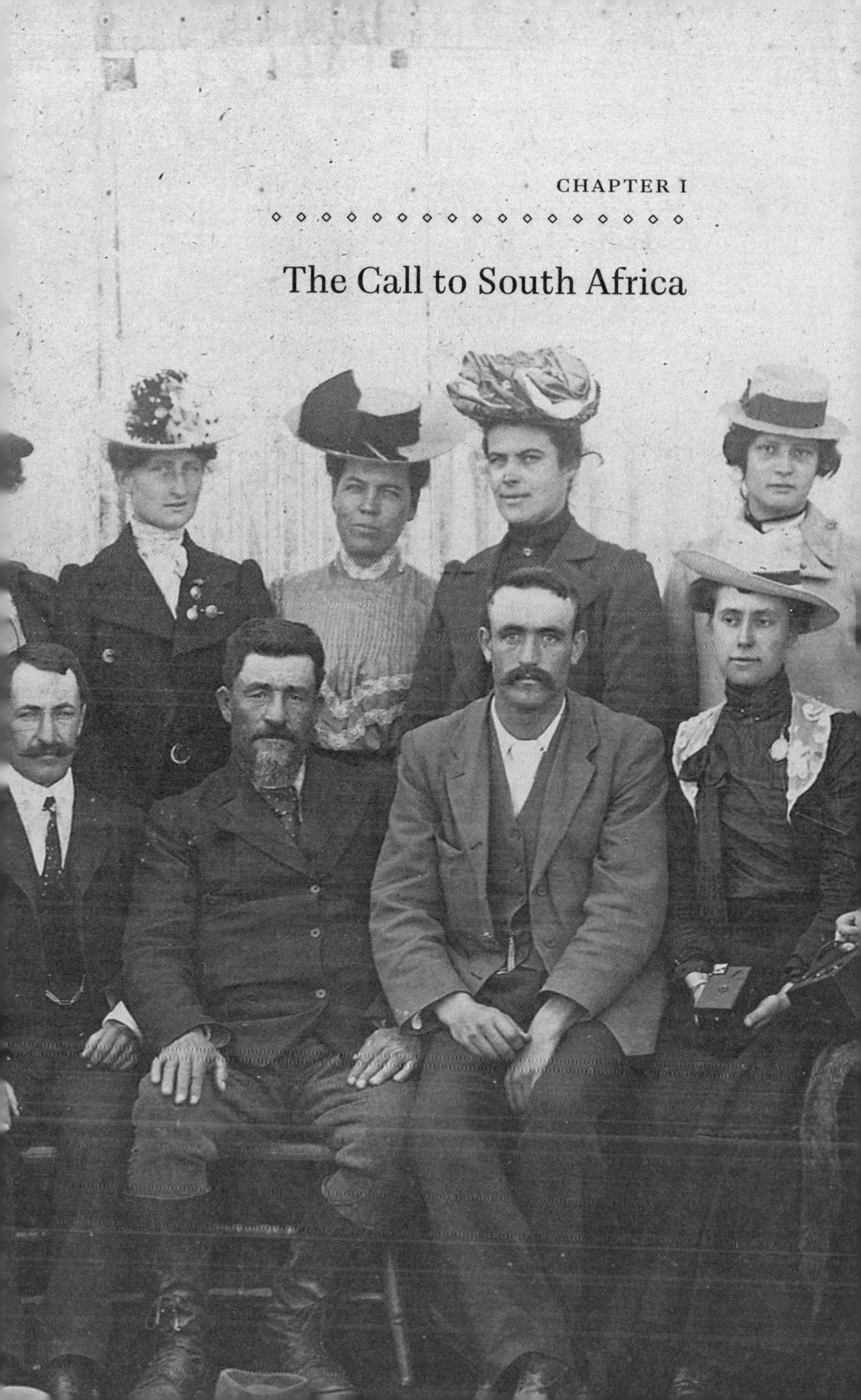

"I WISH I WERE A GIRL. You girls have the best of everything nowadays," said a stalwart Rugby man, an old Varsity[1] acquaintance, as he listened to some of the experiences of the Canadian girls in Africa.

And he was right. Imagine, if you can, forty girls of a hundred years ago being taken on a trip half around the world, fêted *en route* like princesses, all expenses and comforts provided by their Government, and paid besides £100 each for their services as teachers. Or imagine, if you can, forty men of the present day being treated in like manner! Yet such was the way in which forty Canadian girls were treated by the British Government in 1902.

This is how it happened. When Lord Kitchener was appointed Commander-in-Chief in South Africa, towards the close of the late Anglo-Boer war, he saw that so long as the outlying villages and farms were inhabited, guerrilla warfare would continue indefinitely, and he conceived the idea of forming large camps in which to gather all refugees friendly to Great Britain, the women, children and non-combatants from the outlying villages and farms, all Boers who had kept the oath of neutrality taken under Lord Roberts,[2] and any others who would take the oath of allegiance to the British Government. These camps were spoken of indifferently as "Refugee" or "Concentration" camps. The crops and stock throughout the country were then destroyed, and it has become a matter of history how this policy hastened the end of the war. As the various commandos of Dutch surrendered, those who would take the oath of allegiance were sent to the camps, while those who would not—known as "Irreconcilables"—were sent to prison camps at Green Point, near Cape Town, St. Helena, Ceylon, or India.

Naturally these "refugee" camps contained all the poorest people, as well as many of the wealthier who had not fled to Cape

---

1. "Varsity" refers to the University of Toronto.
2. Lord Roberts was the commander-in-chief of the British Forces in South Africa from December 1899 to November 1900. He was succeeded by Kitchener.

Colony or Europe at the beginning of hostilities. As large numbers of the children had never had a chance to go to school, Lord Milner[3] and others in authority thought it an excellent opportunity to help these children by organizing camp schools, and under the circumstances it was deemed advisable to have British teachers. It was Mr. Chamberlain's[4] idea to have volunteers from all parts of the Empire, and each colony was asked to send a certain number. In due time contingents of teachers sailed from New Zealand, Australia and Canada, as well as from the Home Country.

The Canadians were the first colonials to go. As their pathway led through England they naturally had many opportunities which the others missed. The Colonial Office in London had asked for forty teachers from Canada; over a thousand applied. Those chosen were under contract with the Colonial Office for one year's service, with free rations, household necessities, medical attendance, free passage, second-class, to and from South Africa, *via* England, and £100 in cash. The Canadian Government supplemented this by paying for first-class passage to Liverpool; and everybody knows that second-class to the Cape is equal to first on all the smaller Atlantic boats.

The forty girls from Canada were divided into two parties of twenty each, sailing on different dates. Of the party of twenty to which I belonged, not one returned at the end of their contract year, so much were we interested in our work. After that period we were paid by the particular colony in which we happened to be stationed, and our passage home was eventually paid for by the same colony. Of these twenty, one, Miss Sylvia Lee, of Waterloo, Quebec, fell a victim to enteric,[5] and was buried on the veldt; six have married

---

3. Sir Alfred Milner (1854–1925) was British high commissioner for Southern Africa from 1897 to 1905.
4. Joseph Chamberlain (1836–1914) was British secretary of state for the colonies from 1895 to 1903.
5. Enteric is an intestinal disease, usually contracted by ingesting contaminated food or water.

in South Africa, six have returned home, and the remaining seven, so far as I know, are still engaged in their work of teaching. Of the other twenty girls I cannot speak definitely, as they were so widely scattered we could not keep in touch with one another.

Concerning the work done by these forty girls we read in the Government Report of December, 1902:

> "To the judicious selection on the part of the gentlemen at the head of the educational departments in the several provinces is due the admirable result of the undertaking; the entire contingent, it is gratifying to know, having given complete satisfaction, both as regards its personnel and the accomplishment of its purpose. As the request, in itself, was a tribute to the systems of education in the Dominion, so the outcome may justly be regarded as a striking proof of their high standard of excellence and efficiency."

The complete list of the names is as follows:

(1) Sailing from Halifax, by the *Corinthian*, April 12th, 1902:
Miss Katherine McLellan, Toronto, Ont.
" Margaret D. Scott, Hamilton, Ont.
" Florence J. Wilkinson, Toronto, Ont.
" Edna E. O'Brien, Nobleton, Ont.
" Florence Randall, Ottawa, Ont.
" Ruby M. Rothwell, Ottawa, Ont.
" Julia Urquhart, Ottawa, Ont.
" E. Maud MacFarlane, Peterboro', Ont.
" Eleanor M. Yenney, Peterboro', Ont.
" Berta Brydon, King, Ont.
" Libbie Rodger, Belwood, Ont.
" Sara E. Drysdale, Perth, Ont.
" Mabel K. Coffey, Millington, Que.
" Sarah L. Abbott, Montreal, Que.

" Isabel Perry, Montreal, Que.

" Davina Rodger, Belwood, Ont.

" Augusta E. Hoover, Toronto Junction, Ont.

" Georgia A. Grant, Newington, Ont.

" Annie Moulton, Gananoque, Ont.

" E.E. MacBurney, Montreal, Que.

(2) Sailing from St. John, by the *Lake Ontario*, April 19th, 1902:

Miss C. Gertrude Arbuckle, Summerside, P.E.I.

" Maude L. Bremner, Charlottetown, P.E.I.

" Grace Dutcher, Charlottetown, P.E.I.

" Agnes L. Carr, St. John, N.B.

" Annie I. Burns, St. John, N.B.

" Ida E. McLeod, Fredericton, N.B.

" Winnifred Johnston, Fredericton, N.B.

" Mabel V. Elliott, Newcastle, N.B.

" Sophy M. Pickle, Bloomfield, N.B.

" Jessie Fleet, Montreal, Que.

" Sylvia B. Lee, Waterloo, Que.

" Susanna Younghusband, Portage la Prairie, Man.

" Edith A. Murray, Winnipeg, Man.

" Ella D. Crandall, Walton, N.S.

" Ellen M. MacKenzie, Stellarton, N.S.

" Blanche MacDonald, Hopewell, N.S.

" Margaret W. De Wolfe, Halifax, N.S.

" Bertha B. Hebb, Bridgewater, N.S.

" Emma Ellis, Truro, N.S.

" E. Maud Graham, Owen Sound, Ont.

I cannot speak too highly of the kindly way in which we were treated while under the Colonial Office. In addition to the contract salary we were given a daily travelling allowance for incidental expenses; at Liverpool and London ladies were waiting to meet us; at Southampton, mysterious boxes were shipped with us, which later revealed every possible convenience for camp use; at Cape Town we were met and chaperoned up country.

Under the circumstances, our trip to Africa was unique, and scarcely to be duplicated in this generation. Doubtless much of the hospitality heaped upon us girls in London was due to the enthusiasm aroused there by our brave Canadian boys who had preceded us to Africa. The opening chapters, therefore, contain a short account of that trip, written chiefly in recognition of the exceeding kindness of the English people, who impressed us indelibly with the sincerity of their wish to treat the new South African colonies in a spirit of the broadest-minded liberality.[6] The succeeding chapters,

---

6. This interpretation of the British approach to the newly conquered territories of the Transvaal and Orange Free State clearly reflects Graham's loyalty to the British Empire and her uncritical view of the war. In reality the war was highly controversial in Britain. Once it became clear that victory would be neither quick nor painless, and news spread of the concentration camps, the British public grew increasingly critical of the ruling Conservative government's war policies and practices. A significant number of Britons believed the Boers were victims of British incompetence or cruelty, while others defended the imperial war on "backward" Boers and expansion of the empire. After the war, therefore, attitudes in Britain towards the new colonies were mixed: some people felt they had a duty to help rebuild Boer communities and economies; others believed Britain to be superior in culture and its government the bearer of civilization and modernization to primitive societies. As for the government, immediately after the war British authorities were fearful of a possible "Native rebellion" in the region, as African elites, who had participated extensively in the war on the side of the British, fully expected to obtain political and economic rights denied to them under Boer rule. But the British had no intention of improving social and political conditions for Africans, and therefore containing them quickly became the predominant postwar concern. Doing so required uniting the four British settler colonies (Cape, Natal, Transvaal, and Orange River Colony) into one cohesive state in order to be able to effectively police Africans' movements and labour. With the intention of uniting the two white populations, therefore, the British sought reconciliation with the defeated and embittered Boers. For more on British attitudes towards the war, see Arthur Davey, *The British Pro-Boers, 1877–1902* (Cape Town: Tafelberg, 1978), and Steve Attridge, *Nationalism, Imperialism, and Identity in Late Victorian Culture: Civil and Military Worlds* (New York: Palgrave Macmillan, 2003). On African participation in the war, see Peter Warwick, *Black People and the South African War, 1899–1902* (Cambridge: Cambridge University Press, 1983), and Bill Nasson, *The South African War, 1899–1902* (London: Arnold, 1999).

as far as the one on Kroonstad, are an attempt to picture everyday life since the close of the late war, and to correct prevalent erroneous ideas about the South African Dutch. With this aim in view I have given a somewhat chronological sketch of the first year of my life amongst the people. In the later chapters I have attempted to explain the various questions agitating the public mind, in some cases threatening the future welfare of the country. One thing is certain, that most of the glaring faults of the administration are not due to the policy of the Home Government, but to the culpable incapacity of many of the officials, who have obtained their positions, no one knows why. One of the hopeful signs, however, is that many of these men, from various departments, have been dismissed during the past year and a half.

As I look back over the time spent in the new South African colonies, I am forcibly struck by the resemblance of conditions there to the swirling waters of the Niagara. The tumultuous cataract plunges over the edge of the rock with a force which buries it to a depth of a hundred feet below the surface of the river. This surface water, partly concealed by the mist, heaves with a gentle motion, which alone betrays the fierce current beneath, and on it the little "Maid of the Mist"[7] sails securely. But some distance down stream that current rises to the surface and rushes in angry seething rapids to the whirlpool, the most dangerous part of all the river. So it was with South Africa. The catastrophe of the war was followed by a year of calm, when credit was good, and men's deeper feelings hidden by their joy at being home again and renewing old friendships and habits of life. But in the second year, when bankruptcy strode through the land, hidden passions revealed themselves in

---

7. The *Maid of the Mist* is a sightseeing vessel that allows tourists a close-up view of Niagara Falls. On the symbolism of the Falls, see Karen Dubinsky, *The Second Greatest Disappointment: Honeymooning and Tourism at Niagara Falls* (Toronto: Between the Lines, 1999).

racial animosity[8] and general discontent with the administration and the delay in granting the promised self-government.[9] There is no lack of croakers to predict that South Africa has not yet reached her whirlpool. Time alone will show whether or not she is nearing the season of prosperity which will give her the beautiful serenity of Niagara as it flows into Lake Ontario.

The party of girls to which I belonged sailed from St. John, New Brunswick, April 19th, 1902, in the *Lake Ontario*, of the Elder-Dempster Line, after a kindly send-off from Mr. Colson, representing the Canadian Secretary of State. The voyage was an average one, broken by the usual details of a squall, sea-sickness, and games on deck—hopscotch, shuffle-board, quoits, etc. The gentlemen, without exception, tried to make it pleasant for us, even giving us the freedom of their smoke-room[10] on deck, as the number of cattle on board made it very stuffy below.

Amongst the passengers were two clergymen, Rev. Mr. Hastie, Presbyterian, and Rev. Mr. Scovil, Anglican, who took turns in the services on the two Sundays at sea, and were the last Canadians we saw, later, on the pier at Southampton. Another passenger was

8. Here "racial animosity" refers to ongoing tensions between Britons and Boers. After the war the dominant form of racial antipathy in South Africa was between the two white ethnic groups, not between settlers and black people; indeed, it was not until the 1930s that "race" became firmly synonymous with colour and race tensions shifted in the main to between whites and blacks. For discussion of the meaning and politics of race in the early twentieth century, see Saul Dubow, "Afrikaner Nationalism, Apartheid and the Conceptualisation of 'Race,'" *Journal of African History* 33, no. 2 (1992): 209–37; and Susanne M. Klausen, *Race, Maternity, and the Politics of Birth Control in South Africa, 1910–1939* (Basingstoke, UK: Palgrave Macmillan, 2004).
9. The Boers officially surrendered on May 31, 1902 with the Treaty of Vereeniging. Although the British won the war, they immediately aimed at uniting the four white settler colonies in order to be able to control the far larger, subject African population. Therefore, the terms of settlement included the promise of limited self-government to the Transvaal (formerly the South African Republic) and the Orange River Colony (formerly the Orange Free State), granted in 1906 and 1907 respectively, on terms already enjoyed in the Cape and Natal. The four British colonies united to form the Union of South Africa in 1910.
10. The smoke-room was a room set aside for tobacco use and alcohol consumption.

Mr. Gibbs, an engineer from the unfortunate *Lake Superior*,[11] who piloted us through the engine rooms, and along the shaft to the very keel of the ship. Several of us amused the stokers vastly by trying to shovel in coal. There was also a Marconi instrument[12] on board, making experiments, in charge of an electrician who was unable to get any answer until near the Irish coast.

When we reached the cold, foggy sea off the banks of Newfoundland we found ourselves in the midst of a fishing fleet, and some chapters of Kipling's "Captains Courageous" passed before our eyes.[13] We signalled a large schooner to know if she had any mail to send, but she replied that she had not. In the course of further conversation we learned that she was French, and would not return home for a whole year.

During the voyage we laid plans for our sojourn in London, not knowing or dreaming of the way in which that was being arranged for us. The way we acted was rather absurdly characteristic of Canadian or American girls. We decided to organize. Miss McLeod, of Fredericton, was selected chairman, and Miss De Wolfe, of Halifax, secretary. As Miss Carr, of St. John, had formerly lived in London, we asked her if she would kindly act as leader, or guide, for us. We also concluded that as a party of twenty girls could not wander about London without attracting attention, we would wear the stolid expression of Indians, even if the Abbey were to fall at our feet.

As we neared Liverpool the days passed all too quickly, and it was with genuine regret that we had our last "sing-song," and said good-bye to the *Lake Ontario* and Captain Ellis. Everyone felt that the old boat was the last link with Canada.

11. The *Lake Superior* was a ship operated by the Beaver Line that sank without loss of life on March 31, 1902.
12. Guglielmo Marconi had recently developed wireless telegraph technology.
13. *Captains Courageous* was Rudyard Kipling's 1897 novel about a spoiled young American man who is washed overboard at sea and rescued by the crew of a fishing schooner. His time with the fishing crew transforms him into a mature and industrious young man.

CHAPTER II

London

AT THE LIVERPOOL DOCK some ladies met us with the cheering news that we were to have ten days in London. They helped us get our baggage through the customs, which gave us no trouble at all, the officials merely asking with a laugh whether we had any whiskey or tobacco to declare. We then drove to the station of the London and North-Western,[1] where there was a corridor coach reserved for us. Our Liverpool friends said good-bye, giving us each a package of sweetened chocolate to keep up our spirits until lunch-time.

That corridor coach was exciting.[2] We visited from one compartment to another, and decided unanimously that such a car was ideal. Presently lunch was served in the dining-car, the way to which made us feel like a band of exploring Westerners. We had to pass through half-a-dozen coaches, crowded with people, each with its own luggage compartment, a system which we found afterwards to be much more speedy than the American fashion of having all the luggage in one large car. In the middle of some of the carriages the corridor crossed to the other side. The cross-section was arranged with shelves for hand baggage, and the compartments opening in one direction were labelled "Ladies only," while those opening the other way were apparently for gentlemen.

The country along the London and North-Western is mostly in sheep farms, and the small grey sheep with their short legs, in the prim little fields surrounded by hedges, interested us greatly. But meantime a great cloud of smoke in the distance steadily growing larger, indicated that London was near. Soon we streamed into Euston station, where there were more ladies to meet us. One, Miss Mansfield, in introducing herself, told us that she was appointed by the Colonial Office to see that we had a good time in London; a duty she fulfilled most thoroughly and gracefully. When we had driven to

---

1. Graham is referring here to the London and North Western Railway.
2. Corridor coaches were a new development at the turn of the century and facilitated passenger movement on board the train, particularly to and from another recent addition to train travel: the restaurant car.

our hotel we found a pleasant surprise waiting for us in the form of cards to a tea at Miss Balfour's, Downing Street, for the following afternoon.[3]

The rest of that day was a whirl of callers, London friends and some of the first party of Canadian teachers. The afternoon was broken by a trip down to the Colonial Office to report ourselves and to have our cheques cashed for the first month's salary, which was paid in advance.

Thursday morning, May 1st, we started out to "do" London on the top front seats of the busses, when we could get them. It is an excellent way to see things, for the drivers are so obliging in explaining everything. It was the height of the London season, and the city was very crowded, yet the streets seemed quiet to us without the horrid clang of trolley cars. Electric trams, as the English call them, are not allowed to run on the surface except in the suburbs. The crowds at the crossings were comparatively easy to penetrate, thanks to the universal courtesy of the policemen, and also to the excellent system of "refuges." These are elevated lamp-post platforms in the middle of each crossing; all traffic in one direction must keep to one side of them, and all in the other direction to the other side.

In the afternoon, at Miss Balfour's, we met, to our great delight, Lord and Lady Roberts.[4] There were also present Earl Grey, now Governor-General; Lady Edward Cecil, now Lady Salisbury; the Bishop of Rochester, now the Archbishop of Canterbury; Hon Alfred and Mrs. Lyttleton; Mr. and Miss Chamberlain, and a score of other well-known people.[5] We were formally presented to Lord and Lady

---

3. Miss Alice Balfour, the sister of Arthur Balfour who would soon succeed Lord Salisbury as prime minister, was the author of *Twelve Hundred Miles in a Wagon*, a recounting of her travels in South Africa.
4. Lord Roberts had commanded British forces in South Africa from December 1899 until November 1900.
5. The 4th Earl Grey (1851–1917) was an experienced British politician and an advocate of imperial federation who served as the administrator for Southern Rhodesia before his appointment, in 1904, as Governor General of Canada. Lady Salisbury was the wife of

Roberts and a few others, but with the majority we had the fun of guessing who they were from their pictures. A lady was talking to me whom I was admiring as a very handsome, fresh-looking English girl, when a gentleman, whom I recognized as Mr. Balfour, brought us some ices, and from him I learned that the "English girl" was the Duchess of Marlborough. Certainly English air has agreed with her.

After tea we were taken to a large drawing-room, where Mr. Sadler, of the Educational Department,[6] made us a neat little speech, giving us a definite idea of what we were expected to do in South Africa. Then Mr. Joseph Chamberlain gave an earnest address on the dignity and importance of our work, and what it might do for the Empire. After some music Miss Balfour showed us several historic rooms which are never open to the public. First, was the library where Gladstone[7] formerly held his cabinet meetings, a fine room overlooking the garden, with St. James Park beyond the wall. Near this was the Treasury Room, where the Lords of the Treasury are supposed to meet, but where they gather only once a year to appoint the First Lord of the Treasury. There were several mysterious-looking boxes on the table, and at one end a massive chair, last used by George III.

That evening we went to the House of Commons, where the Speaker's and the Ladies' Galleries were reserved for us. As these are at opposite ends of the chamber, we had a fine view of everything. We had heard that this chamber was small, but were surprised to find it so very small that if a large number of members attend, many are obliged to find seats in the galleries, where they may not speak.

British Prime Minister Robert Gascoyne-Cecil (Lord Salisbury). Frederick Temple (1821–1902) served as Archbishop of Canterbury from 1896 until his death. Alfred Lyttelton (1857–1913) was a prominent sportsman and politician who was appointed to oversee South Africa's reconstruction between 1900 and 1903. Mrs. Lyttelton (1865–1948) was born Edith Sophy Balfour and accompanied her husband on his travels to South Africa where she developed a keen interest in imperial endeavours and played a key role in organizing the Victorian League.

6. The reference here is to Michael Sadler (1861–1943).

7. William Gladstone (1809–1898) served as British prime minister on four separate occasions.

The Speaker and the clerks below him with their wigs and gowns looked quite imposing, but their dignity was evidently non-existent for the occupants of the Ministerial bench, who calmly put their feet on the Speaker's table. Indeed, the conduct of the members generally made one think of a lot of frolicsome school-boys. They were lounging about, hats on or off, and if a dull man rose to speak they began to read or talk, and paid no attention whatever. We were unfortunate in not hearing a good debate, only a discussion over a Ways and Means Bill; but had the pleasure of listening to Mr. Balfour, Mr. Lyttleton, Lord Stanley, Mr. Bryce, Mr. Dillon, Mr. O'Connor and our own Mr. Blake.[8] The sergeant-at-arms then led us about the building, and about midnight we saw the members file out for a division.[9]

Next day, Friday, was spent in choosing school supplies to take out with us, and in saying good-bye to the first party of twenty, who were to sail for the Cape the following day. The mail that day brought a shower of invitations which promised to keep us busy in London. In the evening we saw Sir Henry Irving in "Faust."

The chief event for Saturday was a visit to the Royal Mews, at Buckingham Palace. The stables contained some hundred and fifty horses in old-fashioned open stalls. The King's racers were not there, of course, but we saw the ordinary carriage horses, the beautiful black procession horses, and the famous Hanoverian creams,[10] which are not really cream at all, but a light khaki, with manes and tails lighter still, and pinkish eyes. In the harness room were many cases of splendid harness. One set of red and brass, made for George III.,

---

8. Edward Blake was a former leader of the federal Liberal Party in Canada and then served as an Irish Nationalist member of Parliament.

9. Graham is describing a formal vote requiring MPs to leave their seats in the House of Commons and indicate their support for or opposition to a motion by registering their view in person in one of two division lobbies.

10. Hanoverian creams are a breed of horses used to draw the coaches of English monarchs from the early eighteenth century until the early 1920s.

was evidently the model for the handsome red and gold set made for Queen Victoria's Diamond Jubilee, and worn by the creams. In the carriage rooms were a number of perfectly plain carriages, some made on specially easy springs for the late Queen's use. There was also the magnificent red and gold coach for state processions, drawn by the creams, built in the reign of George III., of beautifully carved oak, covered with gold leaf, the body of the coach decorated with paintings, and the upholstery of red. The coach weighs about two tons. In the stable-yard some horses were being exercised with an accompaniment of drums, whistles and flags.

After leaving the Mews we took the Underground for St. Paul's Cathedral, where we had tickets of admission to the crypts, whispering gallery, etc. In the crypts the most conspicuous object is Wellington's great funeral car, made of metal from guns captured in his battles. Amongst the illustrious dead in St. Paul's are Wellington, Nelson, Sir Arthur Sullivan and Turner.[11] In the curious whispering gallery, high up in the dome, a whisper on one side of it may be heard distinctly on the other, a hundred and eighty feet across. Outside of the dome there is said to be a fine view on a clear day, but our visit was paid on a very gloomy day, and all my impressions of St. Paul's are hazy in consequence. We could not visit the Abbey, as it was undergoing repairs for the Coronation.

That evening we went to Drury Lane, where there was a very wonderful spectacular production of "Ben Hur."

Next day, Sunday, I spent in one of the suburbs, with friends living there. A number of the girls, however, went to a tea where they met Madame Albani.[12]

---

11. Field Marshall Arthur Wellesley, 1st Duke of Wellington (1769–1852), was a prominent British military leader and statesman in the early nineteenth century. Perhaps best remembered for defeating Napoleon at the Battle of Waterloo, he twice served as prime minister of Great Britain. Horatio Nelson (1758–1805) was a British naval hero best known for his victory and death at the Battle of Trafalgar. Sir Arthur Sullivan (1842–1900) was an English composer most famous for his collaborative work with dramatist W.S. Gilbert. J.M.W. Turner (1775–1851) was a British watercolour landscape artist.
12. Emma Albani (1847–1930) was a Canadian-born opera singer.

On Monday afternoon we were entertained by Miss Harvey of the Victorian League at the Imperial Institute. I am ashamed to confess that up to that time we knew nothing of the Victorian League or the splendid work it had undertaken along with the Guild of Loyal Women of South Africa, the Daughters of the Empire in Canada, and kindred societies, in furthering patriotism by spreading a knowledge of the different parts of the British Empire. During the afternoon Miss Baden-Powell,[13] Miss Fawcett,[14] and other ladies who had been in South Africa, told us many interesting things of the camp life there, and that we could hire Boer girls and Kafirs to do our housework.[15] The ladies gave us much good advice, and finally embarrassed us by presenting a farewell poem written by the daughter of the Bishop of Winchester. It was rather like getting a medal before earning it.

The poem was as follows:

GODSPEED.

"You who have come from your snowland,
Crossing the main,
Touched on the shore of our Homeland,
Starting again;

"Bridging the width of two oceans,
Weaving a rope
Linking the mighty St Lawrence
To streams of 'Good Hope.'

13. Very likely Agnes Baden-Powell, sister of Robert Baden-Powell, and a thus a key player in the establishment of the Girl Scouts in 1910.

14. Presumably, Graham is referring to Philippa Fawcett (1868–1948), the noted mathematician who played an active role in setting up schools in South Africa between 1902 and 1905. She was the daughter of the suffragist Millicent Garrett Fawcett.

15. "Kafir" was a derogatory term for Africans used by the British and the Boers and derived from the Arabic word for infidel.

"Go from the shore of the Homeland,
Cheered for your start,
Warmed with the grip of her handshake,
Straight from the heart.

"Feel that she glows with your triumphs,
Thrills with your toil;
Longs that the seed which you scatter
May spring in good soil.

"There in the land of the sunshine,
Children, large eyed,
Wait for the light you will bring them,
Drawn to your side.

"Children, the germ of a nation,
Of peoples to be,
Under one Flag, in one Empire,
Prosperous, free.

"Clasp those small hands in your own, then,
Draw them with love,
Tell them we work for one Master—
Our Father above.

"Tell them we look for one Homeland,
We pray the same prayer,
We love the good Shepherd who folds us
So tenderly here.

"Pray that all feuds may be ended,
All enmity cease,
That we all may fight under one Banner-
The Banner of Peace."

Tuesday we were invited to visit Hatfield, Lord Salisbury's[16] famous country-seat, thirty miles north of London. There was a first-class car reserved for us, and we were met at Hatfield station by Lady Edward Cecil, Lord Salisbury's daughter-in-law, who led us about the house and grounds herself. Hatfield House is said to be one of the finest examples of the old style of English country-house. I may not attempt to describe it fully here, but will refer to a rather excellent account of the public rooms, given in *Pearson's*, for May, 1902.[17] A few of the most noted historical features are the "Lion Oak," mentioned in Domesday Book,[18] still in a flourishing condition; the stables, formerly the old Tudor Hatfield where Mary kept Elizabeth a prisoner; and the large tapestries in the stone gallery or cloister. These tapestries, made in Norman times, were formerly full of gold thread, but during the Wars of the Roses the gold was melted out. Hatfield is filled with beautiful things, trophies of travel and gifts from kings and emperors; but what impresses the visitor from America most strongly is the profusion of magnificent carving everywhere in the house. Lord Salisbury being away, we had a glimpse of his private rooms: first was the library crammed with books, simply furnished, with a large window opening on the quaint Elizabethan rose-garden; opening out of this was the bedroom, just a large chemical laboratory with a bed in an alcove; beyond it were bath-room and dressing-room. The serious simplicity of all the family rooms bore out the tales one reads of the simple dignity and kindly generosity of the late Lord Salisbury.[19] After tea and a stroll in the park, we returned to town.

---

16. Lord Salisbury was Robert Gascoyne-Cecil, then prime minister of Great Britain.
17. *Pearson's* was a monthly magazine focusing on politics and the arts.
18. The *Domesday Book*, Britain's oldest surviving public record, was commissioned by William the Conqueror in 1086 as a landholding survey to determine the extent of the taxes he could raise.
19. Salisbury died in 1903.

On Wednesday we visited the Tate Gallery, where we were to meet the Hon. Maud Stanley, who had invited us to tea.[20] In the Tate Gallery are gathered most of the finest modern works from the National Gallery; the Watts collection, many of Landseer's pictures and other famous modern paintings being here. Miss Stanley then took us across Lambeth Bridge to Lambeth Palace, the home of the Archbishop of Canterbury. The late Archbishop, a frail old man on crutches, welcomed us kindly, and gave us the freedom of the house. Such a quaint old place it was, the chapel and all the older parts being thirteenth century. We were taken through shuddery dungeons and corridors in the Lollards' Tower to gaze at the old whipping post with its gruesome associations. The Puritans had destroyed all that was beautiful in the palace, but from descriptions in books the chapel had been restored. We then re-crossed the bridge to Miss Stanley's for tea.

Next day, Thursday, we were invited to Lord Strathcona's country house, Knebworth, twenty miles beyond Hatfield.[21] We left at noon in a special car, Miss Mansfield telling us that there would be a drive of some distance from the station. Carriages were waiting for us, and our road lay through the village, where we were much amused to see the village children running out to curtsey when they saw the carriages from the "big house." Knebworth, the ancestral home of the Bulwer-Lytton family, was leased by Lord Strathcona for a number of years. His daughter, Mrs. Howard, took us at once to the big banqueting hall, where luncheon was spread. Fortunately we were very hungry, or it would have been hard to eat in a room with so many things to attract our attention. Hanging from the rafters

---

20. Graham is referring to Maude Stanley, the author of *Clubs for Working Girls* (1890) and an early campaigner for educational opportunities for working-class girls.

21. Lord Strathcona, a.k.a., Donald Alexander Smith (1820–1914), had enjoyed a colourful career in Canada as a fur trader, financier, politician, and philanthropist. He provided the funds to raise a regiment from Canada, known as Lord Strathcona's Horse, to fight in the South African War.

were tattered old banners, from one of which we learned that there had been a Bulwer in the battle of Hastings, from another that there had been a Lytton in the Field of the Cloth of Gold.[22] While we were still at dessert the village rector came in, who wished to show us the famous old brasses in the church. This was a quaint little building in Norman style, dating back to the thirteenth century—Knebworth itself was built in 1560. Afterwards we went down an avenue of fine lime trees to the lake, and saw a little boat-house, where the late Lord Lytton did most of his writing.[23] Then we returned to the house, the outside of which we admired rather more than Hatfield. It was a brownish sandstone covered profusely with ivy; but the inside, however, was not nearly so interesting, although, as a matter of fact, a description of the beautiful things it contained would fill a volume. After tea we strolled about the flower gardens and then returned to town.

That evening we saw Their Majesties, King Edward and Queen Alexandra. It was opening night at Covent Gardens, and Nordica was singing in "Lohengrin."[24] In the Royal box, besides the King and Queen, were Prince and Princess Christian and the Princess Victoria. We were fortunate in having seats in the gallery above, almost opposite. I never heard "God Save the King" sung so heartily as it was that night.

Next day, Friday, the Colonial Office paid our accounts and gave us our steamer tickets to Cape Town, for the following day; after which we went to the Tower of London, where we were to meet

22. The Battle of Hastings pitted the force of William II of Normandy (or William the Conqueror) against the Anglo-Saxon forces of King Harold II in 1066. The Field of the Cloth of Gold refers to the site of a diplomatic meeting between England's Henry VIII and France's Francis I in 1520.

23. Robert Bulwer-Lytton, 1st Earl of Lytton (1831–1891), was a British diplomat who served as viceroy of India. He was also a popular poet.

24. Lillian Nordica (1857–1914) was an American opera singer who starred in Richard Wagner's romantic opera, *Lohengrin*.

Lady Buller.[25] The guide explained that the original tower, built by William the Conqueror, had been added to until it became a little town in itself, surrounded by a wall and moat. It is really not a tower at all, but a fort, built to guard the port of London. Of all the things we saw in London, the "Tower" made the most profound impression upon us. The walls, eighteen feet thick at the base, hide and contain unspeakable dungeons, where the light of day never penetrates. One must see these places, and the horrible instruments of torture once used there, to appreciate them, and to realize how the world has progressed. Yet the Tower has its lighter side, the guards in their quaint costumes, nick-named "Beef-eaters," the museum with the armor of the old kings, the strong room with the crown jewels.

After leaving the Tower we took the Underground for Lady Buller's home in Lowndes Square, where her daughters and some friends were waiting for us. It was a cozy little tea, where we had the feeling that our hostess liked us just because we were girls, and not because we were Canadians.

As an antidote to the Tower we went that night to the "Toreador," and had a hearty laugh at the antics of Grossmith Junior and Sammy Gigg.[26]

We had invitations also to visit Winchester, the House of Lords, and one or two other places, which unfortunately clashed with engagements already made.

Saturday morning early found us at Waterloo station having an awful time with our baggage. After a nerve-racking experience we succeeded in getting ourselves into our own special for Southampton, and all our belongings into the soldiers' train for the

25. Graham refers presumably to Lady Audrey Buller, the wife of General Sir Redvers Henry Buller (1839–1908), who was relieved of his military command in South Africa in light of the Boers' successful guerrilla campaign.

26. George Grossmith Jr. (1874–1935) starred in *Toreador*, a popular musical comedy, alongside Edmund Payne (1863–1914) who played a character named Sammy Gigg.

same place. There were a number of English people down to see us off, Lady Buller, Miss Buller, Miss Baden-Powell, Miss Mansfield, Mr. Martin, and others; also some of our *Lake Ontario* friends who went to Southampton with us. Miss Baden-Powell gave us each a lovely bunch of cowslips, primroses, forget-me-nots and lily-of-the-valley, a dainty and typical English nosegay.

We reached Southampton about noon, where the docks were already packed with Tommies and their friends.[27] Two transports were to have sailed that day, but as one had been disabled, our boat, the *Avondale Castle*, was to take on seven hundred and fifty men. A transport in the next dock was carrying eleven hundred. Such indescribable confusion it looked! Endless lines of trucks running up and down, countless bales being lowered to the hold by windlasses, hucksters winding in and out selling fruit and fizz drinks to the men, everyone laughing or crying and shouting at the same time—we were exhausted when the order came to cast off, about four o'clock.

27. "Tommies" was a widely used colloquial term for British soldiers.

CHAPTER III

Southampton to Cape Town

AS WE MOVED DOWN Southampton Water the passing boats added to the tumult with whistles and cheers. One conjectured vaguely what the excitement must have been three years before. A huge White Star liner, home from Australia, was moving slowly to her place with flags flying, band playing and a great crowd on deck cheering. Farther on, towards the Isle of Wight, the water was crowded with small craft, bobbing at anchor or skimming along. The bright sunshine over all and the background of soft green English hills made a charming picture to remember old England by.

But when we went below, we no longer felt so calmly happy. We were second-class to begin with, which hurt our Canadian pride; the boat was very crowded and we were to be four in a cabin. Miss Arbuckle, of Prince Edward Island—with whom I had chummed in London—and I noticed an inside cabin with an air-shaft from the upper deck, and made a Canadian rush for the purser. Before the poor man had time to recover from the shock we were settled in the coveted quarters, which proved much more comfortable than the outer cabins, where the girls had to keep their ports closed all through the tropics because of rolling seas. Then again, we Canadian teachers did not fancy our fellow-passengers, and I must confess they did not improve on acquaintance. There were a few nice people, certainly, especially Mr. and Mrs. Raney, taking a little honeymoon trip to Central Africa as missionaries. But there was a party of English teachers on board who found it amusing to sit about the decks on the subalterns'[1] knees, until the officer commanding put a stop to it. We were rather pleased to hear that these called us "the Canadian snobs."

Sunday morning we met for the first time the custom of hot coffee before rising. Afterwards we found it to be universal in South Africa, but Miss Arbuckle and I never became reconciled to it, and each new Kafir girl appearing at 6 A.M. with unspeakable coffee met with a hostile reception. It was only after offering to slay them

1. A subaltern is a junior officer.

if they persisted in bringing it that we could make them understand that we preferred our morning rest unbroken. They all thought us quite mad.

That Sunday morning also we sighted the coast of France, which we skirted closely all day. It was a perfect day, and the Tommies entered heartily into the service held on the forward deck. Their singing was especially good. Mr. Brookes, a navy chaplain bound for Ascension Island, and Mr. Raney took turns in conducting services; while Miss Murray, one of our party who had a charming voice, gave everyone much pleasure by her solos.

On Monday we were well into the Bay of Biscay, which was calm as a mill-pond. There were a number of raw recruits amongst the Tommies, bound for St. Helena, where they were to do guard duty at the Boer prisoners' camp. These were sent to the upper deck in squads for drill, and it was most amusing to see how clumsy some of them could be. They had to go barefoot, to save the decks, and they looked rather self-conscious in consequence. Seeing our interest, the sergeant-major offered to drill any ladies who wished it, and for several days, till the heat stopped it, many of the lady passengers, including most of our girls, did calisthenics, and hopped about on one foot, or did other kangaroo antics, to the great amusement of the non-athletes.

On Thursday, May 15th, we made the first stop, at Teneriffe, one of the Canary Islands. It is a volcanic island with a great peak at one end lost in the clouds. At the other is the little town of Santa Cruz, a dainty pink and white Spanish place nestling amongst the hills, and full of luxuriant tropical trees and flowers. The ship was quickly surrounded by little boats selling fruit, birds, tobacco, Spanish drawn-work and lace. Boys were diving for shillings—pennies no longer; boatmen were mobbing the passengers who wished to go ashore, hucksters were yelling their wares—altogether a scene for an artist. Soon our party was started for shore. We bobbed along in the sparkling sunlight over waves of such a brilliant blue it seemed as if the water would surely stain blue. On shore we met at once one of the characteristics of Santa Cruz—swarms of beggars. They were an assorted collection of all the beggars we had ever met singly or read about. One man had no legs; another had leprosy; the very babies in the gutter piped out in broken English, "I say, gimme a penny." But for all this we enjoyed Santa Cruz, rode its donkeys, raided its bazaars and market, till even the ship men admitted that we had made good bargains. In front of the market I took a snapshot of a characteristic group, fat, swarthy old women with bright scarfs over their heads, sitting in the midst of their wares; others with baskets or bundles on their heads pacing up and down; in the centre a number of donkeys with their yelling drivers.

After the Teneriffe excitement we settled down to the endurance of very hot weather between the Tropic of Cancer and the Equator. It was odd to have the days growing shorter in May, until by the time we reached St. Helena, Sunday, May 25th, it was twilight before dinner. The poor Tommies on the lower decks must have suffered terribly from the heat. We found it so unbearable one night that everyone refused to go below, the ladies taking possession of one side of the deck, and the gentlemen of the other. Fortunately for us the captain was ill with pneumonia at the time, else we could not have mutinied so successfully. One afternoon we forgot the heat in listening to a most interesting talk which Major Barton, the officer in command, gave us on the military schools of Sandhurst and Woolwich. Evenings, the Tommies amused themselves and us by impromptu concerts, the most popular features of which were comic songs, with numberless verses and catchy choruses in which everyone joined. One favorite ditty ran thus:

"Hidin' 'neath the ammunition wagon,
"Hidin' 'neath the luggage van,
When the cannons roar and the battle's on,
I'll be nowhere to be found—not likely."

We reached the Island of St. Helena Sunday afternoon, May 25th, and no one was allowed to go ashore until the next morning, and then only British subjects. The Tommies went first, half of the contingent below decks. The landing there is always difficult, as St. Helena, a bold, bare, volcanic bluff, rises perpendicularly from the water's edge. We thought the little town of Jamestown, nestled in a valley between two great bluffs, quite English-looking. A flight of seven hundred steps leads to the citadel on the right; or one may follow a rocky path, miles long, winding between rough rocks, and clumps of clinging cacti. On top, the view is magnificent, repaying the climb. At one's feet a toy town, and everywhere to the horizon a sky-blue sea. Over the hills behind the town we could see faintly a Boer camp, and farther off still Napoleon's tomb, which we had not time to visit. There were no beggars in Jamestown, and some of the shops were kept by Boers, on parole, happy-looking fellows, speaking good English, to our surprise. Miss Arbuckle asked one fair-haired man if he would kindly point out some Boers to us. "Well," said he, "look at me, I'm one," and laughed heartily at her surprise. There must be some very fertile spots in St. Helena, for the fruits we got there, bananas, tangerines and loquats, were far superior to those at Teneriffe.

After we left St. Helena we found ourselves in a very heavy sea, and, curiously enough, a few who had not been sick the first trip were now laid low. The rest of us put on rubber-soled tennis shoes and practised promenading at an angle of 45 degrees with the deck. With practice also we became quite skilful at dressing with our cabin boxes shooting in and out under our feet like trombones. It grew steadily worse till Saturday night, when we found it so difficult to stay in our bunks that we got up and dressed. Someone ran up the fore companion way to look out, but a great wave came down and flooded two of the cabins, and after that we kept below. It is odd how passengers grow indifferent to a storm. No one was a bit nervous, just chatting between the crashes or reading as the old boat righted herself. In the general din we gradually became conscious of a new variety of noise from the dining-saloon which was not explained until morning. The piano had broken loose and gone waltzing about the room, to be gathered up in fragments later. Daylight revealed also that there were not enough dishes left to go around, and, indeed, dinner-time, for some days previously, had become a vaudeville performance in which the third-class stewards regularly tumbled on the lower deck with the kettles of soup for the Tommies. We used to gather daily to watch this impromptu shower-bath. Naturally we were not sorry to reach Table Bay[2] on June 1st. As no one was allowed ashore till the following day, we anchored outside the breakwater, where we tossed about uncomfortably until Monday afternoon, when we landed in tenders in a drizzling rain.

Meantime a government lighter brought us the news of peace.[3] The soldiers on board were greatly excited, but to our surprise there were no signs of rejoicing in Cape Town, not even a flag flying, and in fact, we heard afterwards that the Cape people were not particularly elated, as they had made fortunes out of the war.

Table Bay was full of shipping riding at anchor, and bobbing up and down like corks. Our first view of the city was not prepossessing. The "table-cloth" of cloud was low down over Table Mountain, and at the foot of the gloomy hills we could see Cape Town straggling along, dirty pink and white in the mist.

With the government officials to examine our permits to land—none but British subjects being allowed ashore—came Miss Nevers, a lady appointed to look after us in Cape Town, and arrange our transport up-country. Military rule remained in force for some five months after the war ceased, and until the end of that time no one was allowed to travel anywhere without a permit, sometimes very hard to get.

---

2. Table Bay is Cape Town's harbour.
3. Boer forces surrendered on May 31, 1902 via the Treaty of Vereeniging.

We stayed in Cape Town till Tuesday evening, and spent the day exploring the city, including a trip to Rondebusch, Cecil Rhodes' beautiful place.[4] June is mid-winter at the Cape, the rainy season, but we thought it a fair variety of summer, as the foliage and flowers were luxuriant. There were quantities of wild calla lilies—arum lilies they call them there—about Cecil Rhodes' place. Cape Town itself was very dirty, and swarming with all sorts of people, fashionable women, dusky Cape girls with gay scarfs on their heads, Kafirs, coolies,[5]—and khaki, khaki everywhere. The houses and vehicles presented the same picturesque jumble, a handsome, modern, cut-stone building jostling a long, low, stuccoed native cottage; in the roadways electric trams, donkey carts, handsome carriages, cabs, ox-wagons and troops of cavalry completed the mix-up. The warm moisture made us long for ice-cream, and the amazement of the shop-men was too funny when we asked for it. "Ices in winter!" they fairly shouted at us. At last we found a little shop near the Parliament Buildings selling a frozen mixture they called ice-cream, and which we ate with much misgiving. It was cold anyway.

In a later visit to Cape Town I found it to be a really charming city, of some two hundred thousand people, with quite up-to-date shops, electric tram service, etc., and ideal residence sections running along the inlets of the sea.

Miss Nevers had allotted us to our various camps, allowing us to pair off as we chose. Miss Carr, who had friends at Pretoria, in the Transvaal, went there at once, and the rest of us left Cape Town Tuesday evening, June 3rd. We were to be stationed as follows: Misses McLeod, Johnston, Ellis and Hebb at Vryburg in Griqualand West; Misses Bremner, Dutcher, DeWolfe and Lee at Bloemfontein,

4. Cecil Rhodes (1853–1902) was the founder of the De Beers diamond company, a strong advocate of British imperialism in Africa, and served as prime minister of the Cape Colony from 1890 to 1896.

5. "Coolies" is a derogatory term for Asian labourers.

Orange River Colony: Misses Elliott, Burns, Pickle and Fleet at Brantford, Orange River Colony; Misses Younghusband, Crandall and Murray at Kroonstad, Orange River Colony: and Misses MacKenzie, MacDonald, Arbuckle and the writer at Norval's Pont, Cape Colony.

CHAPTER IV

On the Karoo

WE LEFT CAPE TOWN about nine o'clock P.M., thus seeing nothing of its outskirts. We were in two first-class corridor coaches sandwiched between sections of a goods train. There was no chance of anyone mistaking our identity, for our coaches were all labelled, "CONTENTS, *Canadian Teachers*." Miss Nevers had thoughtfully stored one compartment with food necessary for the journey, and it was arranged that we should have hot dinner each day at station restaurants.

It had rained nearly all the time we were in Cape Town, and we seemed to have exchanged our normal good spirits for a more than liberal supply of Cape Town mud. We realized at last that we were in Africa, and imagined that we would have nothing but uninterrupted hard work until the return voyage, which we all planned to take together at the end of the year.

But Wednesday morning the sun was shining out of a sky of dazzling blue; the air was clear and crisp, and we hurried out to find our train twisting up through the Hex Mountains, snow-capped and majestic in the sunlight.[1] We had not gone far during the night, for the line, a single narrow-gauge, was badly blocked with trains of homeward bound troops. Besides it was still dangerous to leave the shelter of a station during darkness. Some Tommies yelled at us as they passed us on a siding, "You're going the wrong way; the fun's all over." Gradually the hills, or *kopjes*, grew less frequent, until we stopped for dinner at Matchesfontein, on the great Karoo or sandy plateau which stretches across the interior of Cape Colony.

"Such a country!" everyone exclaimed. There was nothing but great kopjes, covered with boulders, and sandy desert in every direction. The only vegetation was dusty, stunted sage-brush. We wondered where the sheep, with their funny long legs and trailing fat tails, found food, to say nothing of water. And what extremely long legs they had; it was almost impossible to tell a sheep from a goat! But what air! keen, exhilarating, and so clear that every object

1. The Hex Mountains are located approximately 120 kilometres north east of Cape Town.

Top: *Typical Soldiers' Graves.*

Bottom: *Hotchkiss Gun Muffled, to be Drawn near Boer Lines.*

stood out as if magnified. Our eyes felt oddly out of focus. It was no wonder that the war dragged on so long; we were puzzled to see how the British made any gains at all.

The signs of war were all about us. Each side of the railway, for a distance of from twenty to thirty feet, had a continuous network of barbed wire, called an "entanglement." At intervals we passed block-houses, of various size and construction, some of stone, some of mud-brick, some of tin, all well fortified with stone walls and sand bags, and all uniformly desolate, with a sign picked out in white-washed stones "Please throw us your old papers." Next we passed a military hospital, Deelfontein, with a number of white tents, and a large cemetery in which the graves were marked by white-washed wooden crosses.

So the hours of the first day flew past. Kodaks were clicking incessantly and everyone grudged the time necessary for meals, although the keen air and the exercise we got following the train up slow grades made our appetites enormous.

On Thursday we passed many scattered graves, bones bleaching in the sun, heaps of empty tin cans and dead cattle. Once we saw a column on the march. Such a contrast to a parade at home! First came dusty scouts in their shirt sleeves, on scraggy horses with broken harness; then great wagons, called trolleys, drawn by fourteen or sixteen little donkeys, raising a dense cloud of dust; next a mounted guard; then more carts, and finally the men on foot.

At De Aar Junction,[2] where we stopped for dinner, the whole population was rushing out to meet a Dutch commando coming to surrender. The dust there was beyond words. We actually sank to our ankles in it, as in snow. Miss Arbuckle and I, by bribery and persuasion, captured a Canadian flag from some Irish Fusiliers, which had formerly belonged to the Strathcona Horse.[3] As we had

---

2. De Aar Junction is approximately 600 kilometres north east of Cape Town and 140 kilometres west of Norval's Pont.
3. Strathcona's Horse was the Canadian regiment funded by Lord Strathcona.

to wait in De Aar a few hours, we visited the little railway school, in charge of a Cape Colony Dutchman. It was very up-to-date, and somewhat jarred our preconceived ideas of South African schools. During the afternoon the Vryburg girls and Miss Nevers said good-bye to us and took the Mafeking train westwards.

The rest of us then continued our journey on the Johannesburg track. Although the Karoo appeared to be level, it was really a steady upward slope, and before the short twilight had ended it became very cold, and the temperature soon fell below freezing point. But the uniform evenness of the land lent itself to the schemes of the fraudulent engineers who had built the railroad. It was ludicrous the way the track described semi-circles and S's in the most bare-faced manner. On a perfectly flat and featureless bit of ground there were frequent compound curves of this sort, for no other purpose than to increase the mileage of the road, built by day-labor. It is being straightened lately at great expense and inconvenience.

As we were due at Norval's Pont early the following morning, the remaining fifteen of us proceeded to make a night of it. We were side-tracked at Naauwpoort,[4] our lamps were empty and no oil—paraffine they say in Africa—could be had at the station. We all crammed into one compartment—sociability; fastened shutters and doors—security; and burned one candle at a time—economy. There were girls on the seats, on the bunks overhead and on the floor; the folding table serving as platform for performers. Everyone had to do something, no excuses taken, and everyone joined in the choruses. We only stopped when the candles gave out.

Early in the morning of Friday, June 6th, we reached Norval's Pont, on the south side of the Orange River, which divides the Orange River Colony from Cape Colony. The journey from Cape Town had lasted sixty hours, a distance now covered in thirty-six. The four of us allotted to that station, Misses MacKenzie, MacDonald, Arbuckle

4. Naauwpoort (Noupoort) is approximately one hundred kilometres south east of De Aar.

Top: *North-side Block-house at Norval's Pont.*

Bottom: *Orange River at Norval's Pont.*

and myself, felt quite forlorn as the train moved out with the other girls, for we had become very good friends during our long trip together. They were all hanging out of the car windows singing, "Good-bye, Dolly Gray,"[5] till the bridge swallowed them from sight, and left us staring at the long, shining rails, and the Kafir huts beyond the barbed-wire entanglement.

5. "Good-Bye Dolly Gray" was a wartime anthem written during the Spanish-American War. A recording by Canadian Harry MacDonough helped to make it hugely popular during the Boer War. The lyrics are available at. http://www.webquestdirect.com.au/dollygray/dolly_gray_song.htm.

CHAPTER V

Norval's Pont Camp

BUT IT IS NOT IN THE NATURE of four Canadian girls to stand on a station platform at 6 A.M. of a frosty morning and endure the pangs of hunger in silence. We soon unearthed a sleepy coolie—polite little Jimmy—and sent him after hot coffee.

Presently the R.S.O. (Railway Station Officer—South Africa is a land of initials, and the military still controlled the railways) came down. He examined our permits and put us into his office, where there was a bright grate fire, until he sent for carts to take us to the camp, two miles away. Soon a donkey trolley came for our stuff and a Cape cart for ourselves. We learned later that a new Cape cart is quite a pretentious affair, a good one costing £70. It is a square-boxed vehicle, hung high on two heavy wheels, with a very long *dissel-boom*, or tongue. The seat may be drawn forward to accommodate four persons, and the large hood, or tent, as the South Africans say, is covered with white cloth, which sheds the heat-rays excellently. But our first sight of a Cape cart was something different. It was destitute of paint or upholstery, covered with the grime of years, and tied together in places with rope, as was also the very extraordinary harness. And such horses! The hair was all off in patches, from the mange, and they looked fit for nothing but fertilizer. One hurried glance decided us unanimously to walk, and it was only after much persuasion on the part of the R.S.O., and much laughter from the driver, that we finally climbed in. Then to our surprise the horses started off at a spirited pace, and the cart rode quite comfortably. That was our first lesson to judge nothing by Canadian standards.

On the way to the concentration, or refugee, camp, we passed various groups of tents, which the driver told us contained detachments of Army Service Corps, Gunners, Manchester Militia, and Nesbit's Horse.

As we rounded the huge, steep kopje separating the military from the refugee camp, we exclaimed with delight at the picture before us. To the left were enormous kopjes; at their base was the Orange River, winding along between green banks; to the right, and sloping up the opposite hillsides was the camp, with its long lines of tents glistening white in the morning sun. The tents were pitched in regular rows, with broad streets between, edged with lines of white-washed stones for guides on dark nights. The camp officials' and teachers' tents were farther up the slope by themselves. There were also numbers of sun-dried brick huts, and our driver volunteered the information that it had been planned to build many more of these, but that peace had removed the need for them, as many of the refugees were already applying for leave to return to their farms.

As we drove up, Miss Phillimore, the teachers' chaperone, and herself a teacher, came to welcome us; also Mr. Hemans, the Camp Superintendent, Mr. Gunn, the District School Superintendent, and Mr. Erasmus, the Camp School Headmaster. A frowsy head in curl-papers was thrust out of an adjoining tent for an instant, and a muffled voice exclaimed, "Oh, girls, they've made a mistake and sent the mothers instead of the daughters!" an unflattering comment on our appearance after three nights on the train. It's very queer how tent-life affects people. They always seem to think that because they cannot be seen they cannot be heard. These other girls, however, proved to be quite human when we knew them. They were Miss Wilson, a Scotch girl; Misses Odell, Webb, Daniel, Gillingham and Rose, all English.

These teachers already had three marquee tents, and a tin kitchen. A marquee is a long, high, narrow tent, made double, very airy and comfortable in fine weather, and perfectly certain to turn over in a storm. They used one tent as a living-room, and quite cozy it looked. There were pictures pinned to the walls, tennis racquets and hockey sticks standing about, pretty green canvas chairs which they said came in their outfit, some canaries in cages, a book-case and a sideboard made from packing cases, and bunches of wild-flowers on the table.

Mr. Erasmus arranged that Miss Phillimore should take the morning off to show us about, and after breakfast—consisting of porridge with condensed milk, coffee, tinned sausage, and what we mistook for poor brown bread—we visited the school. The school buildings and tents were three-quarters of a mile from our tents, at the farthest edge of camp, where there was plenty of space for playgrounds. Miss Phillimore told us that there were some thirteen hundred children in camp, and that all but the babies went to school. We visited Miss Webb's class first. She was in an old ragged marquee with not nearly seats enough for all. The class, therefore, took turns standing to recite, or sitting to use their slates. Desks there were none. The mud floors were delightfully noiseless, but caused such clouds of dust that we nearly choked. We went next to Miss Wilson's class, in a new tin or corrugated iron building, still roofless. She had benches enough, and her children, in the kindergarten stage, rose politely to say "Good morning." Miss Rose we found in a shelter made of tent-cloth spread over poles. Others were fairly comfortable in E.P. tents, the only reliable sort, but too expensive for general use. An E.P. (European Private) is a square tent, double, white outside, and green or brown inside. It has strong ropes to hold it down, and will withstand the severest storm. Miss Daniel was in a tin building, with a mud-brick addition just finished. She told me I was to have the room where she was then, with one hundred and thirty of her children, and that she was to go into the brick room with the remaining one hundred and seventy. This room had desks—that is there were uprights in the ground, with single planks laid across. Miss Daniel offered to go over my register with me to give me an idea how to pronounce the names; but when I heard a few like Wilhelmina Kachelhoffer and Abrahama Oosthuizen I decided to let my Dutch assistant, Miss Collins, call the roll for some time.

Then the bell rang for recess, and I saw that every child was carrying a mug or basin. Miss Phillimore explained that they all went to the soup kitchen during the cold months, where they were given hot soup at recess. I had a better look at them as they trooped out, and the majority of them seemed to me to be fat, healthy, ragged, dirty, but quite happy-looking youngsters. Evidently they were fond of their teachers from the way they clustered around them, and their pretty manners had impressed us at once from the way in which each class had risen with a smiling "good-morning" as we made the rounds of their class-rooms.

But we were interrupted by a message that the men were ready to pitch our tent, so we hastened back to see the unpacking of those mysterious boxes which had accompanied us from London. The squad of Boers detailed to do the work lived up to the reputation their countrymen had earned for laziness, and at nightfall our tent was not nearly ready, and we had to visit with the other teachers. We learned later that all the men were not of this stamp, and that the educated classes resented the term "Boer," which they said meant a peasant. But these camp squads, however, were Boers required to do a certain amount of work each day—that is, to go through the motions of working for a certain number of hours. It was most amusing to watch them; a squad would do about two men's work, yelling all the time as if they were fighting.

The unpacking of our boxes disclosed that an outfit for two consisted of a large marquee tent with two woollen rugs; two green canvas folding camp beds, with mattresses, pillows and good red blankets, three each; a folding iron washstand, with fittings of enamelled ware; folding canvas lounging chairs, upright chairs and bath; two folding tables, one fairly large and the other a little sewing table; water filter and small mirror; also a canteen containing a little stove and cooking utensils, enamelled dishes, knives, forks and spoons, all packed inside one another into the space of a patent pail. The stove we did not need, as the girls already had the little tin cookhouse mentioned before, with a Dutch woman as cook, and a boy for messages.

We did not sleep much that first night. At nine o'clock a bell rang, the signal for the refugees to put out their lights, after which we heard the night watchmen stumbling round. It seemed as if we had scarcely closed our eyes when a noise like a score of American locomotive whistles galvanized us into life. At the same time the tent began to shake violently, and some heavy bodies were evidently

Public Bake Ovens in Camp.

tangled up in the ropes. A sleepy voice from the next tent explained matters.

"Oh, Josie, there's those donkeys caught in the ropes again! Do chase them off, there's a dear." It appeared that when the camp was wrapped in sleep the little half-starved beasts left their miserable pastures on the sides of the kopjes and often came down to forage for scraps.

After this excitement there was a calm of a few hours, broken just at daybreak by the most doleful sounds I had ever heard. After listening in dismay for some minutes, and wondering if it was a funeral, I suddenly realized that it was the Boers at their sunrise devotions. Apparently they were singing psalms, a custom universal amongst the poorer classes. At sunset again they have similar exercises, but always in the same extravagantly doleful manner.

Next day we went for a walk through the lines, and saw the tents with their sides up for the regular Saturday inspection. The officials, doctors and line nurses were making their rounds. We were surprised and pleased to find the women quite friendly as they stood about chatting, most of them knitting. "Mittag" was the word of greeting, but when we spoke to some of them they smiled, shook their heads and said, "Verstan nie."[1] Every woman and girl wore a "kappe," or sun-bonnet, and a mother-hubbard apron, usually of dark dingy print. On the central street were the general bake-ovens, formed in long low mounds of sun-dried brick, the fuel for which was provided by the Government.

We kept straight on to the Camp Hospital, which was in one corner, separated by a high wire fence and a gate with a lock. In the enclosure were a number of E.P. tents and a new building just finished, of tin, lined with fitted hardwood. The "Sisters"—nursing sisters, the English call the nurses—some half dozen in number, were very friendly, and gave us some tea. Apparently every occasion in South Africa is an excuse for drinking tea or coffee. The Sisters told us that they had found the fence a necessity to isolate contagious cases, the Boers being too ignorant to stay in quarantine. At first, if anyone had measles or diphtheria, the whole camp got it, largely through carelessness, thus giving credence to the stories of neglect and ill-treatment. The line nurses, several of whom were young Dutchwomen, went through all the lines every day and reported all cases of illness. At that time there were not more than a dozen in hospital, although the camp numbered about thirty-five hundred people. We learned also that the greater number of the people in the camps were of the poorer classes, which accounted for their dirt and susceptibility to disease. It is perfectly true that numbers of the children had been found sewn up in their clothes. Such people were never so well off in their lives as when in camp, for

1. "Verstan nie" means "I don't understand" in Afrikaans.

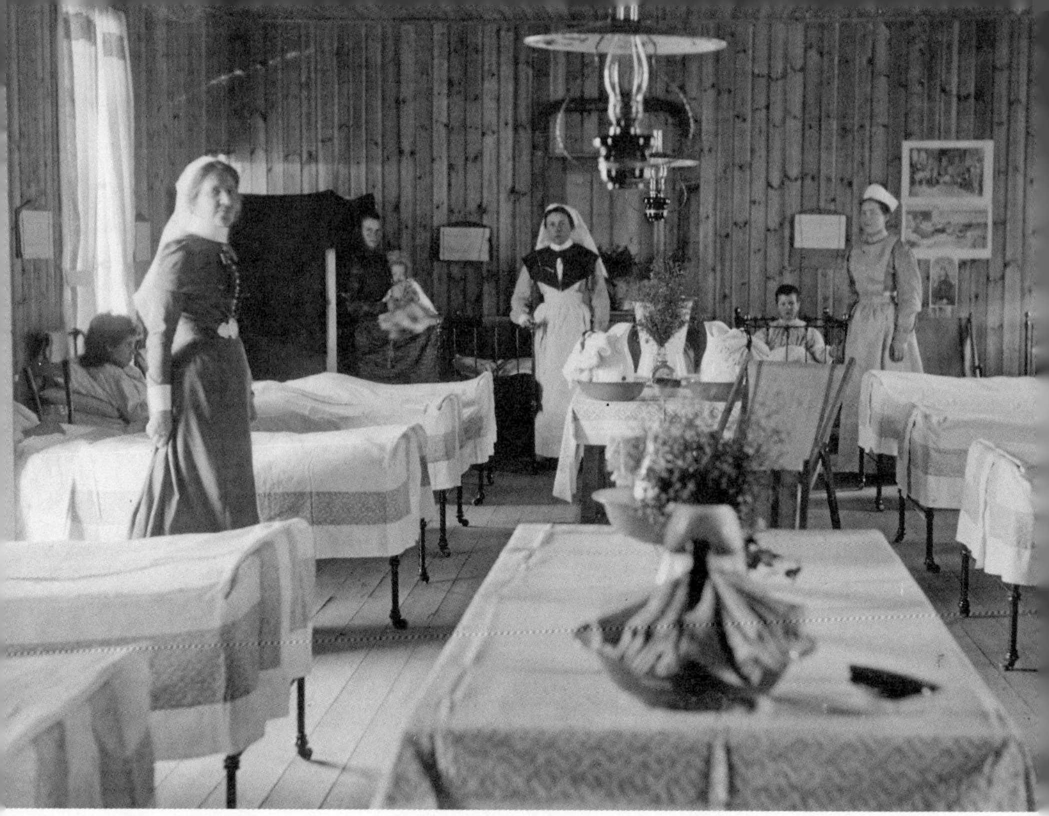

Children's Ward in the Camp Hospital.

they received lessons in cleanliness and sanitary living which must have been beneficial to their children at least. As we went back to our tents I asked what the peculiar smell was along the lines, and was told that it was caused by the weekly "smearing" of the floors with manure water to harden them. The doctors winked at this custom, for although offensive, it was not particularly unsanitary, and had always been the custom in the poorer houses.

In the afternoon some of the Sisters from No. 10 military hospital came up to call, also some officers. The girls could not get Miss Arbuckle's name right; one of them convulsed us by calling her Miss Carbuncle. We also learned that four Canadians were considered too great an addition to Norval's, and that Miss MacDonald and Miss MacKenzie were therefore to go on to Springfontein, where the need was still greater. They were not to go for a few days, however, as a house was being built for them, which was not quite finished.

On Sunday Dutch service was held in the big unfinished tin school, the Government paying a Dutch minister, Mr. Malerby. English service was conducted by the military chaplain in the railway schoolhouse, and Colonel Leyden of the Manchesters[2] kindly sent up a cart for any of the teachers who wished to attend. There was a special service this Sunday of thanksgiving for peace, in which Monday was proclaimed a public holiday.

The officers of Nesbit's Horse celebrated by giving a fine picnic in the bend of the river. A gorgeous spread it was, too—fresh butter, yeast bread, chicken in aspic, and similar luxuries from the canteen. To appreciate fresh butter, one should use the tinned variety for a little while; and to appreciate yeast bread, I would advise a trial of the sort of thing we were living on, made by our Boer cook, known as sour-dough bread, and tasting like-wise. It was heavy as lead, yet we ate enormous quantities of it, for tent life made us so hungry. We could have bought yeast bread at the station shops, but it was sixpence a pound, and we required at least four pounds a meal, which meant bankruptcy.

Our housekeeping arrangements were rather complicated. The girls took charge in turn monthly, and kept careful accounts during that time. The Government paid for the cook, who refused to do anything else but cook, so we had to hire other help; also it allowed us ten shillings a month washing allowance. Then we had "rations" the same as the camp people, and also certain "hospital comforts." Rations included fresh meat, usually Australian frozen beef, vegetables from the big garden, candles, one each per day, flour, salt, sugar, and similar things. Hospital comforts meant paraffine for our hanging lamps, fresh fruit, one quart of fresh milk, jelly powders, bacon, bovril and corned beef, suggestively known all over South

2. The "Manchesters" refers to the Manchester Regiment of the British Army.

Africa as "bully beef." Yet we were always hungry with living in the open, and bought quantities of things besides. The officers also brought up many a welcome present of *spring-buk* (venison) or cold storage fish from Cape Town. We were fortunate also at Norval's in having excellent water, brought down in pipes from springs in the kopjes.

Tuesday morning, June 10th, found Miss Arbuckle and myself at work in the schools. The hours were from nine to one-thirty, with recess from ten-thirty to eleven. The regulations called for twenty minutes of religious instruction at the opening of school, in Dutch; but as our Dutch assistants took charge of this work, it gave us an extra twenty minutes in bed—very acceptable on the frosty mornings.

We found it difficult to dress to suit the weather. The nights and early mornings were frosty, so that we enjoyed our warmest clothing when school began; by noon the sun's rays were so hot that cotton blouses were comfortable. Then it always became windy in the heat of the day, and sometimes the dust was so thick that we had to close school early, a welcome respite, as the roof of my tin room used to pound up and down with the wind in a deafening manner.

Let me describe my school-room, and an ordinary morning's routine. I would arrive when the class was finishing a morning hymn, usually a Moody and Sankey,[3] of which they were very fond, and of which they knew several in English. "Dare to be a Dan-e-el," was the favorite. Then, at first with Miss Collins' assistance, I would call the roll, and Miss Collins would write out a list of absentees for the truant officers, who made the rounds every morning. While she was doing this, I went around and examined feet, hands, necks and ears; specially dirty children were sent back to their tents to wash, and any with veldt sores were sent to the line nurses for treatment.

3. Graham refers to the itinerant evangelical duo Ira David Sankey (1840–1908) and Dwight Lyman Moody (1837–1899).

The children suffered dreadfully from chilblains[4] and these veldt sores, similar to boils, caused by bad blood and poor food. The poorer Dutch women hadn't the faintest idea of cooking anything properly, even when they had good materials; the rich, hot soup given the children by the camp, at recess, being the only nourishing food they had, in many cases. The soup was of the best, and many a time we teachers took it in preference to our own lunch sent down from our kitchen. The veldt sores were especially hard to heal because of the dust and dirt.

My class was Primer II., and when I had finished this inspection, the big cupboard was unlocked, and the slates given to half a dozen little ones to pass around. All slates, pencils, books, etc., were supplied by the Government, a system which is still in force, except in high schools charging fees. I had also a number of picture rolls of different sorts which were hung to the scantling, on which the corrugated iron walls were nailed. It was a great relief when the sun began to warm the air so that the windows could be opened. These had no glass panes, but the frames were filled with pieces of calico tacked in.

Meanwhile the class was carefully copying figures or letters, from large models on the blackboard, a portable one some three feet square, standing on an easel. I went around to correct the work, and those who had done well were allowed to draw on the side of the slates marked in kindergarten squares.[5] Those who had done badly were obliged to do it again. Then they laid down their slates and sat straight for a reading lesson off the big reading sheet. This usually caused a number of benches to collapse. These were made to fold,

---

4. Chilblains are ulcers affecting the extremities and are caused by the rapid warming of skin exposed to cold temperatures.

5. The children's drawing slates were incised with a grid, "kindergarten squares," to facilitate the copying of geometric shapes—a pedagogical approach developed by the German educator Friedrich Froebel (1782–1852).

and had a disagreeable way of folding without warning, catching some poor unfortunate little toes, on which there would be a great outcry, and after peace was restored the lesson went on. After that everyone was getting tired of sitting, so the class stood to sing. They were very fond of this, and it was a reward for good behaviour to be allowed to choose favorite songs. The kindergarten action songs proved the quickest way of teaching English, and I found it wonderful how quickly they memorized a new song.

By this time the recess bell was ringing and the headmaster went to each class in turn to dismiss, so that the soup kitchen might not be mobbed. The favorite games at recess were marbles for the boys, and skipping with a long rope for the girls. Curiously enough, the girls seemed to have far more energy than the boys. After recess there was a lesson in reading from the small books, followed by a simple lesson in mental arithmetic, and spelling. After that they had a few minutes at memorizing a new verse, then a simple, very simple little story, and an illustrated talk about something in Nature—animal stories being the favorites. When I could not make myself understood, Miss Collins explained the new word. Then it was nearly time to dismiss, so we sang again until the bell rang. The highest reward for the day's work was to be allowed to carry teacher's clock back to her tent; a lesser reward was the carrying of a coat or book; and there was always a lively row as to who should hold her hands. And such pathetic little presents they brought to school—a ragged ostrich feather, a battered old Christmas card, a gay cover of a cigarette box, a green quince—treasures to be received with delighted thanks.[6]

Another of the teachers' duties was to report to the officials all ragged children, in order that the reason of the raggedness might be inquired into. If the family was very poor clothes were given out of the stores. Of course there was a great deal of imposition practiced;

6. A quince is a fruit roughly resembling a cross between a pear and an apple. Green quinces have not fully ripened.

Saturday Inspection of Tents.

in scores of cases the children were persistently sent ragged and barefoot in the cold weather, and the new clothes hidden away for such time as the family would leave camp. I remember one case in particular which amused us greatly. The man had never ceased complaining of great poverty, and had been given an unusual amount of free supplies. When he left camp he unearthed a bag of gold from the floor of his tent, bought all he wanted, and paid thirty-five pounds for a horse he fancied. Even in times of peace it had not been uncommon for a Boer to secrete his money in this way, as the more ignorant had a deeply-rooted prejudice against banks.

We found that as a general thing the little girls were cleaner and neater than the little boys, and they all wore quaint short-fingered mittens, for down to the poorest, dirtiest little tot there was a general horror of having face and hands sun-burnt. The boys were odd wee men. They wore soft, shapeless felt hats with brims down;

their clothes were most frequently made of mud-colored corduroy, the coats cut high in the neck and collarless; while their knickers were always made with a large, neat patch of a different color on the seat, the legs reaching nearly to their boot-tops. All the children wore *veldt-shoene*, home-made shoes, rather shapeless, but comfortable, as the leather was very pliable.

But I would be very sorry to confirm the rather wide-spread belief that all those in the camps were dirty. Far from it. Of course *all* the poor people were gathered into them, making them seem, at first sight, like the poor section of any large city. But even of the very poor some were scrupulously clean; indeed, some quite well-to-do people were of the dirtiest. Curiously enough, or perhaps naturally enough, the dirty ones were also the ignorant ones, unable to speak any English, their children being quite unschooled. All this class benefited by the camps. They had free schools, free medical attendance, wholesome food, and were obliged to be decently clean. But there was also a large class who undoubtedly suffered many hardships in camp, though some say not so great as they would have suffered had they remained in their homes after the destruction of stock and crops. However, they did suffer, and greatly, as some are bound to do in every war. There were in our camp numbers of people whose homes I afterwards saw—beautiful places, with numbers of servants—and it is simply nonsense to pretend that it was not a fearful trial for such people to live huddled together in a bell tent, or a mud room, doing their own work, and carrying their own wood and water in all sorts of weather. For instance, there was one family of mother, father, and three daughters, living in a mud room, whose home was a large house with piazzas back and front, standing in a beautiful orchard, irrigated by an artesian well; the house inside finished with hardwood floors and ceilings; amongst the remains of destroyed furniture, two pianos, one a grand, the other for common use. But such is war.

And again, as regards food, I know that Norval's Pont was more fortunate than some of the other refugee camps. Norval's farm, and also Schalkwyk's across the river, were well irrigated, and had fine vegetable gardens, tended by the men in camp, from which generous rations of vegetables were issued three times a week.

But I have wandered far away from that first day in school, and now must "resoom and continoo" as Samantha Allen says.[7] The morning had been hazy, and as the day wore on the clouds rolled up, and the wind increased so that everyone predicted an unusual storm. Towards bed-time it grew very cold, and began to drop rain. The other girls advised us to loosen the tent ropes in spite of the wind, for our tent being new would shrink greatly in the wet. I went to bed with a thick old serge dress, and a pair of high rubber boots close by. It wasn't half an hour till the rain poured down, and up went the side of the tent next [to] Miss Arbuckle and Miss MacKenzie, the pegs popping out of the ground like corks out of ginger-beer bottles. We dressed in record time, got out our oil-cloth sheets, and put as much under them as possible. By this time the wind was blowing a hurricane and it was beginning to snow—and thirty-six hours before we had been enjoying a picnic in cotton shirt-waists! What things we could not cover we carried over to the mess tent, which seemed quite solid, and left our old marquee to collapse as soon as it liked. It did so in about ten minutes. By that time relief gangs were out all over the camp, and some men pulled the tent cloth well over our trunks and furniture. Between the noise of the storm and the shouting of the people the uproar was deafening. We asked the other girls if they meant to get up and dress. "Oh, no!" they said; "our old marquees have weathered out lots of storms." But towards morning we got our revenge, for their tents went down on them in bed, and everything was soaked. We managed to keep the mess-tent standing by taking turns at hammering down the pegs. In the morning half the tents of camp were down, and there was much discomfort, the people crowding into the school-rooms for

7. Samantha Allen was the title character in a series of books by the American humourist Marietta Holley (1836–1926).

shelter, which ended school for that week. The camp officials lent us teachers their mud-brick mess-room, where we camped until our tents dried. The military camp fared still worse. There they had nothing but bell tents, which were lifted clear by the wind and went flying up the kopjes, with their contents after them.

They say it never rains but it pours! To add to the discomfort, fuel was scarce, and to cap the climax for us, the cook was sick, so we took turns cooking. In the afternoon the sun came out, and Captain Reid, of the Nesbit's, kindly came up with a squad of men to help with our tents. Presently a lot of Manchesters followed suit, and soon we had crowd enough for a barn-raising. The fun quite made up for the discomfort. In a few days everything was dry, and nothing but the mud-stains on the tents told of the storm.

After Miss MacKenzie and Miss MacDonald left for Springfontein, Miss Phillimore came to share the tent with Miss Arbuckle and myself; and a lasting friendship sprang up between us, in spite of the fact that our Canadian ways and manner of speech were a never-ending source of amazement to her.

About this time we were ordered to take a census of all the children in camp, and fill out papers answering such questions as "Was je pa's nom?" "Was je ma's nom?" "Was je Plas nom?" and so on—and after days of labor the papers were never asked for by the Education Department.

Towards the end of June there was great excitement one day. A big commando[8] had surrendered and had come into camp. The wives refused to believe that peace was signed, and said they would not believe it unless they heard it from General Christiaan De Wet[9] himself, called their husbands and sons "Hands-uppers,"[10] and proceeded to beat them with brooms or any other convenient weapon. To pacify them, the Superintendent, Mr. Hemans, said

8. Graham is referring to a Boer military unit rather than an individual.

9. De Wet (1854–1922) was the most successful commander of the Boer guerrilla forces.

10. The term "hands-uppers" was given to Boers who voluntarily surrendered to the British.

Vegetable Garden, Norval's Pont Camp.

he would telegraph for De Wet, and the latter came two days later and spoke very sensibly to both parents and children. It was most pathetic, too, and before he finished everyone was in tears. He spoke in Dutch, though to us he used fairly good English. He said he had done his best in the war, no man could do more. They had all fought bravely, and were fairly conquered, and now instead of wasting their energy in useless grumblings, he advised them to take advantage of the schools, to work their farms well, and to show the world what good stuff was in them. We thought, however, he did a very unkind thing in Miss Arbuckle's room. Her assistant, a nice little Dutch girl, went up to shake hands, but De Wet drew back, saying, "Your uncle was a traitor who surrendered with Cronje, and I cannot shake hands with such people."[11] The poor girl cried bitterly.

---

11. General Piet Cronjé surrendered to British forces at Paardeberg in February 1900

The next excitement was a party out at Schalkwyk's farm, given by the Nesbit's Horse, a force of South African volunteers, who had orders to disband. We girls drove out in a big van drawn by twelve donkeys, our first experience of Kafir driving, and very exciting it proved. One boy sat on the driver's seat, while another ran alongside cracking a great stock-whip with a lash twenty feet long, both yelling constantly "mach ho" (get up) and other unintelligible words. All *sluits* (ditches) were taken at the dead gallop to gain enough impetus to take us up the opposite slope. The whole surface of the veldt is scored with these dry waterways.

We had not expected anything but work in the camp, and I had provided myself with photographic materials for leisure moments. As a matter of fact there was always something going on. Someone was sure to drop in for afternoon tea, after which there would be tennis, at which game the Dutch people are experts. The military had polo, until the Nesbit's left, taking their horses along. And everybody played field hockey. Miss Arbuckle and I kept out of that rather loftily at first, it looked so rough and dirty, until one day a Dutch girl asked Miss Arbuckle to supply in her team. She did so, and came back hot, dusty and enthusiastic, while I poured out tea, feeling consciously superior in a fresh pink blouse. A few days later another teacher asked me to supply for her, and I too came home hot, dusty and enthusiastic. An English gentleman had furnished the camps with materials for games, hockey, tennis, etc., some of which we did not use until the town schools were re-opened. We also had several concerts in the big tin school shed, some of which were given by local talent in aid of the orphanage, the best part of such entertainments being that everyone joined lustily in the choruses.

Towards the end of June we were told to prepare for a ten-day trip to Johannesburg on June 30th, for a Teachers' Convention. Mr. Sargent,[12] the Director of Education, had planned this convention,

---

12. Graham is referring to Edmund Beale Sargant (1855–1938).

to bring together all the teachers, Dutch, English and Colonial, from all the colonies of South Africa. The railroads promised free transportation, and the residents of Johannesburg offered to billet as many as possible. It was a tremendous undertaking, especially so soon after the war, but the idea was one of the best. Mr. Sargent deserved all possible praise for carrying it out to a successful issue. It was the one scheme of Mr. Sargent's with which no one found fault.

CHAPTER VI

Johannesburg and Pretoria

EARLY IN THE MORNING OF JULY 1ST we arrived in Johannesburg, in a wretched condition. Apparently the cars had not been cleaned from the outbreak of hostilities. Our train, an enormous one in two sections, was crowded with pedagogues, most of them awful-looking females.

The approach to Johannesburg through long groves of tall Australian blue-gum, or eucalyptus, trees, was very pretty after the monotonous bare plain from Norval's northwards. These trees were grown to furnish poles to support the underground levels of the mines.

We had each been given numbered badges for identification, which we found very necessary, as the big station was simply packed with people. Miss Arbuckle and I were claimed by a young gentleman with a smart horse and trap, who drove us to his uncle's, the late Mr. Freeman-Cohen's, where we found the Bloemfontein Canadians, Misses Lee, Bremner, Dutcher and De Wolfe. During our stay of ten days in this beautiful home, Mr. Cohen and his family could not have been kinder to us if we had been their best friends.

The sessions of the convention, held in the big gymnasium of the Wanderers' Club, were interspersed by popular lectures and concerts, amongst others a lecture by General Baden-Powell on "Scouting."[1]

Johannesburg presented even greater contrasts than Cape Town. It had a population of about sixty thousand, but, for its size, had more fine houses and public buildings. But the pavements were very rough, and the roadways one sea of red dust. The unceasing cry in "Joburg" is, "What shall we do with the dust?" The city was beautifully decorated for King Edward's coronation, which should have taken place on July 3rd had it not been for His Majesty's illness. In the big market square were a number of arches, Indian, Australian,

1. Robert Baden-Powell had recently drawn upon his military experience in southern Africa to publish *Aids to Scouting for NCOs and Men* (1899), which would be revised and published as *Scouting for Boys* (1908). The Scouting movement formally began in 1907.

Canadian Coronation Arch, Johannesburg.

American and Canadian, surrounding a statue of the King, erected by South Africa. As the cables were rather hopeful, people indulged in fireworks that evening, but saved the holiday and regular celebration till later.

Two of the features of Johannesburg are the coolics and the rickshaws. Numbers of these latter have their stand in front of the big post-office, and are drawn by native Kafirs, or Indian coolies with extraordinary head-dresses. Another girl and I stood until we were tired, trying to get a snapshot, but they proved as wily as brook trout, and kept turning their backs when we attempted to press the button.

One day the convention was adjourned to pay a visit to the mines. We visited the Village Main Reef, and the City and Suburban. The party I was with was hurried past the native compound, with the remark that it was "a dirty place." This remark occurred to me months later when visiting the diamond mine at Jagersfontein, and noticing the contrast in the better condition of the natives there. We then descended six hundred feet to the second level in a sort of rough elevator, used for carrying ore to the surface. As there was no gas to fear in these mines, everyone carried a candle, and we watched the Kafirs for some time loading the ore on trucks which ran along a narrow rail to the elevator. Our guide explained that there were eight levels below the one we visited, and that the vein of gold sloped down far enough to allow the sinking of the shaft twice the depth it was then. After ascending to the surface again, we visited the great smelters and saw the refining machines at work, also the assaying process. This mine yielded about ten ounces of gold to a ton of quartz, which was considered a good average. Then we had afternoon tea in the officials' mess, and retraced our dusty road to the city.

On the seventh of July, Lord Milner gave a garden party to the convention at his beautiful place a few miles out of town. Our party of six from Mr. Freeman-Cohen's went together, of course, and Miss Carr and Miss McLeod were also with us that day. Lady Lyttelton, whose husband, General Lyttelton, had just taken General Kitchener's place as Commander-in-Chief, recognized us as having been at Miss Balfour's reception in London, and presented us to Lord Milner. On learning that we planned to visit Pretoria she said that she would like to have us to tea at the Residency there.

We spent all day Wednesday in Pretoria, which was a much smaller, quieter and more settled-looking town than Johannesburg. The streets had many fine trees, well-watered, for the city had an excellent irrigation system, sending little streams of water along the ditches. We visited the *Raadzaal*, the old Dutch parliament, on the market square, and sat in Kruger's big chair in the council room.[2] Then we visited Kruger's house, used as headquarters of the South African Constabulary, with Colonel Steele,[3] of Montreal, in charge. The living rooms were just as Kruger left them, even to the big Bible on the sitting-room table. Miss Carr took us to the school where she was teaching, and where Winston Churchill and some others had been imprisoned, and had effected their much-talked-of escape.[4] It did not seem to us as if very wonderful ingenuity had been required.

After dinner we visited the Zoological Gardens, which contained an excellent collection of South African birds and animals, including the *wildebeste*, or South African buffalo, now found only in protected herds. After that we went to General Lyttelton's, the Residency, a very handsome two-story brick house, quite American-looking, standing in large grounds. Lady Lyttelton showed us the dining-room, where the peace contract had been signed.[5] Then we had tea on the lawn, where the General joined us, saying that he had been in our North-West rebellion of '85.[6]

While in Johannesburg we met a number of Canadian men, and most of us found some acquaintances. Amongst others who called one night was Dr. Parry, who graduated in the same year as myself from Toronto University. It was very jolly meeting these people, and made us feel how small the world is after all.

---

2. Paul Kruger (1825–1904) was a founding member of the South African Gereformeerde Kerk (Dutch Reformed Church) and president of the South African Republic from 1883 to 1900. During the South African War he fled first to Mozambique and then to Europe.
3. Sam Steele, a leading officer in Canada's North-West Mounted Police, had earlier been appointed as the commanding officer of Strathcona's Horse.
4. Churchill had been captured by the Boers while working as a newspaper correspondent.
5. The Treaty of Vereeniging was named after the town where negotiations occurred; the actual signing of the treaty took place at Melrose House, what Graham called the Residency, in Pretoria. Melrose House was requisitioned as the headquarters for the British forces after Pretoria was invaded in June 1900 until the treaty was signed in May 1902.
6. The North-West Rebellion pitted the Métis, led by Louis Riel, and Aboriginal peoples against the Dominion of Canada.

At a dinner-party at Mr. Freeman-Cohen's we met a number of very interesting people. The gentleman who took me in had been a chief intelligence officer under General French.[7] According to him French was the greatest hero of the war; an opinion I heard confirmed by many other men of different regiments, and also by civilians. From one end of the country, indeed, to the other we were amazed at the different rating given to the various leaders from what we were accustomed to in newspaper reports. General Buller, for instance, was spoken of in terms of the highest praise. Men said he had been set to do an impossible task, and under the circumstances no man could have accomplished more. Others, again, who had received unstinted praise from the outer world had no reputations worth speaking of in Africa. One of the most interesting bits of literature it has been my lot to read was "Unofficial Despatches," a book published by a London reporter whose work was censored, being too rashly accurate to be palatable.[8]

Another surprise in "Joburg," as people usually call it, was to find a first-class opera house, and an actor like Wilson Barrett playing "The Sign of the Cross."[9] There was a special convention night, when we packed the building. Altogether we all felt vastly ashamed of our preconceived ideas of Johannesburg, which we had imagined to be a rough mining town with few of the comforts and none of the luxuries of civilization.

Saturday morning, July 12th, we left Johannesburg and stayed at Bloemfontein, for some reason or other, from 10 P.M. till 10 A.M. Sunday. Miss Arbuckle and I went to early service in the Cathedral, a large barn-like building outside, but quite handsome inside, after

---

7. John French, commander of the 1st Cavalry Brigade during the South African War, came to prominence in battles to relieve the Siege of Kimberley and at Paardeberg.

8. Graham is very likely referring here to Edgar Wallace's *Unofficial Dispatches* (London: Hutchinson, 1901).

9. Wilson Barrett (1846–1904) was a British actor and playwright. *The Sign of the Cross* was his most successful production.

which there was plenty of time to see the town, which numbers about twelve thousand. The main street, Maitland, running past the Market Square, had some fine shops, but the paving was the worst we had seen yet. Each man built his own piece of sidewalk, and some were high and some were low, some wide and some narrow. People generally kept to the middle of the road, the usual way in all small towns. The Government Buildings were much superior to those in Pretoria, standing in large, well-kept grounds, with a fine statue of the late President Brandt in front.[10] To this man is given most of the credit by both English and Dutch, for the excellent system of government in the Orange Free State, a system not yet equalled by the present administration. The Raadzaal was a handsome building, surrounded by a lofty portico with polished marble pillars. Besides these there was nothing of note in Bloemfontein.

The railroad journey from Pretoria to the south of the Orange River Colony is the dullest possible, the land being an almost unbroken plain; therefore, when we saw the kopjes increasing in size and number we knew we would soon be home. About nine P.M. we pulled into the familiar Pont station.

10. Presumably Graham is referring to J.H. Brand (1823–1888), who served as president of the Orange Free State from 1864 until his death.

CHAPTER VII

End of Camp Life

DRIVING UP TO OUR QUARTERS, we saw great changes in the camps. The number of lights in the military camp showed that it had grown, although the Nesbit's and Gunners had broken camp before we left; but, in the meantime, the Manchesters, seven hundred men, had been gathered in from their detachments, and were awaiting orders to embark for home. The refugee camp, on the other hand, had shrunk greatly. Large numbers of families had *trekked* during the holidays, leaving big gaps in the lines, and when school re-opened I found only a hundred left in my class. From this time on the shrinkage was continued, until by the time my own orders came to move on, I had only twenty left.

On Coronation Day we had a holiday. Every child was given a bottle of lemonade, a bag of candy—sweets, as the English say—and an orange. I doubt if many of them realized what the treat was for. There were also sports for young and old, and some quite attractive prizes offered for the bigger events. The most amusing item on the children's programme was an obstacle race in which each competitor, after crawling through a barrel, had to eat a crumbly biscuit and drink a bottle of ginger beer. The sputtering was indescribable, and the vanquished realized at least that haste was not the best policy. The military camp celebrated on the following day so as not to interfere with our programme. Some of their events were open to the ladies, as the egg-and-spoon, the steeplechase, etc. The steeplechase was most absurd; a gentleman, blindfolded, ran at full speed down the course and over green hurdles, guided by reins tied to his arms and held by his lady driver.

About this time a challenge to a hockey match came over from Colesburg, of Cole's Kop and Suffolk Hill memory.[1] The team was to

1. Colesburg is approximately thirty-five kilometres west of Norval's Pont. Intense fighting between the British and Boers occurred in the area in early 1900. Suffolk Hill was the site of a key Boer victory on January 6, 1900; General French gained a good deal of favourable publicity for co-ordinating the use of lyddite to destroy a Boer maxim gun stationed on Cole's Kop in February 1900.

be a mixed one, five ladies and six gentlemen. I had been practising industriously, and was rewarded by a place on the team. August 2nd was set for the match.

When the day came, everyone who could get off came along with us, so that we quite filled an empty goods van—freight car we say—and reached Colesburg about noon. Carryalls[2] were waiting to drive us to our hotel, where a number of the Colesburg team were waiting to welcome us. They entertained us at dinner and treated us right royally all day. The game was not called until four o'clock, so we had plenty of time to see the town, a typical country village, clustered about a large central market-square, the houses one-storied, of mud-brick, limed over white or pink, with wide verandahs, and shaded by pepper-trees or blue gums. All the houses were built on the street, with gardens behind. There were no sidewalks, and whites, blacks, horses, donkeys and oxen mingled indiscriminately in the roadways. There were some quite good general stores, which we raided in hilarious fashion. As I was housekeeper that month, I had a long list of household wants to work through, from new dish-cloths to lamp glasses. The others entered on a regular orgy of shopping. One giddy subaltern bought up all the white kid gloves in town and proceeded to run a corner on them. Retribution, however, overtook him swiftly, for when he tried to fit them on himself they all split up the back, "Unhasting, unceasing," as Goethe says. Everyone borrowed from everyone else, and I haven't the foggiest idea how we ever straightened out accounts.

About three-thirty we gathered in vans to drive to the recreation grounds, within view of Cole's Kop, where the grand-stand was already filled. Our girls were feeling nervous because one of our best players was not on the team, but had come simply as a supply. However, we soon saw that we could more than hold our own. The Colesburg team did some splendid individual work, but could not break our

2. Carryalls are horse-drawn carriages.

combinations. We scored every time from the right wing. When little Carroll, right half, sent the ball in to Miss Webb, inside right, who in turn shot it out to old Barlow, outside right, he never failed to dribble it past a half dozen opponents. Poor Mr. Barlow! His death was the first break in the friendship of those days. At half-time the score was two all, and with the change of sides, wind and sun would be in our favor. Tea was served at half-time; and during the second half everything came our way until, when time was called, the score stood eight to two for Norval's. The Colesburg team promised to play the return match in a few weeks, but the weather became so hot and dusty that we had to drop hockey. However, several of the girls, and the mother of one of them, came to visit us later on.

After an excellent supper we started back to Norval's, which we did not reach till nearly midnight, as the speed of a goods train is not breathless. There a final excitement awaited us. We were held up at the station by a sentry, and not one of us had his or her pass, but luckily Captain Smith, a staff officer, was along and got us through. So ended a day to be marked with a white stone.

The rules regarding passes were amusing. After the war, until the end of martial law, the authorities enforced the regulations with spasmodic severity.[3] All refugees were strictly forbidden to leave the boundaries of camp without a special pass, and this was regularly enforced; we teachers, however, could go where we pleased in daylight, but were required to have a general pass for the evenings. The military were not allowed in the refugee camp without a special pass, but, as our tents and tennis court were at the boundary, this rule was not incapable of being stretched.

Towards the end of August camp life was not so pleasant. The refugees were moving out as fast as they could get their wagons in

3. Martial law is a set of regulations used by occupying forces in a conquered territory as well as in times of insurrection or dire emergency. Transvaal Martial Law was proclaimed by the British in September 1900.

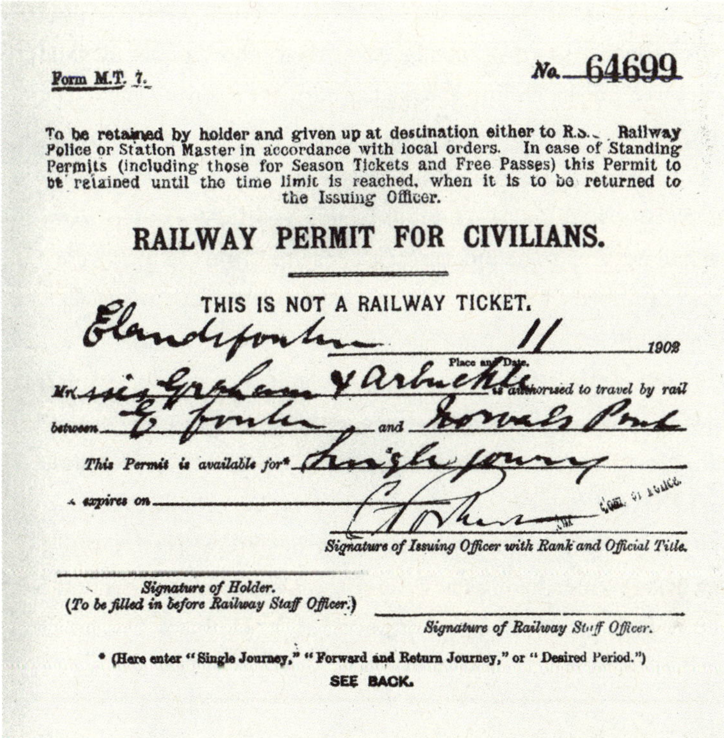

Form M.T. 7.

No. 64699

To be retained by holder and given up at destination either to R.S. Railway Police or Station Master in accordance with local orders. In case of Standing Permits (including those for Season Tickets and Free Passes) this Permit to be retained until the time limit is reached, when it is to be returned to the Issuing Officer.

RAILWAY PERMIT FOR CIVILIANS.

THIS IS NOT A RAILWAY TICKET.

Elandsfontein 11 1902
Place and Date.

Mrs Graham & Arbuckle is authorised to travel by rail between E'fontein and Norvals Pont

This Permit is available for* Single journey

& expires on

Signature of Issuing Officer with Rank and Official Title.

Signature of Holder.
(To be filled in before Railway Staff Officer.)

Signature of Railway Staff Officer.

* (Here enter "Single Journey," "Forward and Return Journey," or "Desired Period.")

SEE BACK.

Fac-simile of civilian's permit.

readiness. Each family, on leaving, was given free seed and a month's provisions, also stock at cost price, by the Repatriation Board. This was entirely separate from the Compensation Board, as I shall explain later.[4] School had become a succession of good-byes. In our own camp the circle was broken by the departure of Miss Odell for Bloemfontein. Also the weather was changing and we no longer had a procession of brilliant, cloudless days, warm at noon, and cold at night. August is always characterized by endless dust storms, which usher in the clouds for the September rains; in a good season it rains the greater part of September, thus soaking the ground, and

4 See Chapter XI

filling the dams to overflowing. An ordinary shower does no good whatever, for the ground is baked as hard as brick, and the water simply runs over the surface and is lost.

There was considerable fun going on in the military camp, however, for forty officers and seven hundred men waiting for orders to move on had nothing to do but amuse themselves. And the men were most exemplary. I did not hear of a single instance of an officer, or a Tommy either, in that camp, doing anything objectionable. The men were taken out every day for long route marches, and on pay-nights the officers started a series of concerts to keep the former out of mischief. The N.C.O.'s (non-commissioned officers), managed these, and everyone helped. Two of our girls, Miss Daniel and Miss Wilson, sang very nicely, as did also a few of the hospital sisters. Naturally the best features here, as in the Refugee Camp concerts, were the comic songs, in which everyone joined in the choruses. One absurd account of the trials of a man in the Yeomanry had for chorus:

"Oh, you don't catch me on a gee-gee's[5] back again,
It's not the sort of place that you can doze on,
For the only 'orse that I think that I can ride
Is the one that the m'ssis dries the clothes on."

These concerts were held in the big engine-house at the station, used also at that time for Sunday service. There was scarcely anyone in camp who could play, and I was gradually called upon to play everything, from the hymns in the military service to "vamping" accompaniments to unheard-of-songs, without music. I drew the line at that. One prime favorite, often "sung by request," was "Because I Love You," and the reason of its popularity was characteristic of the life in camp. One of the staff officers had become engaged to one of the English teachers, and thereafter subalterns

5. A "gee-gee" is a horse.

and men made his life a burden to him. Every order given was respectfully received, it is true, salutes given and "Yes, sir," uttered in the regulation wooden tone, but—every subordinate turned away to carry out his orders to an accompaniment of "Because I Love You." And the worst of it was that there was absolutely nothing to be said about it.

A new element of interest in the refugee camp in August was the return of many prisoners of war from St. Helena and Ceylon. Whenever these men signified their willingness to take the oath of allegiance they were taken back to South Africa, and put on an equal footing with the other Dutch in regard to supplies of stock, seed, etc., from the Repatriation Board. All whom I met expressed regret that they had been so slow in taking the oath, saying they had never dreamed that the British would have shown such clemency.

There was in one corner of the refugee camp a comfortable orphanage, the main building of sundried brick surrounded by several E.P. tents, and sheltering some forty-five little orphans whose fathers had been killed in the war. It was supported partly by the English and partly by the Hollander Government. I say "Hollander," because all through South Africa that word is used to distinguish the people of Holland from the Dutch people of Africa. The children there were healthy and hearty and well-cared for in every way. About the end of August there was a big farewell picnic for them, our last picnic on the banks of the Orange River. We drove out in the big donkey trolleys, and for anyone suffering from a torpid liver, let me recommend a ride on a donkey trolley. Such a jolly picnic it was! I think those teachers who expressed the opinion that the Boer children were dull and disinclined to play did so before they got acquainted with their charges. They were shy with strangers, and were never so quarrelsome and boisterous as American children, but they were just as fond of fun as any children I ever met, and at picnics, such as this orphanage one, showed a knowledge of many a game I had never heard of, though they played one game called "rounders," which is almost the same as our baseball.

Orphanage in Norval's Pont Camp. In her photo album, Graham wrote under this picture, "Orphanage building and tents, sheltering some forty orphans. They had every attention possible."

The people were now leaving camp by hundreds every day. Miss Webb and Miss Wilson had received notice to leave for Bethlehem[6] on September 1st. Miss Daniel and Miss Gillingham were to go a few days later to Jagersfontein,[7] and Miss Arbuckle and myself, at the same time, to Fauresmith.[8] The Manchesters also had orders to leave September 1st. So, from end to end, the camps were in confusion. Just as things were at their worst, Mr. Gunn, the Superintendent, called me one morning as I went to school and said that he had just had word that a party of Australian girls had come over to teach, and that the camps would have to billet them until the town schools were ready. He had been asked to accommodate six. We arranged that I should stay at home and plan with Mr. Robertson,

6. Bethlehem is located approximately 130 kilometres south of Johannesburg.
7. Jagersfontein is located approximately fifty kilometres south of Bethlehem.
8. Fauresmith is located approximately fifteen kilometres west of Jagersfontein.

our assistant Camp Superintendent, for their entertainment, while he would go to the station to meet them. Six visitors! And two of our girls had all their own things packed and were sharing ours! Indeed for some time it had been a standing rule at our occasional dinners, that everyone should talk fascinatingly between courses, so that no one should notice the delays owing to the fact that all the dishes had to be washed. Mr. Robertson, however, proved to be a trump. He had an E.P. pitched in an incredibly short time, furnished it with hospital supplies, and sent us some school benches and tables for the mess-tent. Meanwhile I rushed from office to shop with an order for extra rations, and then to the kitchen where the cook railed at having to cook them. Soon the Australians came. They saw, they smiled—a sickly smile—and they retired to their E.P., where they raised their voices in one prolonged wail. Miss Gillingham thought someone was ill, and rushed over with a kettle of hot water, but they told her no—"boo-oo"—they were only homesick. And for one awful week they floated about the camp in dressing-sacks and wrappers, red-eyed and doleful. Then they were sent on to Springfontein with the remaining refugees from Norval's, which was to be finally closed about the middle of September.

Events crowded thickly in those last few days, but the most highly-colored one was the Manchester auction sale, held in the Refugee Camp. The auctioneer was an Irish captain, famous for his comic songs and stories. He kept the crowd in a gale of laughter over the rubbish he sold!

Meantime the Repatriation wagons had been out Fauresmith way and returned. The drivers amused themselves hugely at Miss Arbuckle's and my expense, telling us we would find baboons in the houses and not a soul who could speak English.

On September 12th we left camp in the midst of the long-threatened rain storm. Our party of six consisted of Misses Daniel, Gillingham, Arbuckle, Mr. Gunn, Mr. Robertson and myself. Our boxes had preceded us by a few days to Jagersfontein Road, where a traction engine of the Jagersfontein Mining Company was to haul them out to Jagersfontein and Fauresmith. We girls were to stay over night at Springfontein Camp, and drive from there in Cape carts, accompanied by Mr. Gunn and Miss Pugh-Jones, a camp inspectress, who had visited us a short time before. But the storm increased so in violence that the roads became impassable and we were obliged to stay some days at Springfontein. We girls camped there in a big unused hospital ward, along with our friends the Australians, who, now that they had recovered from their homesickness, proved to be exceedingly bright and pleasant. However, I heard afterwards that very few of them remained longer than the year in South Africa; so they probably disliked the country to the end.

There was at Springfontein, doing guard duty for the camp and surrounding blockhouses, the unfortunate regiment of Irish Fusiliers which had shown the white flag at Nicholson's Nek, and had been punished by being taken off active service.[9] The poor colonel had become a broken-down man, so deeply did he feel the disgrace. Everyone said that he was absolutely innocent, as was the majority of the regiment, for some fool subalterns had put up the flag in a moment of weakness. It was not known exactly who had started it, but suspicion rested strongly on one youth, who, if guilty, was not man enough to confess for the sake of his regiment. There was also in Springfontein a very large number of refugees, many of them in houses. The authorities gradually gathered there all who had no farms to return to, and were thus enabled to close the neighboring camps. Government works were then started at Springfontein to give these people employment.

As the Springfontein government store was better than the one at Norval's, Miss Arbuckle and I supplemented the month's supplies which we had laid in. Mr. Gunn was greatly amused at the amount of food we were taking, but he didn't know the Canadian girl's appetite. As a matter of fact we finished all the vegetables and nearly

9. The Boers inflicted heavy casualties on the British at Nicholson's Nek, north of Ladysmith, in October 1899.

Travelling in an Open Truck.

everything else except the bags of flour and sugar, in two weeks. Mr. Sinclair,[10] of cricket fame, then Superintendent of Springfontein, kindly gave us a soda sparklet bottle, an indispensable article in the hot weather.

We could not get carts after all at Springfontein, but had to go on to Jagersfontein Road station. The mail train was four hours late, as usual in those days, and this delay would prevent us from reaching our destination before dark. There was a goods train ready to start, however, but the guard's van was full of paraffine tins. In this train was an open truck half-full of meal bags, covered with sail-cloth, and as the day was warm, sunny and dustless, we girls

10. J.H. Sinclair (1876–1913) was widely viewed as the South African colonies' best all-around cricketer at the turn of the century.

suggested climbing into it. It was no sooner said than done, and a few minutes later saw us and various bundles and rugs, our fox-terrier Nellie, and Miss Daniel's birds all perched on top of the open truck. Mr. Sinclair took my kodak and snapped us, for we looked just like a Boer trek. We reached Jagersfontein Road about eleven o'clock—thirty miles in two hours—only to find that all our stuff was still there, as the traction engines had broken down in the mud. There were there also a number of Norval's refugees, who had left some time before, delayed likewise for lack of transport. They told us that they were bound for Smithfield, but the roads that way were still hopeless. Poor Mr. Gunn was wearing a worried look, when we caught sight of the good-natured face of Mr. Van Niekerk, an old Norval's Ponter, now driving a Repatriation wagon between the Road and Fauresmith. He said he could make room for a few of our smaller boxes, so we each chose a steamer trunk and a roll of bedding, and that was the last we saw of the rest of our belongings until the 9th of October. Then we drove off in two Cape carts, and I did not see the railroad again for eleven months.

CHAPTER VIII

Fauresmith

OUR CARTS WERE DRIVEN BY CAPE BOYS, who spoke English very well, and were thus able to tell us what we wanted to know. This was really our first acquaintance with the veldt, for at Norval's we had been surrounded by high kopjes. We had a thirty mile drive ahead of us, to Jagersfontein, and then some six miles more to Fauresmith.

For the first two hours the road was perfectly flat, and the country absolutely featureless. At noon we reached Fischer's Farm, where we "out-spanned" and ate our lunch. There were people living in the farmhouse, which was in fairly good condition compared with others we saw later. In the afternoon we passed several farms, most of them deserted and the buildings destroyed. All along the road there were burnt and battered articles of furniture and skeletons of animals. We saw now for the first time what war did to the prosperity of a country, for all this section had been under fire repeatedly. Along the railroad, of course, things had been repaired quickly.

This Jagersfontein road, like all roads on the veldt, was simply a track leading from one farm to another. The land was an immense open plain, used for great stock runs, the only enclosed fields being the house gardens. In the distance a clump of fruit trees, a green oasis in the general brownness, marked our approach to a new farm. Cattle kraals[1] and gardens were surrounded by low stone or mud-brick fences, or hedges of prickly pear, the ordinary cactus which grows wild all over South Africa.

We saw a number of large, dignified birds stalking about, something the shape of the pelican. Our "Boy" said the Dutch name for them meant policeman, and that they were highly prized because they devoured the locusts. Around some of the carcasses also were gathered solemn-looking vultures, the scavengers of the veldt. They gather in a circle about the carcass, guarded by sentinels, and apparently at a signal all begin the feast together. There is a heavy penalty

1. Kraals are enclosures.

Fauresmith School.

for shooting one of these birds, and they seem to know it as well as people, for they have not the slightest fear of man.

As we neared the kopjes which indicated Jagersfontein, the ruins beggared description, and we were glad that twilight began to veil the landscape. Sunset amongst the kopjes is very beautiful. The long shadows have violet and opal tints, never seen in the north, but darkness follows so rapidly that one has need to hasten if there is no moon. We began bumping over a villainous stretch of road just as darkness fell, and saw that we would have to remain in Jagersfontein over night. As we drove to the school-house we met a large number of people in the streets, but could not see the town clearly.

The school-master, Mr. Rowan, was comfortably settled in the school-house, which means in South Africa a residence, the school being a separate building. We girls stayed over night in the school-house, Mrs. Rowan giving us two empty rooms to camp in. Mr. Gunn put up at the Methodist parsonage, a cozy bachelor home. Jagersfontein was full of people, had several shops open, and hoped to have the diamond mines working soon. The road-bed for a railroad to Springfontein had been laid before the war, and that work was to be resumed as soon as more pressing matters were attended to. Jagersfontein has since become one of the leading towns of the colony.

The next morning we went on to Fauresmith, over a shocking road; evidently nothing had ever been done to improve the condition of any of the roads, and a skittish horse, or a dark night, would lead to certain destruction. Miss Daniel and Miss Gillingham came along to see what our place was to be like. We reached the town at noon and were delighted at its appearance. It was very pretty, lying in the valley between big kopjes, with large, well-built houses and plenty of shade trees. Most of the people there had been very wealthy before the war, but very few had yet come home; the streets were littered with rubbish, broken furniture, wrecked pianos, empty tins and dead animals everywhere. Many fine houses opening on the street had large gardens behind, but were badly broken also. In the Market Square all the shops had the shutters up, and the big hotel was almost in ruins.

Arrangements had been made for us to board with one of the three English families, because the school-house was out of order; but Miss Pugh-Jones advised us to stick to our original plan of keeping house, and to insist upon having the school-house repaired; accordingly we arranged to board for two weeks only.

After dinner we went to school. Some forty children and about a dozen grown-ups, including Mr. Bam, the Dutch minister, were there to receive us, and greeted us very kindly indeed. They were nice-looking children, some of the girls as handsome as any I have ever seen, and all neatly dressed. Miss Arbuckle was to have only the higher classes, for she had never tried teaching little ones, and we divided as equally as possible. My class of nineteen soon increased to sixty, and by the middle of November reached eighty-five; the whole school numbering a hundred and fifty. In that class there were at least four distinct grades; first, the smallest ones, just beginning school, who could not speak a word of English; next the A B C class, who had made a beginning in camp; and finally, Primers I. and II.

The school had suffered very little in the war, but there was absolutely nothing in the way of supplies except twenty cracked slates and two small, portable blackboards. It is still a mystery to me how the schools there had been run without blackboards, yet in the Orange Free State they had been excellent. This one in Fauresmith had been equipped with an up-to-date workshop for the Sloyd manual training, while nature study and sewing, still novelties with us, had been on their curriculum.[2]

But with these meagre supplies we had to teach for nearly four weeks. Luckily we had a box of slate-pencils from Springfontein, and the children brought us scraps of chalk which they had picked up in camp; I printed short reading lessons on slips on paper, we divided the broken slates, and managed somehow. At first I used to dismiss the smallest ones at the end of two hours, and take the bigger ones out-of-doors for Nature talks, until some of the mothers complained that they were wearing out their shoes too quickly. Of course it would have been impossible to have kept school open under such circumstances if the children had not been very good. In spite of our camp experience, we used to say day after day, "It's quite impossible that this can last; they're just watching to see what sort we are." But after a while it was borne in on us that the children were liking us and that they had no wish to give us trouble. Every morning there was a crowd waiting on the front door-step, and we were mobbed by the girls trying to "walk with," as they said, in order to put their arms around our waists.

Meanwhile Mr. Watts, acting school trustee, was making every possible effort to have the school-house put in order, although every inch of him expressed disapproval at our madness in wishing to keep house. This school-house, typical of the better-class houses, contained eight rooms, kitchen, pantry and bath-room, all on the ground floor, with a verandah in front eighty feet long and twelve feet wide, shaded by honey-locust, poplar, and pepper trees. There was a small garden

2. Sloyd was a system of manual training emphasizing handicrafts.

at the back, with a good hen run, three Kafir rooms, and two large cisterns supplying the bath. We had everything cleaned, but used only the wing containing the kitchen. I wish I could describe the interior of that house, as it was typical of all the houses in town. It had been sacked in turn by troops of Yeomanry, Highlanders and Colonials; Driscoll's Scouts seemed to have been the chief offenders, to judge by the autographs on the walls. Every bit of furniture was more or less smashed, every mirror was in fragments, every mattress ripped up and the feathers and hair scattered. Every dish was broken, and all this mixed up with hats and clothes and kitchen dishes made an indescribable mixture fully six inches deep over all the floors. In one room was a good organ in fragments. Yet this house was not so bad as some others, in which doors, floors and windows were also smashed. To complete the desolation we found a dead horse in our yard, and in the adjoining house a heap of dead sheep.

The town library had been sacked, and all the silverware in town looted, the search for which was the cause of much of the destruction. Furniture, of course, was used for firewood, there being no wood on the veldt. Of sixty-two pianos, only two escaped, and some had had the key-boards ripped out and the hollow space used for feeding-troughs for the horses. Three pipe-organs were smashed. It seemed, indeed, as if the spirit of destruction had seized both sides equally, for Dutch and English agreed that what one side had spared, the other had destroyed. Around Fauresmith there had been a large number of families who had taken and kept the oath of neutrality under Lord Roberts. These had been severely scored by De Wet in his book, and had suffered chiefly at the hands of their own neighbors.[3] One old lady showed me her dining-room suite, from which the leather had all been stripped to mend the uniforms of a Dutch commando. I asked an officer why they smashed all the mirrors, and he said, "If you had been on *trek* for six months,

3. See C. De Wet, *Three Years' War* (New York: Charles Scribner's Sons, 1902).

Top: "Maple Cottage," the Fauresmith School-house.

Bottom: Ruined House opposite the School-house.

without a chance to shave or have a hair-cut, you wouldn't ask that question."

Yet the uncomplaining way in which both sides set bravely to work to clean out their ruined homes made a deep impression on us. For the moment, it seemed as if joy at being home had swallowed up all other feelings. There were a few indeed who were disposed to whine incessantly, and accuse their neighbors of stealing their goods, and knowing that we visited everywhere, would bluntly ask us did we see such-and-such a piece of furniture in so-and-so's house. But to offset these there were others who made a joke of the debris, and pointed with laughter to the work of Driscoll's Scouts in shooting out the eyes of the enlarged crayon portraits of their relatives.

Fauresmith was the chief town of the District of Fauresmith, containing the magistrate's house, court-house and jail. It was also headquarters for the South African Constabulary for the District, under command of Captain Dawson. The men had been using the school as a barracks before our arrival, which they naturally resented.

This town contained many of the influential families of the old Free State, furnishing members for the Volksraad[4] and generals for the war, so we did not expect a cordial reception. Indeed Mr. Gunn advised us to make the first advances ourselves, advice which we followed literally, with some laughable results. However, from our first hour in the town, we met with nothing but the greatest kindness and hospitality, and everyone seemed glad to have school going again.

Besides the famine in school supplies, we had a very limited wardrobe. Not dreaming of separation from our boxes, we had simply packed in the easiest manner, and for one long month Miss Arbuckle and I shared and schemed to make things do. There was a trying ordeal to face at the end of the first week. Mrs. Dawson, the captain's wife, had arranged an informal concert—no charge—to bring people together. Miss Taylor, our hostess, assured us that

---

4. *Volksraad* is the Afrikaans term for "people's government" and refers to the parliament of the South African Republic.

Fauresmith Girls. In her photo album, Graham identified these as, left to right, Miss Fannie Eilenberg, Miss Meintjes, Miss Watts, Miss Annie Meintjes, Miss Emmie Eilenberg.

everyone expected us to be there. Friday afternoon found us sewing frantically in anticipation, and Friday night finished our discomfiture when the usher gave us the very front seats. The programme was good, however, and we quite enjoyed the informal evening afterwards when refreshments were served and we met everybody. Mrs. Dawson introduced an S.A.C. officer, Captain Poussette, of Sarnia, in whom I discovered another fellow-student of old Varsity—one more instance of the smallness of the world. He was in command of a Canadian troop of S.A.C. stationed thirty miles to the north of Fauresmith, and he told us that there was another troop of Canadians forty miles east of us, at Edenburg, under Captain Powell, of Ottawa. This news made us feel quite at home.

On October 1st our house was ready, and we decided to move in and make shift with some bits of the old broken furniture, which

Mr. Elfers, the former headmaster, had commissioned Mr. Watts to sell. This Mr. Elfers was a Hollander, highly spoken of by both English and Dutch. It was thought inadvisable, however, to retain him in the government schools, and he was afterwards engaged by the Dutch church to take charge of an orphanage. The people of Fauresmith were quieted by promises of a headmaster from an English university, but it was seven months before anyone came. By shutting out all teachers suspected of pro-Boer feelings, the Educational Department paved the way for the Separate Schools which were opened later; for when the Dutch synods succeeded in stirring up their people to support such schools, they had all ready at hand a large body of able and thoroughly disaffected teachers. However, I anticipate, as I intend to deal with this grave question of Separate Schools in a later chapter.

Our house, which we christened "Maple Cottage," promised to be very comfortable. There was a grate in the sitting-room, and an almost uninjured range in the kitchen, presided over by a neat and smiling Kafir girl, hired for us by dear old Mrs. Beddy, who from first to last "mothered" us in the kindest way. Her name should have been first in the list at the beginning of this book, only she died long since. Maria, our Kafir, could speak no English, and we could speak no Dutch, so we smiled sweetly and relieved our feelings in French. Our Kitchen Dutch soon equalled Maria's English, and we found her very teachable. She was beautifully clean, but cooked things in the Dutch way, potatoes with sugar, and mutton with cloves. Miss Arbuckle and I at once arranged a division of labor. She was to keep the school registers and accounts, while I was to be housekeeper and keep the house accounts. The Government was now giving us a cash living allowance in place of rations. My first problem was to get fuel. I found that everywhere off the railroad people burned *messe* (dried manure) because coal was not to be had; so I made a bargain with one of the big boys to bring me a bagful every week. This substance burned as evenly as charcoal.

As soon as we settled in Maple Cottage we proceeded to carry out two plans we had formed. The first was to give a picnic to all the smaller children; and the second was to give a tea to the mothers and the members of the upper classes. The picnic was like any other picnic, of course, but the tea made a perfect sensation. We blundered innocently enough, but we should have found out the customs of the place. It seemed that a formal tea was an unheard-of function, and many of them expected a sit-down supper. Then it never occurred to us that a tea could be given without having the blinds drawn, and our silliness only dawned upon us when a few of the younger people asked us timidly why we had candles lighted. However, they all seemed to enjoy themselves, and certainly the sitting-room and dining-room looked exceedingly cozy in the candle-light. The ceilings and floors were of hardwood, and Maria had polished the latter with a mixture of paraffine, candle-grease and turpentine until they shone. We had brought over several benches from school and covered them with our red blankets, and there were masses of roses everywhere. It was the rose season, and the children brought us the most magnificent roses from their gardens, the same as our most expensive hot-house varieties.

As soon as the town ladies heard we were in our house they hastened to call. They nearly all spoke perfect English, with a slight accent, noticeable chiefly in their "g's" and "ch's," which they made guttural. But their kindness did not stop at calls. They sent us presents of flowers, home-made bread, fresh butter and an occasional egg, which things were not to be bought at any price; and we had invitations everywhere. At that time also we heard the origin of the baboon stories. It seemed that after the evacuation in December, 1901, the baboons had come in from the neighboring kopjes and had ransacked the houses; the doors had apparently banged shut on some of them, which were afterwards found dead in the houses.

If those Fauresmith houses could have spoken what a history they could have told of those vacant months; of the repeated

Top: *House Ruined in the War.*

Bottom: *A Commandeered Church, used as a Stable.*

attacks on the town from the block-houses on the surrounding kopjes, with the Dutch making their last stand in the big church tower; of the burning of the shopmen's goods in the market square; of the women grinding corn in the coffee-mills to make coarse bread; of the long *trek* of the refugees to the various camps, or the coast; of the endless succession of Highlanders, Dutch commandos, Yeomanry, more Dutch, Driscoll's Scouts, Remington's, Constabulary, all looting and all destroying. And other towns had a similar story.

Then we got acquainted with the Constabulary and heard their side of things, to add to the tales we had already heard at Norval's, Springfontein and Johannesburg; how one of their sergeants, a quiet little Australian, had been imprisoned in a Boer laager,[5] stripped naked, and sent back on foot across the burning veldt to his own camp, miles away, which he had reached almost dead; and how in one little village of Dopper Dutch, the women and children had mobbed the house of the only English residents, in the absence of the father, and told the wife and girls what the Dutch intended to do with them and the likes of them as soon as they had driven the English into the sea—and then fired on the house; and how—but these things are better forgotten.

We first met a number of these S.A.C. at Mrs. Beddy's. She told us afterwards that, as several of the town girls had refused flatly to meet the troopers, she was quite nervous about inviting us lest we should spoil her evening. But we found them to be exceedingly gentlemanly and well-behaved fellows, and we were much too democratic to see any reason why we should not associate with them. Some of them, to be sure, had considerable difficulty with their "h's," but many others were gentlemen's sons. When General Baden-Powell first organized the force, his idea had been to attract "gentlemen rankers," hence promotion was to be entirely from the ranks. A third-class trooper's pay nearly equalled that of a subaltern

5. A *laager* refers to a number of wagons organized in the form of a circle; from inside Boers could shoot at enemies while being protected by the wagons.

of the line, while a first-class trooper had more. The work was to be somewhat similar to that of the North-West Mounted Police, but with less individual responsibility. Every week the men went out on patrols, of one, two, and three days in succession, taking rations with them. They had to find out if any arms or ammunition were secreted about the farms, keep a census of all farm inhabitants and stock, see that stock was properly branded, issue and oversee the passes of the Kafirs;[6] and some of the men became welcome guests in distant farms because they were thoughtful enough to carry out parcels and mail.

After Mrs. Beddy's party, a few who were not there made the most laughable attempts to meet us. One man came down to borrow a rat-trap which he heard was stored with Mr. Elfer's stuff. Another wondered if we had a piece of elastic to spare; he could not get any in the shops. Another, passing the door, dropped a loaf of bread on the step. Without thinking, I exclaimed, "Yeast-bread!" He laughed, apologized, and said, "I'm the cook of the sergeant's mess, and they won't miss a loaf." He insisted on giving us one, saying they got it from Jagersfontein, which had much better shops than ours. He offered to tell "old Dave" to bring us some when he drove over for the S.A.C. supplies twice a week, and in due time "Old Dave" appeared, driving a square thing he called a Scotch cart, drawn by four mules in a fearful tangle of old harness and rope. And a staunch friend "Old Dave" proved to be. Twice a week until he sailed for England, months later, he never failed to leave us our order of bread or anything else we wanted from Jagersfontein. Then he inherited a little property, married his fiancée of ten years' standing, and settled on a Mexican ranch.

The sergeant-major told us his story, and stories of the others, too; for none of these men, English-like, could be induced to talk of

6. The pass system required that African men carry with them proof of employment. Those caught without passes faced fines or imprisonment. For Graham's description of this system, see Chapter X.

themselves. The nickname "Old Dave" was self-evident, but malaria had weakened and aged him beyond his years, so he was not required to go on patrols, but did the light jobs around the barracks. We often saw him sitting on the ground in the sun, surrounded by old harness, which it was one of his duties to mend. This was a man with a dozen titles floating around in his family. He was also a gentleman in the best sense of the word, but lacked initiative. I never saw such a change in anyone as in him when he got his legacy. He came in to say good-bye in a fine suit of tussore "civvies," and positively swaggered down the street. Then there was "Sandy," who broke in and trained all the horses, and whose father was said to have speculated away a huge estate in Australia.

But the sergeant-major's best stories centered around a tall, handsome fellow, who had signed on at nineteen, long and lanky. He had grown up in a beautiful home, but suddenly finding himself poorer than he had expected to be, thought he saw his chance in the S.A.C. First night in quarters he knelt to say his prayers, being the sort of lordly youth whose surroundings did not particularly interfere with his personal habits. Naturally he was greeted with a shower of boots, brushes, jacks, etc., which rendered devotions impossible. Then he got up—he stood six feet one in his socks—and offered to fight any or all individually who were spoiling for a scrap. After he had thrashed two or three, British fair play was satisfied, and he returned to his interrupted devotions. Nor did the prestige thus gained suffer on the battle-field. One day the officer commanding found it necessary to send a message to another division, across a stretch of open veldt exposed to the enemy's sharpshooters. He called for volunteers. The tall youth drawled his willingness, and cantered across as coolly as on parade-ground, with showers of bullets pinging the ground alongside. His turn apparently had not come, for even his horse escaped with only a slit ear.

A few days after the "mothers' tea" there was a public holiday, St. Weden's Day. This was one of the Dutch holidays retained by the

British; another was Dingaan's Day in February.[7] Miss Arbuckle and I were out for a walk when we heard a horse thundering behind us. We stepped aside, but the rider pulled up and dismounted.

"Excuse me!" said he. "But I'm a Canadian, and I was looking out of the mess window when you passed by, and I knew you were Canadians by the way you got up street as if you owned the town. The fellows said you were the new teachers, and I just *had* to come and speak to you. I hope you'll pardon me, but I haven't seen any but Dutch girls and Kafirs for three mortal years."

We murmured some reply, but he dashed on—"I guess you're the same Canadians Captain Poussette told me about. I'm in his troop."

All this in an accent one could cut with a knife. Yet we felt our pride in our country swelling as he stood there, six feet of well-developed young Canada, with fair hair and blue eyes gleaming out of his brown skin. The unconventionality scarcely occurred to us, we were becoming so accustomed to the friendly veldt fashion of greeting all strangers.

The friendship thus begun proved most useful to us, as our new friend constituted himself advisor-in-chief as to which men were worth knowing, and which were to be tabooed. Captain Poussette certainly had his hands full with twenty-one, some of whom adorned the district jail during the greater part of our stay in Fauresmith. And they weren't a circumstance to the Constabulary in Edenberg, under Captain Powell. The latter was transferred, and a new captain, whom they disliked, was put over them. They mutinied, and at kit inspection would fling their rifles out of their tents,

---

7. Graham is likely referring to Weenen's Day that commemorated the massacre of about five hundred *Voortrekkers* (Dutch and Afrikaans for pioneers) in present-day Kwa-Zulu Natal near the town of Weenen (Dutch for weeping) on February 17, 1838. The *Voortrekkers* were travelling northeast from the Cape and were searching for land in Zulu territory when the Zulu leader Dingaan ordered the killing. Dingaan's Day (or Day of the Covenant) was an annual celebration to mark the *Voortrekkers'* victory over the Zulus on December 16, 1838 at the Battle of Blood River, so named because of the blood of three thousand Zulu warriors that ran that day.

and tell the Captain to come and look at them if he wanted to. They were disbanded at once and sent home. Yet everyone gave these men the greatest praise for their coolness and skill in battle, but it seemed as if they lacked self-control in time of peace, especially when they got whiskey. One night two men out on parole spied some whiskey in a Dutchman's house. They immediately helped themselves, turned the Dutchman and his family out-of-doors, and proceeded to make a night of it. Before the end of the year we were shamed into the feeling that Canada had sent across the scum of the Eastern Provinces, though some of the men were of the very best, and one could fully sympathize with the feeling which led one of them to remark that the voyage on the S.A.C. transport was "a month in hell."

But I must turn to a more cheerful topic. In the second week of October our boxes came from Jagersfontein Road. The big schoolboys made a bee of unpacking, and I never imagined that slates could look so attractive. We stored the school books on the sitting room shelves for safety, and the various games around the hall. A neighbor called the latter the Fauresmith Gymnasium. Along one wall were arranged racks of hockey sticks, tennis rackets and Indian clubs,[8] and on the other side were croquet, cricket and our own saddles. Miss Arbuckle had arranged that the senior classes should control the play-ground, on a sort of self-government principle. This worked admirably, and the boys turned to work manfully to put the tennis court in order. Only the larger ones were allowed to play cricket, hockey or tennis, the smaller ones having rounders and basket-ball, which I had brought myself from Canada. The little ones had simply the ordinary children's play which was all they required.

School now began properly, and we felt that we could accomplish something. We had a very large supply of pictures, colored and plain, which we used to decorate the class-rooms, and which gave

---

8. "Indian clubs" were wooden clubs used for exercise and juggling.

great pleasure to the children. Apparently there had always been an incredible lack of pretty books for children throughout the country, even our biggest scholars having never heard of our best known children's books, such as "Alice in Wonderland." A roll of colored Sunday School pictures, sent out by Dr. Briggs, called forth a chorus of ecstatic "ohs!" from my class.[9]

Other people in town were also getting supplies, so that the houses were gradually regaining a home-like appearance. Martial law was at an end, and a daily post cart connected all our chain of towns on the Kimberley Road, Luckoff, Koffeefontein, Fauresmith and Jagersfontein, with the railway. Until October the mail had reached us only once a week, by S.A.C. carrier. It was the custom as soon as the mail was sorted to ring the market bell, when all the inhabitants rushed to the post-office like boys to a dog-fight.

By the end of October the absentees were nearly all home from the Coast, and the school had grown beyond our strength. We were constantly agitating for a kindergarten teacher, and also a Dutch teacher, so that we might comply with the regulations, which called for about four hours of instruction in high Dutch every week. But it was the middle of November before the kindergartner came, and Christmas before we had a Dutch teacher. People were grumbling loudly by that time. Still they tried to make it plain to us that they did not hold us responsible, and, indeed, we were helped in school by Miss Bam, daughter of the Dutch minister, during an illness of Miss Arbuckle's. Miss Bam was kindness itself, and simply laughed at the mention of pay.

About this time the farmers were discouraged by a flight of locusts, the only one I saw during my stay in Africa. The heavy rain of September had caused the seed to spring up in a gratifying manner, and the trees promised much fruit. In a single night everything was lost. It was nearly time to dismiss school one day when the windows

9. Graham is likely referring to Charles A. Briggs (1841–1913), the liberal American Presbyterian scholar and theologian.

were suddenly darkened by numbers of what looked to us like enormous flying grasshoppers. The children gasped, "Locusts!" They knew what it meant, and became so excited that we let them go. Everyone immediately started killing as many locusts as possible, which was curiously easy to do, for it seemed as if they became stupid when they alighted, and very few remained flying about singly. They settled on the ground in even rows, quite close together, in the same direction in which they had been flying, and ate up absolutely everything. The Constabulary tried to exterminate the next brood, by watching the hatching places, and, as soon as a brood began to crawl, the men inoculated some of the insects with poison. The remainder fed on their carcasses and also died. The reports on this method of extermination were very encouraging. That one flight, however, deprived us of all the first crop of fruit and green vegetables, a terrible loss in the hot weather just coming on. No more rain was due until after Christmas, hence it was useless to sow fresh seed.

In consequence of the failure of the harvest there was danger of famine amongst the very poor, and to guard against this the Government wisely decided to keep the Repatriation office, or Government Relief office, as it came to be called, open until after the next harvest. This office was to inquire into all cases of distress, to supply work when possible, or to give supplies outright.

When I use the word "harvest," I do not mean such a harvest as we have in America, but a supply of vegetables, fruits and rough hay for the stock. The grain of the country came from the section bordering on Basutoland, and most of the hay from the northern Transvaal.[10]

10. Basutoland was the kingdom of the Sotho established in 1824 by Moshoeshoe during the *difaqane* (Sotho for "scattering"), a period of severe political upheaval and migration in southern Africa in the 1820s and 1830s. The British annexed Basutoland to the Cape Colony in 1871 and in 1884 it became a British High Commission Territory. In 1966 Basutoland gained independence from Britain and was renamed the Kingdom of Lesotho.

It seemed to us that the children faced the hard conditions with surpassing bravery. Many a girl came to school with a bright smiling face although she had no dinner to look forward to but a slice of bread and molasses; many a boy had to do a good day's work before the school day began. I recall one family especially, of which I had two girls and a boy in my class. The family consisted of father, mother, and six children. The father's sole earnings were the few pounds he picked up by driving an occasional Repatriation wagon. Suddenly the eldest girl and the boy left school. On inquiry I learned that the boy had enteric—typhoid fever—the mother was in bed with lumbago,[11] and this girl was sole nurse and cook for the family. They were by far too poor to keep a Kafir girl. Yet, when the children returned to school, the girl was very little behind in her classes, having managed amidst her multifarious duties to find time to study; nor had her home duties been neglected.

On the King's birthday a shocking accident occurred, which had, however, the effect of showing how strong a link of friendliness was uniting all classes at that time. Our town was playing Jagersfontein in a cricket match, and the men came home in inky darkness over the bad road I have before mentioned. Sergeant-major Doris' horse ran into a remnant of barbed-wire entanglement, throwing his rider against a stone. He never regained consciousness. The sergeant-major had been a most strict disciplinarian, and many of the men professed to hate him; yet even these stood pale with emotion at his funeral. He was buried with full military honors, the most affecting of all funerals. Even some of our Dutch friends had red eyes. A few of the most exclusive townspeople, who had refused to meet the troopers, stripped their gardens of their finest flowers; while the whole town observed a week of mourning as for a personal friend. The service was conducted by Rev. Mr. Thorne, of Jagersfontein, an

11. Lumbago is intense lower back pain.

old gentleman who had lost everything in the war, and had formerly lost all he had in the Transvaal war of 1883.[12]

Mr. Thorne was a peace hero. The Fauresmith rector, Mr. Stevens, a man about whose name there clustered endless tales of life-long sacrifice, had died during the war, the rectory had been burned, and the people were too poor to support another rector. Mr. Thorne, whose little church was filled twice a day with men from the mines, might have been excused if he had paid no heed to us, yet at infinite discomfort and labor to himself—for he was an old man—he drove over to us on Sunday afternoons, in all sorts of weather, and held service until Easter-time. Anyone who has been obliged to cross the veldt at two o'clock of a summer afternoon, when all the South African world is in bed, can appreciate what that meant. At Easter the Mission Board helped us out with a rector of our own.

The Dutch church, of Presbyterian doctrines and order of service, held meeting in the mornings only. There was some sort of young people's prayer-meeting at night, but many of the young people came to the English service.

Towards the end of November the kindergarten teacher came—Miss Blair, a Scotch lassie, one of the sweetest and most unselfish girls it has been my good fortune to know. She found everybody talking concert. Mrs. Dawson was getting up one to raise funds for renovating the town hall, and we were drilling the children for closing exercises. There was no piano in the school, which made it uphill work. However, we knew that things usually come to those

12. Graham is likely referring to the First Anglo-Boer (also known as the Transvaal) War of 1880–1881. In the 1860s and 1870s the Transvaal was encroaching on the land of neighbouring African kingdoms and one in particular, the Pedi kingdom, was having success at rebuffing the Transvaal. In 1876 the Transvaal lost a costly war with the Pedi kingdom and was facing bankruptcy. Britain considered the Transvaal's weakened state and inability to conquer African militaries a threat to its strategic and economic interests in the region and so in 1877 it annexed the republic. In 1880 the Boers rebelled and defeated the British in humiliating fashion. Wishing to disengage from the conflict, the British signed an armistice and the Boers regained self-rule in 1881.

who hustle while they wait. By the time we were ready for rehearsals in the town hall, the non-commissioned officers of the S.A.C. had kindly offered us their old mess piano, and Mrs. Dawson cheerfully lent us her good one for the concert.

Two days before Christmas the arrival of a second-hand piano changed Maple Cottage into a home, and from that date it was more than ever "The Young People's Club-house," as a neighbor christened it. It was indeed a sort of neutral ground where the different cliques might meet without injury to their pride, as several new elements were then agitating Fauresmith society. These were a few families and some young men and women, all friendly to the British, who had recently returned from Europe, or Cape Colony, and boarding-school. One young gentleman, whose sisters had been particularly cordial, had just graduated in law from London University. Another gentleman and his wife were from Edinburgh, whose university has always attracted a large number of South African Dutch. These were an exceptionally handsome couple who had had no little amusement at a Scotch tea given in their honor. An Edinburgh lady remarked to the gentleman, "I don't see any Boers, here yet, do you? I was told there would be some." "No," said he, looking around—he could easily see the whole room—"I don't see any Boers anywhere." Just then his hostess rushed up and introduced him and his wife as her two South African Dutch friends.

Everything considered, the town was becoming too British in tone for a few ultra-Dutch, called in Cape Colony Afrikanders, and they formed a little clique of their own. A few old Anglo-Africans scoffed at the apparent friendliness of others, remarking, "Just wait till the compensation claims are paid, and then you'll find out how much their friendship is worth. They don't think it wise now to show their real feelings." Such gloomy prophecies made us feel unhappy, but I fear they contained a percentage of truth. No doubt other causes were at work, but the fact remains that in many communities, living in the utmost concord during the first year of peace, there has since been nothing but strife. In Colesburg, for instance, where we had spent such happy hours, the same people who had entertained us had joined opposing cliques, boycotting each other in society and business.

Just before Christmas the Government Compensation Claims Board, whose work will be considered more fully in a later chapter, opened an office in Fauresmith. Our late assistant superintendent at Norval's, Mr. Robertson, was secretary, an instance of the way in which one was always meeting old friends in Africa. Although the country is so large, the population is small and constantly moving about, and one is soon impressed with the "knowability" of everyone, as Kipling says of India. All persons who had vouchers for stock used or claims for compensation were to present them to this office for investigation. Mr. Robertson thought that a month would be sufficient to finish the work, but it proved to be so complicated that a year saw it still incomplete. The delay had a bad effect on business, as people had already stretched their credit on the strength of their claims.

On Christmas eve all the neighborhood gathered at Mrs. Truby's (the wife of the postmaster), to "sing in" Christmas. We were told that this was an old Dutch custom, and a very pretty one we thought it. But with the mercury in the nineties every day it was hard to realize that it was Christmas time.

Contrary to expectations, I did not feel the South African heat so oppressive as the midsummer heat in Ontario. The air is so clear and dry, and the nights usually so cool, that I found it quite bearable. Sunstroke in ordinary times is rare.

Christmas morning we were feeling rather depressed, when we heard Joanna coming down the passage. Maria, our first Kafir, had left us some time before, because of illness, and Joanna, or "Janiky," as she called herself, was a continual source of amusement. She was an older woman, an excellent cook, but always talking to herself and apparently enjoying some joke at our expense. These Kafir girls were like mischievous children. One day Maria was caught in the act of imitating to the life the walk of a certain young lady who was rather conceited, and after that we were constantly getting her to imitate all our friends, and ourselves included. So when we heard Joanna chattering in an excited way we prepared for surprises. In she came, her arms full of bundles. "Hi, missy, missy looi (lazy), ho, missy upstand, hi, hi, hi!" and she waited expectantly. The largest parcel was an immense box of sweets for the three of us. While we were exploring the parcels with our spirits up a hundred per cent., there came a great clamor at the door; the verandah was full of children to wish us merry Christmas.

The day passed off delightfully. A clergyman passing through to Kimberley held morning service, which was followed by an informal reception at Mrs. Philip Voortman's. A thunder-shower in the afternoon cooled the air, thus enabling us to do full justice to the fine dinner waiting for us. Several neighbors had sent in samples of plum-pudding, and our own was an absolute success. The sergeants' mess had sent us a present of some chickens which the late sergeant-major had destined for our Christmas. We had invited a few other exiles to share the feast, and Joanna had filled the kitchen with a hilarious gathering of her cronies to devour the remains. Mrs. Beddy, knowing that our oven was defective, insisted upon roasting the chickens for us, and I fear that there wasn't much left for Joanna. After eating nothing but lean hill mutton for three months, until Miss Arbuckle declared that she was ashamed to look a sheep in the face, chickens tasted indescribably good. In the evening Mrs. Meintjes and her daughters and some other neighbors dropped in for a "sing-song." Miss Lulu Meintjes, who was to teach Dutch in school, was a charming singer, and an exceedingly handsome girl.

The day following Christmas—Boxing Day, the English call it—was another public holiday. An immense picnic was held at *Groen Kloof* (green valley) farm. Those of us who had saddles rode, and the others went in a big *trek* wagon with a tent, drawn by a dozen oxen. Several engagements were the result of that picnic, but the first wedding was our own Margaret Blair, who married Mr. Chas.

Schickerling some months later, and is now living on a beautiful farm near Fauresmith.

This farm of *Groen Kloof* was occupied by an especially bitter anti-British family. One of the daughters, a little fair woman with golden curls, was quite a noted character. She was well educated, and had been a Boer ambulance nurse. During the war she had been a spy, was caught and sent down to Cape Colony; whence she worked her way to the front again without a pass, was caught again and put in Springfontein Camp. There she made such a disturbance that she had to be put in the "irreconcilable" lines.[13] She was an excellent seamstress, and we made her acquaintance over some work. One day, as we sat sipping coffee at the farm, she began railing at the English, calling them "white devils." We said:

"Why do you talk like that? We are British, remember."

"Oh!" she answered, "you may be British, but you are not English. You are Canadian, and we like Canadians—you come from a big free country and you are not stiff."

We finished our coffee with rather mixed feelings.

The Dutch farmers, in fact, assured us that they took the liveliest interest in Canadian farming interests, and I heard much from them of the progress of the Dutch deputation to America to study farm methods. Everyone approved highly of the policy of the Bloemfontein Government in seeking to improve the farming conditions of the Orange River Colony. Generally also the Canadian soldier boys were well spoken of by the people. They never failed to tell us what looters they were, but I rather think they admired that quality; at any rate they "got on well with them," to use their own expression.

Not only on the farms, but everywhere, coffee is an institution of South Africa; everyone drinks it before rising, again at eleven o'clock, and at four o'clock instead of tea. Usually it was good, but sometimes it was unspeakable, and to refuse it was to give great

---

13. "Irreconcilables" was a term given by the British to Boers who refused to take an oath of neutrality.

offence. There was another farm near Fauresmith which we often visited and where the coffee-pot was always on the stove. When the liquid became weak more coffee was put in, and when the pot refused to hold more water, I suppose the grounds were emptied out. The lady of the house was a jolly old soul who could speak no word of English, and who was so fat that I always held my breath when she reached the door. One day I was out there with some of the village girls, one of whom had been accepting various attentions from a young Englishman. "Why do you smile on that pauper?" cried the old lady. "See my son, he would marry you gladly; and look at the beautiful farm, and the stock! What foolishness!" The girl's cheeks would have toasted bread.

The Christmas holidays lasted five weeks, and shortly after school began again Miss Blair had a peremptory telegram ordering her immediately to the Railway School at Bloemfontein. She was greatly upset, but there was no one to give an explanation, as Mr. Gunn was no longer our inspector, and we did not know who was in his place. Then a letter came advising us that Miss Phillimore would take the kindergarten. It was delightful to have Miss Phillimore again, but we knew that she intended sailing for England in a few weeks, so this arrangement would be merely temporary, and in March the kindergarten would be upset once more. It had grown to such an immense size that it was very difficult for a stranger to take hold of the work; so after much writing to the Department, Mrs. Van der Post, a lady in the town, was hired as assistant to Miss Phillimore. Meanwhile Miss Blair used all her powers of persuasion in the head office, and when Miss Phillimore left for England she was sent back to Fauresmith. This was one example among dozens of the foolish waste of money by the Department in shifting teachers, often contrary to the expressed wish of the people of the towns, to say nothing of the frequent upsetting of the classes. Whenever a teacher moved a private cart had to be hired to take her to the railroad, as the post carts carried only hand baggage. And the Department, of course, had all expenses to pay. The only explanation we could ever get for it was found in the shortage of teachers; whichever schools clamoured loudest for help got it at the expense of others.

All our classes were very full in March, the beginning of autumn. The farm children had come to town to take advantage of the free schools, because there was little to do on the farms. An almost unbroken drought, from September, had killed the seed of the second crop, and we heard pitiful tales of the sheep dying by the thousands for want of water. It was said that all the stock given out by the Repatriation Board died that year. In town we were fortunate in having an excellent supply of water from springs in the hills. It was almost impossible to get fruit, for it had simply shrivelled up and dropped off the trees. A few farms like Botany Grove (Mr. Schickerling's) had magnificent fruit, because their gardens were irrigated, a fine object lesson of what could be done with irrigation from extensive dams.

We had no little amusement out of these big farm boys. Several had served on commando and had forgotten almost all their former schooling, but were quite content to start over again with the little ones. Indeed, such was their desire to make up for what they had lost that they had to be chased out for recess. One day a little man knocked at my door, and ushered in a big, overgrown boy. He said:

"Miss Graham, I bring you my boy Gert. He goot boy, but no school—tree, four year. He fight goot, and work by the farm. Now, you beat him, beat him hard, make him learn." Poor Gert, eighteen years old, and only fit for the Third Reader! But he did his very best.

In March, also, the town was thrown into a flutter of excitement over the approaching wedding of Miss Winnie Rorich, whose father had made a fortune from diamond mines found on his farm. She was one of the most popular girls in town, and was to marry a Mr. de Villiers, who, as the name signifies, was descended from one of the old French Huguenot families which had first settled the Cape. There was quite a sprinkling of these French names amongst the children, such as Olivier, Joubert, Roux, Bilgnaut, De la Rey, etc. Half the town was invited to Miss Winnie's wedding reception, after which she and Mr. de Villiers drove away to the Road in a carriage all decked with white ribbon, and followed by an escort of a dozen other carriages. The spirit of a wedding is the same the world over, and the guests left behind spent the rest of the day picking rice out of their hair.

It was from Joanna, the cook, that we learned some new wrinkles in the conduct of a wedding. Having secured permission one day to go to one the following morning, she electrified us at breakfast by appearing in a bright yellow gown, with every individual strand of her wool frizzed out on end, and surmounted by an artificial wreath. Asked the meaning of this frivolity it transpired that she was to be bridesmaid. "Bridesmaid!" we shrieked. She had a pickininny[14] eight years old. Further questioning elicited the astounding statement that the bride had been married by Kafir rites some twenty years before, that her own grown-up daughter was to be the first bridesmaid, and that in the intervening twenty years she and her *mann* had saved the requisite fifty pounds for a grand Christian wedding, with a sumptuous breakfast and a week's revelry afterwards; and that this programme was rather a popular one amongst the Kafirs.

Easter brought several changes to our little world of Fauresmith. Rev. Mr. Downton, our rector, came and began his work on that day, and we felt very important at the thought of having our own clergyman at last. Also the long-talked-of headmaster arrived from Scotland. This led to the removal of Miss Arbuckle to Bethlehem, and she left amid the universal regret of townspeople and children. I don't know which of us felt it more, she at going, or I at staying behind. However, she was not to be thrown amongst total strangers as Miss Wilson and Miss Webb, from Norval's Pont, were still at Bethlehem, and Miss De Wolfe, a Canadian from Halifax, had recently been moved there from Kroonstad.

14. "Pickininny" is a derogatory term for a child of African descent.

Our Cook Joanna.

We observed the spirit of Easter Day by decorating the graves of all soldiers, British or Dutch. This work was carried on all over Africa by the League of Loyal Women, an organization similar in aims to the Daughters of the Empire in Canada.

Easter also marked the end of the warm weather, and the beginning of what proved to be a very severe winter. In May and June there were several degrees of frost nightly, and one day in June there was a flurry of snow. That sounds meaningless to Canadians, but if you will reflect that most of the people were too poor to buy fuel, or even warm clothing, you will understand that there was much suffering. It brought a lump to my throat to see my children morning after morning in cotton frocks or jackets, with brave smiling faces, and their little fingers so swollen with chilblains that they could scarcely hold their pencils. The continued drought and the delay in the payment of compensation claims had strained credit to the utmost, and only the wealthiest were free from worry.

So the time slipped by until the July holidays with no special developments of any sort. The compensation claims were gradually being paid, and the Relief Board was selling off its stock and supplies preparatory to closing its office. The social life of the town, aptly likened to that of a summer resort by Miss Phillimore, had exchanged the milder summer sports for polo, field hockey and paper-chases on horseback. Being so near Jagersfontein we had quite a large circle of young people, and every day of the winter holidays had something special.

Meantime I had received my orders to march on, and was looking forward with regret to the time when I should leave Fauresmith, when a horrible accident rang down the curtain on my life there. From the time of the headmaster's arrival Miss Blair and I had been boarding; and on the day before I left Fauresmith a young man who sat opposite me at table was killed at polo, and the last thing I did in the town was to play the funeral march in the service.

CHAPTER IX

Kroonstad

MY NEXT STATION WAS AT KROONSTAD, the seat of the Orange Free State Government after the occupation of Bloemfontein by Lord Roberts, and next in size and importance to Bloemfontein. It is very prettily situated on the banks of the Valsch River.

Two incidents of my journey there stand out as peculiarly characteristic of life on the veldt. The first occurred at the noon "out-span" on the way to the railroad. The halting place was a ruined and deserted farm, where already another cart had stopped, of which the occupant was preparing his picnic lunch on a rug spread on the sand. He was a commercial traveller, evidently, to judge by the enormous boxes roped in careful balance before and behind his Cape cart. When my boy had led off the horses to water and I was laying out my own lunch, I could see my fellow traveller taking furtive glances in my direction. As I had no fresh fruit he had a chance to break the ice by offering some of his, and in a few minutes we had arranged to re-spread our lunch together while our boys looked on at a respectful distance, awaiting their share. A pretty pair we were, too! He was a red-headed Scotchman, with his face burnt to the same fiery hue; while I was tanned almost as brown as a Kafir from the out-of-door life I had been leading with hockey, tennis, or paper-chases on horseback every afternoon. With my white Panama, bound with a dull red puggaree,[1] I might have posed as a western cowboy-girl just off the plains.

The second incident was on board the train—the first I had seen for eleven months. In the same compartment was a pretty English girl, just out, with the typical English complexion of cream and roses. She was wearing a dainty travelling costume of grey serge, with a little white Alpine hat, which altogether presented such a contrast to my dust-stained garments as must have made a Zulu laugh.

Kroonstad was a new type of town, much busier than Bloemfontein. My new headmaster, Mr. Noakes, who met me at the station, informed me that they were having a boom, and that people were

---

1. A puggaree is a scarf or cloth to further protect the wearer from the sun.

paying from seven to nine pounds a month for cottages of five rooms, while others were still obliged to live in tents. As time passed on I failed to discover any sufficient reason for the boom, as did likewise many of the business people. There were all sorts of rumors in the air of new gold finds, valuable coal deposits and precious stones. They did indeed find coal of an uncertain quality at Vereeniging, some distance from Kroonstad, and some indications of gold, but the precious stones, on investigation, proved to be bits of colored glass scattered about by sharpers.[2]

Prices, moreover, were still exorbitant during that second year after the war, owing to the droughts. Eggs sold at two shillings a dozen, fresh eggs at four shillings, and strictly fresh eggs at nine shillings on the market; butter was from two to three shillings a pound, and milk fourpence a pint; bread was sixpence a pound, but meat was only ninepence, as it was brought in quantities from Australia. Clothing became quite reasonable in price, but Kafir labor was the only cheap article on the market. It amused Canadians vastly to hear South African ladies grumble because a good Kafir cook wanted a pound a month, while a fair one could be had for ten shillings, all Miss Arbuckle and I had ever paid. Of course the girls expected old clothes, and carried away all the leavings from the kitchen to their "location" homes every night.

Kroonstad was the centre of a circle of military camps—the second battalion of "the Queen's," the Fifth "Mounted Infantry" two regiments of Hussars and some Gunners, who contributed largely to the gayety of local society with gymkhanas,[3] polo, races, band concerts, balls, etc. Yet the social life lacked entirely the spontaneity and unity characteristic of the previous year at Fauresmith. People were beginning to feel the shortage of money keenly; banks were calling in their loans, causing numbers of people to become bankrupt; all classes were blaming the Government, as people usually do,

2. Sharpers are thieves or con men.

3. *Gymkhanas* are equestrian competitions.

for their woes, and Dutch and English were not only drawing apart, but were dividing into numerous cliques. Individually, however, I found the people of Kroonstad more hospitable, if possible, than the people of Fauresmith had been. The inhabitants were about half and half British and Dutch, with many nice families of both races. Amongst the Dutch there were a number of retired farmers, old people who had sold their land to the Government at the close of the war and were living on their money.

In the government schools the majority of the children were British, as the Dutch had a large Church school. The government schools were three in number, two free and one a fee-paying, or High School, in which I was an assistant. I pass over this topic here, as it is dealt with in the chapter on education. In fact, the chief problems which were agitating society that year are all discussed under their various heads.

A few months before leaving Kroonstad, several of us made a determined and rather successful attempt to bring the various factions together by means of field hockey, the most popular pastime of the last three winters. The club had a membership of nearly a hundred, drawn from all the cliques of town; the ladies' club, of which I was captain, included a school-girl eleven, and had about equal numbers of Dutch and English. We arranged a regular schedule of games, the gentlemen playing alone three days in the week, the ladies two days, the remaining day being devoted to a mixed game. On ladies' and mixed days tea was served on the grounds by members of the club in turn; and as there were always a number of spectators, the hockey field became a sort of informal social club.

On the day before I left Kroonstad hockey interest reached its climax. The gentlemen had challenged the ladies to a match, the former to be handicapped by wearing skirts. All the town was on hand. During most of the first half everyone was too helpless with laughter to do much with the ball. A well-known colonel, centre forward for the gentlemen, was arrayed in a white skirt with a train which he had managed to fasten straight in front, with the obvious result that when he attempted to follow the ball he tripped and went rolling down the field. An elderly doctor, playing half, worked so hard that his skirt was in ribbons and himself so exhausted that he went straight to bed at the end of the game. It didn't take the younger gentlemen long to learn how to sprint in spite of the skirts, and it would have gone hard with our team had it not been for our right back, Miss Bouwer, who was simply unapproachable. Making allowance for the umpire's partiality, I think the score stood fairly one all.

CHAPTER X

The Kafirs and the Labor Question

IN THIS AND THE FOLLOWING CHAPTERS I shall try to give an account of the chief topics of interest in the new colonies, some of which still present unsolved problems.

The Kafirs are an important element in South African life, outnumbering the whites five to one. The term Kafir is applied to all the blacks indiscriminately although it belongs properly to the most numerous race, which is gradually absorbing the others. None of them are so coal-black as some of our American negroes, who are usually superior in physique.

The Cape boys are almost yellow, and are said to be half-breeds. The Kafirs and kindred tribes are a clear brown, and the Hottentots somewhat darker and altogether most inferior-looking. The blacks of the Orange River Colony come mostly from Basutoland, lying to the east, strictly reserved from white settlement, and protected by the British. There are various mission stations there, and it is reported that Basutoland is most fertile, and rich in minerals. None of the natives who come out for service will give one any information about the country, but become suspicious at once when questioned. Nor can one blame them. They have the same feeling of ownership of all South Africa that the Red Indians had of America, and in fact have often been heard saying, since the war, that when all the British soldiers would leave the country it would be their turn to get back their land. And so old settlers who have lived through the horrors of former native wars, feel very uneasy at the gradual withdrawal of the troops. The Dutch, moreover, have reason to fear the Kafirs, for in the old days they oppressed them. Many a Dutchman has told me unblushingly that the Kafirs had no souls and were only fit to be slaves. Indeed, during the year after the war scarcely a Dutch family could keep a Kafir servant, for the Kafirs had received much larger pay than they were accustomed to from the military, and as their wants are very simple, had saved enough to keep themselves for a year in idleness; hence they would work only when they chose. The quality of the work also depended largely on their personal liking for their employers. Several times I tried to get my girls to do odd jobs for a neighbor, but they would look annoyed and say, "Missy—scelum (bad)." After much coaxing, however, they would go, but would do the most slip-shod work. If a mistress got the reputation of being fussy, inefficient, or hard to please, no capable Kafir would work for her. They had, in fact, a most complete system of boycott in such matters.

One of the unexplained things amongst the Kafirs is their system of communication. Many a time we got news from distant parts of the country before the same items came by paper or post. Another quaint thing was their desire for long holidays. The most industrious of them would suddenly express a longing to go back to Basutoland, and "sit" so long as savings would last. They would hunt up a good substitute on these occasions, and at the end of the appointed time would reappear, and go on with their work quite cheerfully. Cheerfulness indeed is their prevailing characteristic, but they can sometimes squeeze out genuine tears in the most amusing way. We discovered that whenever anyone was moving away, the Kafir girl would become demonstratively affectionate. She would weep copiously and express an ardent wish to go with "missy." When she thought her victim's feelings were sufficiently worked upon, she would smile through her tears, like a rainbow through the clouds, and ask insinuatingly, "Missy want dat?" pointing to some coveted article. It was so funny that she usually got what she wanted.

One of our most amusing evenings in Fauresmith was spent at the closing exercises of the Kafir mission school. Our party rashly accepted front seats, being filled with a vain-glorious ambition to pay grave attention to everything on the programme. The opening number was an anthem, rendered by a dozen dusky beauties in gorgeous raiment of red and yellow, and an equal number of the more sombre sex in ill-fitting blacks, ranging from ordinary serge to some one's cast off evening coat. The chorus was trained by the sol-fa system, and sang without accompaniment, reflecting great credit on their teacher, a native with a really fine face. We gave the well-merited applause with great vigor. After that a succession of recitations, given with varying degrees of agony, to say nothing of the toilettes, was rapidly undermining our gravity, when the appearance of Sam, the butcher's boy, proved to be the last straw. Sam was a long, loose-jointed Kafir, with protruding head and splay feet. He shuffled on to the platform, pulled down his waistcoat, smoothed his coat-tails, adjusted his collar, and after several convulsive breaths emitted a stentorious "Come!" Apparently the key did not suit him, for after repeating his former programme to the minutest detail, he again shouted, "Come!" in a different key. By this time our party scarcely dared breathe, lest someone should explode with laughter. After a third and final effort, Sam succeeded in finishing his invitation. "Come into the stilly night," he sang, and finished it manfully, whereupon we encored him, and after that there was no holding ourselves at all.

The treatment of the natives by the Government up-country is not the same as in Cape Colony. There they live freely amongst the whites, having practically the same privileges, politically and otherwise. But in Natal[1] and on the veldt they are too numerous,

---

1. In the colony of Natal, located below Zululand alongside the Indian Ocean, and the two Boer republics, Africans were denied economic, social, and political equality; for example, the franchise had always been limited to white males only. In contrast, the Cape Colony had a history of relative non-racialism. When the Cape established representative government in 1853 it introduced a non-racial franchise (for men only) with income and property qualifications that were low enough to ensure most white men qualified and high enough to ensure most (but not all) African men did not. Natal was originally the Boer republic of Natalia (1839–1843) and was conquered by the British in 1843, and from the outset the small British settler population had a hostile relationship with Africans. The development of capitalist agriculture required farm labour and African peasants largely refused to work for wages on white-owned farms. Consequently, the colonial government—after first recruiting thousands of indentured labourers from India—began a process of proletarianizing Africans by imposing on them a battery of taxes, fines, and duties to be paid only with cash. In the years immediately after the South African War, there was a recession in Natal and the colonial government responded by expropriating additional African land for British sugarcane agricultural production and imposing yet more taxes on Africans to raise revenue and force more peasants into wage labour. As an official in the British Colonial Office in London observed at the time, "If Natal liked to revert to medieval methods of taxation I do not see that it is any business of ours" (Marks, *Reluctant Rebellion*, 142). For more on tense British–African relations in Natal after the South African War, see Shula Marks, *Reluctant Rebellion: The 1906–8 Disturbances in Natal* (London: Clarendon Press, 1970).

and for the most part too ignorant, to be allowed such freedom. Since the war the Natal regulations have been followed very largely throughout the Orange River Colony and the Transvaal, and are not widely different from the regulations of the late Republics. In the first place, the Kafirs are not allowed to live intermingled with the whites, but must keep to themselves in "locations," or settlements, at one side of a town or farm. Secondly, no Kafir is allowed to wander about the towns or country without having in his possession a "pass," signed by his employer, renewed monthly, to certify that he is in regular employment. At nine o'clock, throughout the country, a curfew bell rings, after which any Kafir found outside the location, without a special pass, is liable to fine or imprisonment. The necessary arrangements are easily made when it is desirable to have the Kafirs stay at one's home overnight; but they prefer to go to the locations, being above all things gregarious in their habits. It was found that the house-servants, washer-women in particular, evaded the law by sharing up washes and lending their passes. To prevent this the Constabulary now visit the locations to search out all who have no passes and send them back to Basutoland, a step rendered necessary by the frequency of petty thieving to support idlers in the location.

The Kafir girls make excellent laundresses, but their methods are sudden death to delicate fabrics. All the washing is done in the river beds, on the flat rocks, the dirt being worked out by constant pounding with small stones. The clothes are then spread on the thorn bushes, always found along the banks of streams, and what the stones spare the thorns finish.

Some people say that the Kafirs are dishonest. Personally I never had the slightest cause for holding such an opinion. In the mines, however, they have to be very strictly watched, and, even so, thousands of pounds' worth of diamonds are stolen every year, and are sold by the illicit diamond buyers.

Native labor is, of necessity, one of the main features in the conduct of the mines. A visit to Jagersfontein diamond mine, during my year in Fauresmith, afforded an opportunity of comparing the treatment of the Kafirs there with what we had seen in the Johannesburg gold mines. This mine was afterwards held up as a model by the *Bloemfontein Post*, and cited as one which had no difficulty in getting all the native labor it required.

Mr. and Mrs. Debell, the manager and his wife, entertained a party of us at dinner, and took us for a most interesting walk about the mine. We went first to the great pit where the diamonds were found. It was then excavated to a depth of over a hundred feet. As we looked down the Kafirs were preparing for the noon blast, and were scurrying under shelter like rabbits into their burrows. They wore oddly-braided straw Kafir hats, and little else; and when the blast was over heaped the broken clay in buckets, which were drawn to the surface by pulleys, there to be dumped into small trams drawn by donkeys along narrow rails to the pulsator. There it was spread out to be softened by the sun and air, after which it was sifted for stones.

When the men quit work for dinner they vanished into a hole in the inside of the pit. Mr. Debell explained that that was the mouth of the tunnel leading to the native compound, and that the natives down below were not allowed to have any communication with those working on the surface. He then took us to the compound to see them fed. It was a large area enclosed by a high whitewashed wall of mud brick, and surrounded by a continuous ring of mud brick rooms, also white. The natives were coming up from the tunnel past an overseer who checked them off. We followed them to the kitchen, a long room having a row of six iron kettles built in over fire-holes. Each kettle was as big as a barrel, and all were full of mealie meal mush (Indian corn, or cornmeal mush). Each Kafir had a pail, and as he filed past received a shovelful of mush, which is the Kafir's staple diet. None of them seemed to have any difficulty in making away with about three pints of mush in one meal. Besides mealies, each one was allowed as rations a certain quantity of bread, meat and vegetables. There was also a store where these and other articles, of guaranteed quality, were sold at strictly cost price. The rooms were kept beautifully clean, and there was a hospital ward with free attendance. There was also in the compound a search room, where departing Kafirs were carefully examined for stolen stones; a favorite device was to swallow them, for which scheme the search room programme provided a strong emetic.

The Kafirs signed for a definite period, usually three months. During that time they were not allowed out of the compound on any pretext whatever. That they appreciated their fair treatment, and that they understood perfectly the reason of this detention, was proved by their readiness to sign on again at the expiration of their terms. We heard from various sources that other diamond mines did not treat their Kafirs so well; but, however that might have been, the agitation for Chinese labor was confined almost entirely to the gold mines of Johannesburg.[2]

As a matter of fact, what is known as the labor problem never assumed large proportions in any instance outside of the mines. It is true that farmers had difficulty in getting help, and projected railroads were hindered by the scarcity of native labor; but everyone recognized the fact that such scarcity was merely temporary, due to the fact that the Kafirs were for the moment independent, owing to the relatively large amounts they had earned during the war. Therefore, when Johannesburg made such an outcry about their

---

2. Even before the war, mine owners were complaining about a shortage of workers and clamouring for more cheap African labour but many men (especially those living in the Cape and Natal) avoided working in the mines because of low wages, dangerous working conditions, and ruthless disciplinary practices. During the war, the Chamber of Mines (est. 1889) began recruiting tens of thousands of Mozambicans but still more workers were needed, especially immediately after the war when the mining sector rapidly expanded. Therefore, mine owners once again turned to Asia for workers, this time China: between 1904 and 1906 at least sixty thousand Chinese men worked in South African mines. Unlike indentured workers from India, however, Chinese workers were not allowed to settle in South Africa. For more on the mining industry's labour recruitment during and after the war, see Alan Jeeves, *Migrant Labour in South Africa's Mining Economy: The Struggle for the Gold Mines' Labour Supply, 1890–1920* (Montreal and Kingston: McGill-Queen's University Press, 1985).

native labor having fallen to seventy thousand, as opposed to ninety thousand before the war, it scarcely caused a ripple of interest in the southern colonies. Agitators came down from the Rand,[3] for and against Chinese labor, and could scarcely draw a meagre hearing. Everyone laughed at the amount of political capital made out of the question in the British House, for even the strongest opponents of the Chinese did not for a moment imagine that there could be any possibility of enslaving them; and even their strongest advocates did not promise that the relief in the financial situation would be anything more than a temporary one. Everyone knew that the big syndicates were trying to consolidate the Rand mines, and it was to their interest to make things appear in the worst possible light.

In Johannesburg itself, however, the excitement was intense. Men who attended some of the public meetings there told me that the disorder in them beggared description. One night an anti-Chinese meeting was advertised for a large hall; the pros filled the building, wrecked all the furniture, and yelled without cessation for four hours. Similar scenes took place on the other side.

The Dutch people, who look upon the mines as the ruination of their land, the first cause of all their troubles, being the chief attraction for the "Uitlanders,"[4] took comparatively little interest in the discussion from any standpoint.

---

3. The Rand was the colloquial term for the Witwatersrand, the area in the Transvaal where gold was discovered in the 1880s.
4. *Uitlanders* is an Afrikaans term for "foreigners" and here refers to the thousands of white mine workers from other parts of southern Africa and the world that flooded the Transvaal after the discovery of the goldfields in the 1880s. Migrant mine workers were mostly British and they quickly outnumbered the Boers; in the 1890s there were an estimated sixty thousand *uitlanders*, double the number of Boer Transvaalers. The Transvaal government feared losing control of the republic to the British if *uitlanders* had political rights and therefore it denied them the vote. This was a major source of resentment on the part of emigrant white mine workers (there was, of course, no question of extending any political rights to African workers). British colonial authorities pressed the Transvaal government to amend the policies on *uitlanders* but it refused, stoking hostilities between Britons and Boers that would ultimately explode into war in 1899.

The Chinese, however, won the day. The arrival in South Africa of large contingents of these deprived numbers of Kafirs of their work in the mines, but as the Government promptly made use of the latter to push on the construction of public works, chiefly railroads, the first result of the importation of Chinese has been beneficial.

CHAPTER XI

Repatriation and Compensation

REPATRIATION AND COMPENSATION were terms on every man's tongue during the whole period of my stay in the country, terms rather vague to the people of the outside world. Various references have been made in previous chapters to the work of the Repatriation Board, Relief Board, and Compensation Board. These boards were quite distinct in the nature and scope of their work, but, as they frequently had offices in the same rooms and were managed by the same men, it is small wonder that there was much misunderstanding of their character even in Africa itself. Stated briefly, the Repatriation Board sought to reinstate the farmers on their deserted homesteads; the Relief Board, to relieve distress caused by the long droughts and delays in payment of compensation money; while the Compensation Board tried to untangle the very complicated question of the amount owed to the former burghers[1] for stock used or destroyed, as shown by scrip tallies, vouchers, or military receipts.

Naturally, the Repatriation Board was the first to organize, which it did immediately on the signing of peace. It will be remembered that at that time the whole of the farming community was absent from the farms, of which the stock had been used or destroyed, and the buildings in many cases burned. A sight which frequently met the eye was the large sheep kraal—walled enclosure—heaped full of slaughtered animals. People say continually, "Why all this destruction?" The answer is that just as long as the Boer commandos were able to obtain supplies on the veldt, just so long did guerrilla fighting continue. The Boer commandos also destroyed what they could not use, to prevent supplies falling into the hands of the British. When peace was signed, the British nation undertook the stupendous task of re-instating the farmers, setting them going, where necessary, in matters of seed, implements, stock and building material; a month's food being included in the supplies issued. If a man had sufficient ready money to pay for the supplies they

1. "Burghers" is another word for citizens.

were furnished to him at cost price, but if he could not pay he took what he wanted and had the amount credited to his compensation claims account, to be reckoned with after the farms were resettled.

Repatriation depots were opened in all the district towns—a district corresponding to our country—and were under the supervision of the resident magistrates. Each depot had its own stock of supplies and employed regularly a number of clerks, both English and Dutch. It had several large *trek* wagons constantly on the road, driven by Dutchmen. As soon as these wagons had finished the work of carrying the farmers and their goods to their respective homes—about Christmas, 1902—the oxen, numbering fourteen to a wagon, were loaned out to the farmers for ploughing.

But these efforts of the most humane of governments were rendered almost futile by the long drought, lasting from June, 1902, till January, 1904. During that time the Government, with unheard-of generosity, converted the "Repatriation Depots" into Relief Depots, no longer under the supervision of the magistrates, but controlled by special clerks, trained in the Repatriation service, and known as District Administrators of Relief. These men were assisted by clerks, usually belonging to the district in which they worked. As the Relief Depots occupied the same premises, employed the same clerks, and used the same stores as the Repatriation, people naturally continued to speak of them as "The Repatriation." In fact, the Repatriation became almost as much an institution as the magistrate of the post office. There was the essential difference, however, between their work and that of the Relief Board, that while the supplies issued by the former were often charged to the purchaser's account, nearly everything given out by the latter was absolutely free, and had nothing to do, later, in the settling of compensation claims. The Relief Board was, in fact, simply a temporary government charity.

Connected with each Relief Depot was an administrator, one or more clerks, English or Dutch, conductors, drivers, and native boys to do the rough work. There were large stores on hand of tinned meats, and all kinds of staple foodstuffs, also wagons, oxen and ploughs. Under its direction an occasional sale was held of imported cattle to enable the farmers to refill, at the lowest possible figure, the gaps in their stock, caused by drought or disease. Subsidiary depots were also established at the smaller villages, in charge of the special justices of the peace. In most cases wagons were sent at intervals from the depots to such substations with rations for issue as required.

Thus, so far as the actual investigation of reported distress and the issue of relief was concerned, the arrangements of the Government were very complete. Another branch of the work, however, was the seeking out of distressed persons. The South African Constabulary were instructed to do as much as possible in that direction while out on patrols, but after all it was a matter which might reasonably be trusted to look after itself. People do not usually sit down and wait for starvation to come to them.

Besides the terrible drought, which wasted three seedings and killed cattle and sheep by the thousand, the chief cause of the widespread distress was the delay in payment of compensation money; a delay which was deplorable, but was almost unavoidable under the circumstances, so complicated had the claims accounts become. Some men had mixed their receipts for purchases by the military with Government vouchers for stock removed or destroyed, and expected to be paid the full amount; others had forfeited their vouchers by breaking their oaths of neutrality; others again, misunderstanding the nature of compensation, had used up most of their claim in buying stock from the Repatriation, and then expected to be paid the original amount in cash.

What is compensation? There is, to begin with, one class which is sanctioned, if not required, by international law. That is the payment by invaders of a reasonable price for all goods taken from the invaded country as supplies. But such a scheme as was projected by the British Government marked a new epoch in the history of warfare. In the terms of surrender £3,000,000 were promised to assist those persons who surrendered under Lord Roberts' proclamation, or to compensate British subjects, foreign subjects, and natives.[2] The granting of this sum was purely an act of grace on the part of the authorities for the partial relief of sufferers—partial, for it was an obvious impossibility for the most generous of nations to do away entirely with the effects of a three years' war. An equitable allotment of this large sum proved to be utterly beyond the power of the Compensation Boards, and therefore, towards the close of 1903, a Central Judicial Commission was appointed at Pretoria to receive and classify the reports of the local officials. This commission was the visible result of Mr. Chamberlain's visit to the country, during which he assured the people that the Government intended to keep the promises made to them.[3] The complaints one heard, however, showed that many people overestimated the nature and extent of those promises, and considerably under-estimated the number of claims that had to be dealt with under them.

When the Claims Boards began their work, about January, 1903, they were met at the outset by undreamed of difficulties. The first class of claims examined were those under the class acknowledged by international law. It will be remembered that, at the beginning of the war, payment for goods commandeered was made in cash, but, as the money so paid often found its way into the Boer treasury, this method was discontinued and receipts were given. These receipts, through ignorance of international law, caused many heart-burnings. The liability of the invaders in respect to payment for

2. On March 15, 1900 Lord Roberts issued a proclamation intended to induce Boers to quit the war by granting amnesty to those who surrendered and took an oath of neutrality. Farmers who did so were issued a protection pass that would safeguard their property from looting by either warring Boers or British, although in reality protection was unreliable. Farms were looted by compatriots who considered the *hensoppers* ("hands-uppers") traitors and by the British who, when supplies were low, requisitioned food and horses as they saw fit. See Johannes Gerhardus Boje, "Winburg's War: An Appraisal of the Anglo-Boer War of 1899–1902 as It Was Experienced by the People of a Free State District" (DPhil, University of Pretoria, 2010), especially Chapter 3, "The Failure of Protection," 123–74.

3. Joseph Chamberlain toured South Africa from December 1902 to February 1903.

commandeered goods is limited to a fair, average market price—not the price that such articles would fetch in the stores in war time, or even in time of drought. Of course that means that in selling to the military the farmers and storekeepers made smaller profits than if they had been able to sell in the ordinary way. But as, in selling at all, they escaped the destruction which overtook so many others in the course of the war, they were, in fact, to be congratulated on having got out of the mess so cheaply. No one could expect that a war would not interfere seriously with his business. Many of the commandeering officers, however, had in their inexperience ignorantly entered up entirely false values on the receipts handed out, having written down practically whatever the farmers asked. These receipts, therefore, had to be redeemed on a new estimate of the value of the goods in time of peace, and often with no relation to the amount which appeared on the notes themselves. Hence many claimants complained that they had not been paid the full value of their notes, although they had really received a fair average price for the goods.

Other claimants, again, mixed up the vouchers given for stock removed from their farms, lest the Boers should get it, with receipts for commandeered goods, and expected to have these vouchers paid in full by the military, a total misconception. Purchase notes, or receipts, were paid in full, being a government debt, but vouchers for stock removed or destroyed only entitled the claimant to a *share* in the compensation money named in the terms of surrender.

At the time the commission met in Pretoria over two and a half million pounds sterling had been paid out on account of these military, or commandeering, claims. But the other class, under the terms of surrender, proved to be even more difficult to deal with. In reinstating the people in their homes a very large sum had been expended in the work of repatriation; and it was not until the second year after the war that the claims of this class were investigated in a thorough manner, a most unfortunate delay. Even if it had not been possible to hasten the payments, an official assurance as to the approximate time when they might have been expected, and some idea of their probable proportion, would have been most useful. The latter would have been a beneficial disillusionment to some claimants—notably the "wilde Boer," or poor farmer, who was expecting impossibilities. Others, who ought to have known better, incurred debts on the supposed strength of their claims, which later reduced them to the verge of bankruptcy.

There was one class especially which suffered keenly by the delay, and whose condition might as reasonably have been described as "distressed" as that of those poorer people who received aid from the Relief Depots. There were many families of the middle class, accustomed to comforts and a measure of refinement, who were reduced to a state, only bordering on poverty, it is true, but probably felt by them more keenly than actual poverty by those accustomed to it. One man, for instance, on a fairly large farm, said, eighteen months after peace had been signed: "If I had £200 now—and my compensation claims are many times that—I would have a prospect of success. If I do not get my compensation within two months, I must give up and go insolvent. It will be hard to hold out as long as that and quite impossible to keep on longer." His situation was that of hundreds throughout the country.

Even the general payment of a small proportion of the claims would have been a great help in that hard season of 1903–4. It would have enabled the farmers to buy a little more stock, would have circulated a little ready money, and thus would have given business in the towns a distinct lift. A leading Englishman in Kroonstad was wont to say that if he could have laid his hands on fifty pounds cash he would have guaranteed to clear half the town of debt by putting this money in circulation. As it was, everyone owed everyone else, and no one could start the cash ball rolling. In face of such a situation the reports in outside papers that South Africa was enjoying a boom had a decidedly sarcastic ring.

The commission, however, set to work in a systematic way, and it was gratifying to see that British subjects were looked after first, which quieted the fears of those who had an uneasy feeling that they might be served in the same way as were the loyalists of 1882.[4] Next came the protected burghers,[5] to whom in a few districts a fair percentage was paid, pending the full payment of their claims. These districts were gradually increased in number until the whole country was covered. In the last class came the "wilde Boer." Altogether, between repatriation and claims, it was estimated that the Government had paid out some six millions of pounds by Easter, 1904.

One disheartening result of the payment of the claims was that many of the educated townspeople threw off the appearance of friendliness which they had worn during the first year, or year and a half, following the war, and revealed themselves as rank Afrikanders. In northern Cape Colony, indeed, this tendency was most marked. In the little town of Colesburg, for instance, where I

---

4. In 1877 Britain annexed the Transvaal, with a population of approximately forty thousand Boers at the time. Encouraged by repeated reassurances that Britain would never relinquish the Transvaal, about five thousand uitlanders, most British, settled there and many made major investments in land and businesses. In December 1880 the Boers rebelled, sparking the First Anglo-Boer War (1880–1881). Most British loyalists stayed during the hostilities, secure in the belief of continued military protection. However, the Boers defeated the British at the Battle of Majuba Hill in February 1881, a humiliating loss, and afterwards the British decided to sign an armistice rather than become further entangled in what was likely to become a costly war. The loyalists, who were furious over the armistice, demanded full compensation for the depreciation in value of their properties under restored Boer rule, and for property lost during the war. But in the months following the armistice, the British sought a settlement that would first and foremost improve relations with the Transvaal government in order to prevent Boers across the region from joining together in a united front. Therefore, Gladstone's Liberal government agreed to pay only for loyalists' direct losses (lost or destroyed property) and not indirect losses (falling property values and loss of trade). Loyalists felt betrayed politically and economically, and "sacrificed on the altar of improved Anglo-Boer relations" (Laband, "Burying the Union Jack," 9). See John Laband, "Burying the Union Jack: British Loyalists in the Transvaal during the First Anglo-Boer War, 1880–1881," *History of Intellectual Culture* 4 no. 1 (2004): 1–19.
5. The term "protected burghers" refers to Boer republican citizens who voluntarily surrendered to the British. In return, the so-called "hands-uppers" received protection from retaliation and impressment by Boer forces.

had paid two delightful visits during my first year, there was instituted a most unpleasant social and commercial boycott of the Dutch against the English.

One can only hope, therefore, that the passing years will soften this feeling and lead to a prosperous, united South Africa.

CHAPTER XII

Paupers and Government Relief Works

INCREDIBLE AS IT MAY SEEM, there was not such a thing as a beggar throughout the length and breadth of the new African colonies during the year and a half following the war. After that an occasional unfortunate drifted down from Johannesburg. Yet there were thousands of landless people who, in the ordinary course of events, would have been utterly stranded after the war. These were the very poor, very dirty and very ignorant folk, who had passed the most comfortable days of their lives in the refugee camps. Under the Dutch régime they had been known as "by-woners"—squatters—and seemed but little higher than the Kafirs in the scale of civilization.

The wealthy farmers, with great sheep runs miles in extent, required a large number of shepherds, and they had found that the most paying method was to allow families of these poor Dutch to squat on their land, in return for which privilege they gratefully herded the flocks with the aid of Kafirs. Each poor man was allowed to use a little plot of ground for the cultivation of such vegetables as his family required; any surplus going to the nearest market, and bringing in almost the only cash such a family ever possessed. Plenty of fresh air was the only luxury these people had. They lived in little mud-brick huts with mud floors and walls, calico ceilings and tin roofs; usually these had but two rooms, a living room and a sleeping room. It was commonly said that they never took off their clothing until it wore out; certainly numbers of their children were found, in camp, sewn up in their clothes. Small wonder the mortality was great amongst them when any epidemic disease broke out!

Obviously this class had nothing to lose by war or any other catastrophe, but, on the other hand, they had nothing to return to after the signing of peace. Their erstwhile wealthy patrons were in straitened circumstances, awaiting their own turn to be replaced on their land by the Repatriation Department, and fully able, with the aid of their own children, to care for their very limited flocks.

Here was a large problem facing the authorities—What was to be done with the "by-woners?" As a temporary measure some of the refugee camps were kept open for almost a year after the close of the war. In Chapter VII., a passing reference was made to Springfontein as a gathering place for the remnants of various neighboring camps. It was one of a small number which were made such centres and the ordinary life of the refugee camps was maintained in them, with free schools, church and hospital. As the men were well-paid for work on the new railroad being built to Jagersfontein, it is not surprising that under such fair treatment there should have sprung up in the minds of these people a strong feeling of loyalty to Great Britain.

One could only hope that such a sentiment would have a beneficial effect on another class who inhabited these belated camps for a vastly different reason. They consisted of considerable numbers of women and children left in the various camps because their husbands and fathers were still away in the prison camps refusing stubbornly to take the oath of allegiance, and known as "Irreconcilables." These women and children, therefore, had to be provided for unless taken in hand by relatives, and many of them remained under the care of the Government for more than a year following the war, and others for still longer periods. It is interesting and hopeful to note that each party of irreconcilables, on returning to South Africa, experienced the liveliest surprise at the friendly way in which Briton and Boer had settled down side by side; and in the majority of cases expressed strongly the wish that they had taken the oath of allegiance sooner.

As soon as the repatriation work was well under way, the Government proceeded to carry out certain plans for the better treatment of these poor folk. To keep them on indefinitely in the refugee camps, feeding and clothing them at the public expense, meant simply to pauperize them for ever. Therefore, it was proposed to establish several centres known as "Relief Works," where necessary public works would provide ample and suitable employment for all. Food and clothes would no longer be doled out, but fair wages would be paid for all work done; the Dutch clergyman, the hospital and the school, however, would still be provided free.

One of these industrial camps was on the government farm of Strydfontein, six miles from Kroonstad, and as one of the hospital nurses, Sister Blew, was an old friend from Norval's Pont Camp, I made frequent visits there.

During the time I was stationed in Kroonstad there were about twelve hundred people living at Strydfontein, in a village of corrugated iron huts, built on a long slope, the huts rather close together, each with a yard in front and behind. The road from town led past the military camps over a stretch of rolling veldt, magnificent grazing land, and as soon as we passed the height of land hiding the last camp, we never failed to find on the road stray couples from the Works, making love in the most nonchalant way. Of course the people in Strydfontein were under no supervision, as they had been in the refugee camps, but were free to come and go, work or starve, as they pleased. The Government merely provided the work, but no one was forced to do it.

Whenever we went out to Strydfontein in the afternoon, the view was very prepossessing. As we cantered down the long slope facing the village, its tin houses shone like silver in the sunlight; and the green trees on the next farm, a favorite picnic ground, made a delightful break in the uniform brownness of the veldt. But a closer view of the Works was not so pleasing. The women, freed from the enforced cleanliness of the refugee camp days, had relapsed into slatternliness; their yards were untidy and their huts filthy. Most of them had a few chickens, a pig and a sheep, and it seemed a matter of indifference whether the animals were in the pasture, the yard, or in the house. The men did not seem so dirty, while the children had to conform to a certain school standard of cleanliness. All were dark-skinned, in some cases showing obvious traces of a dash of Kafir blood. Such children were dull and phlegmatic.

Still following the main road, we passed in turn the school, a decent building used on Sundays for church, the teachers' E.P. tents, inhabited by four Australians, the tennis court, and the hospital. The latter was a mud-brick building with a large airy ward, kitchen, dining-room, and lean-to bedrooms for the two nurses, Sisters Williamson and Blew. Contagious diseases were isolated in E.P. tents. There was no resident doctor, the district doctor from Kroonstad having charge of the Works as part of his duties. There was very little illness, however, most of the cases being the dressing of wounds received in accidents at the Works. Beyond the hospital, the road suddenly turned down a steep hill and brought one into view of a wide flat valley with the immense dam and irrigation works, furnishing employment to the village above.

Strydfontein was one of the farms bought by the Government after the war and retained for experimental purposes. It contained an immense level valley, through which trickled a tiny stream, fed, in the rainy season, by numbers of tributaries whose beds were dry at other times. The largest of these water-beds led through a narrow valley into the lower and larger one. Nature thus apparently afforded an excellent opportunity for experiments with irrigation systems, for nothing appeared simpler than to build a dam across the end of the small valley, thus transforming it into a huge natural reservoir.

Accordingly, engineers and skilled masons took up their abode at the mouth of the valley, and the people who had been brought in from the refugee camps round about were given work on the huge dam. In Kroonstad the progress of the work was followed with such interest that afternoon outings usually included a trip to "the dam." Indeed, it became most disconcerting to strangers in town to hear everyone talking glibly of "the dam engineers," "the dam hospital," and so on. The works included also the construction of a great sluice-way, leading from above the dam to the irrigation ditches below, in which the water could be turned on or off at will.

About Christmas, 1903, the dam and the sluice were finished. The former, an immense pile of masonry and cement, was calculated to resist the force of a thirty-foot flood; the latter had bored its difficult way through almost solid rock. Altogether the works at that time, in material and labor, had cost, it was said, £70,000.

Then the rains came—no gentle summer showers—but the tremendous downpour which caused the deplorable loss of life and property in the Bloemfontein floods.[1] The dam filled so rapidly that engineers and people alike were eager to test the possibilities of the new system of waterways. But an unforeseen contingency arose. In South Africa, twenty-four hours after it stops raining, the surface of the land is usually hard and dry again, owing to the rapid evaporation in that dry atmosphere. But, contrary to expectations, the land at the foot of the dam, outside, became filled with bubbling springs; and—there was no possibility of doubt—the water inside was rapidly lowering its level. Alas for the engineers! Investigation showed that the soil was full of pits of quicksand, impossible to detect during the drought. These caused the water to soak far below the dam, as into a sponge; it then oozed up again on the outside. Pumping engines were hastily set to work and the most vigorous attempts made to clean out the holes, in the hope that there might be a chance of strengthening the dam underground, to a sufficient depth to stop the leakage. Vain hope—the pits appeared to be bottomless—and when I left Kroonstad, en route for Canada, it was thought that the whole scheme would have to be abandoned.

Since coming home the news has reached me that the settlement has been broken up and the people scattered; some found employment in the old way with farmers; others drifted into the towns; others were given government work elsewhere, and a few remained to work on Strydfontein.

Other and smaller works undertaken elsewhere were more successful; but all had the same aims, to carry out valuable experiments testing the resources of the country, or to improve the means of transportation, and at the same time to benefit the thousands of unfortunate landless men.

1. At least twenty people died and over 170 buildings were destroyed by the flood in January 1904.

The more one learns of the attitude of the British Government towards the Dutch people of South Africa since the war, the stronger does one's patriotism become. Never in the history of the world did one nation show such clemency to another; never did a government make such stupendous efforts to obliterate the traces of war; never have those in authority made such wise and generous plans to mitigate the sufferings of the poor. What matter if an occasional undertaking has failed in the execution, or if an occasional official has failed to realize the responsibility of his position; the more thoughtful people throughout the country acknowledge to-day the unparalleled generosity of the British nation. Many an old Dutch resident has said to me with a smile that had the Afrikander cause been successful the English would have been treated very differently.

"We meant to take all their land and property, and then drive them into the sea," said one old lady over her coffee-cup. "Yes," added her husband, "and these lazy beggars of Kafirs wouldn't be lording it over us as they are with their missions and silly notions. They're only fit to be slaves."

Undoubtedly the triumph of the Afrikander cause would have been a long step backward in the history of South African civilization. Without taking into account the immediate cause of the war, its justice or injustice, everyone acknowledged that the conflict had to come sooner or later; and every student of history knows that nations, like individuals, are subject to the universal law of nature—there must be progress, or the offender is pushed to the wall. Olive Shreiner[2] aptly says that the average Boer, in his mental and moral outlook, is a child of the seventeenth century. The future glory, therefore, of the South African Dutch depends on the rapidity with which they get in line with the march of modern progress.

2. Graham is referring to Olive Schreiner (1855–1920) who wrote extensively on South African affairs, including *An English South African Woman's View of the Situation* (1899).

1901

CHAPTER XIII

Education and Church Schools

THROUGH THE INFLUENCE of the humane treatment received at the hands of the British Government there promised to spring up, generally, amongst the Dutch a feeling of kindly friendship towards the British.

Both Dutch and British agree that if the predikants[1] of the Dutch Reformed Church could have been muzzled for about two years after the war untold mischief would have been prevented. But these men—so called Christian teachers—left no stone unturned to stir up the animosity of their charges, to work upon the credulity of the ignorant classes, to foster resentment at local irregularities of administration or delays in payment of compensation money; matters which might reasonably have been expected to right themselves in course of time, and which did right themselves in the majority of cases. In this respect the Cape Colonials were ringleaders, and incited their kinsmen of the Orange River Colony and the Transvaal to rancorous expressions of discontent, which, if left to themselves, they would probably never have thought of.

Up-country, one had not far to seek for the reason of the predikants' ill-temper. With all due allowance for a certain percentage of misguided patriotism, the quarrel resolved itself into a mere matter of money. Under the Republics the Dutch Reformed Church was all-powerful, the central and most imposing buildings of almost all the small *dorps*[2] being the church and parsonage. Each minister received a substantial grant from the Government, a free house, and an extremely good local salary besides; in addition to which were the perquisites of his office, practically all the food and fodder required for his house and stable, and his wedding fees. He did not leave the latter to the generosity of his patrons, but had a sliding scale of prices for the different days in the week, ranging from one to five pounds. But after the war the predikant found his bank account shrinking alarmingly. The gradual stoppage of the government

1. The *predikants* were church ministers.
2. *Dorps* is Afrikaans for villages.

grant was the first blow; the big salary had reached the vanishing point, owing to the poverty of the people; and, finally, marriages were few and far between.

Yet, foolishly perhaps, no one paid any attention to the grumblings of the predikants in their various gatherings until the end of 1903, when the appearance of Church schools in various localities, and the publication of some of the doings of the Transvaal Synod, opened people's eyes. This latter body, as a matter of fact, overreached itself, and drew forth loud protests from some of the more progressive Dutch. The occasion of the outburst was the visit paid to South Africa by delegates of the Scottish Church who proffered the hand of friendship to the Dutch, at one time members of the same communion. The following is an extract from the answer made by the Dutch Synod of the Transvaal:

"When our churches and parsonages were mercilessly burnt down and our church registers incontinently destroyed; when they armed the Kafirs against us, who time after time murdered women and children; when they made a portion of our people disloyal to us by the promise of pay and plunder; when they locked up our women and children in murder-camps and sent out the lie to the world that they went there for protection of their own free will; when they did not give these helpless ones sufficient daily bread, after having made all that belonged to them a prey to the flames; when they mutilated our cattle in the most barbarous manner; when our beautiful land was converted into a wilderness; when our ministers, simply because they were true to their country and people, were thrown into foul prisons, banished from the country, and loaded with every disgrace and scorn; when men did things to us of which the world knows not yet; when we were given over wholly powerless into the hands of our enemies—then, yes, then was the time to help and encourage us and to act with us, who were at one with you in the highest matter, not for one hour longer to suffer us to be trodden upon, dispised, ruined, murdered; but just then you preserved a deadly silence."

Such a document spoke for itself and showed clearly the spirit of the irreconcilables. Naturally, such men were continually trying to find weak points in the new administration. Such a point they thought they discovered in the Education Department, yet they had to agitate unceasingly for over a year before they succeeded in collecting enough money to start a few separate schools, and rumor said that much of it came from Holland. At the time of Mr. Chamberlain's tour through South Africa, in January, 1903, though opportunity was afforded for any farmer or other resident to bring forward anything that he thought a grievance—an opportunity of which they availed themselves to the full—not a single complaint was made with regard to the schools. Press representatives who sought to get the views of the country people on the schools found the farmers voluble enough on the weather, the crops, compensation prospects, and every other matter of interest in the country, but they had simply nothing to say about education. The dispute, apparently, lay between the predikants and the Government, the farmers' share being simply the signing of petitions to oblige the predikant.

Shortly after Mr. Chamberlain's visit, there was a great outcry made in Cape Colony that the British Government was trying to suppress the teaching of Dutch in the schools, and was seeking, in other ways, to stifle all Dutch sympathies in the children. I was still in Fauresmith at that time, and one of the most influential ladies there, whose male relatives were all leaders in the Dutch cause, said to me:

"Miss Graham, I have been much puzzled by the reports in the Cape Synod about our schools. They say that you are not giving Dutch lessons, as the people were led to suppose. Now, will you please tell me exactly what you are giving in our school."

I explained to her that each class had about three hours of high Dutch teaching in the week, and might also have the daily Bible lesson in Dutch, if their minister cared to give it to them; that I understood the English clergymen in various places were taking advantage of this opportunity of Bible training, but that the Dutch were not.

"Well," she said, "what you tell me is exactly what my son says, and I cannot understand at all why anyone should grumble. When I was a girl at school we hadn't any more Dutch than that."

"But," I continued, "didn't you have any of your ordinary subjects taught in Dutch—arithmetic, for example?"

"No," she answered, "never, unless the teacher happened to be too ignorant to make full explanations in English. We always looked down upon those who could not speak English fluently, and therefore it was used habitually in school. No, I cannot understand at all this attack on the schools."

But the attack was kept up, and the agitation spread, until to-day there are numbers of separate schools throughout the country, an unceasing and increasing menace to its future unity and prosperity. Always the shibboleth has been, "More time for the Dutch language."

Was the Education Department blameless? Why could it not hold its own, as other departments did in the face of attack? Of all possible misfortunes, surely the worst is that the children of this generation should grow up alienated from one another, and hostile, as children of rival schools invariably are.

So far as organization went, the Department had many admirable points, some far in advance of corresponding ones here in Canada. During the first year and a half after the war, the Orange River Colony and the Transvaal had a common head, Mr. Sargent, Superintendent of Education; but the Bloemfontein and Johannesburg offices and accounts were kept entirely separate, under assistant superintendents. Later, each colony had its own superintendent, but otherwise the system remained the same, with everything centralized in the two offices. The Bloemfontein superintendent had under him a number of inspectors, usually four—this for a population no larger than that of the city of Toronto.[3] Under them were the teachers, graded and paid according to their

3. Toronto's population in 1900 was approximately 208,000.

certificates, experience and skill, and not according to the size of school in which they happened to be placed, a method of settling the salary question, which I cannot praise too highly. At the head of the schools there was the Normal School in Bloemfontein, where candidates were trained free, with a Domestic Science course if they wished; there was also a Girls' High School, and a Boys' High School doing efficient work. One heard rumors occasionally of a Technical School being founded, patterned after the one in Johannesburg.[4] In the country, where the old buildings were inadequate, temporary tin houses, or E.P. tents, were put up to accommodate the classes. Pending the establishment of self-government in the colonies, when each town would hire its own teachers independently of the central office, local school committees, with advisory powers, were appointed in each town. The school programme gave to the teaching of high Dutch practically the same time which had been allotted to it before the war.

All this was most excellent, and ought to have been successful had there been anyone in authority with any sort of executive ability. But from the first the Education Department struggled along under men of mediocre talent, and sometimes more than mediocre stupidity. It was hampered also by the personnel of some of the teachers sent out from England. Evidently those who were responsible there for the selection of teachers for South Africa were ignorant of the class of children who would be in attendance at the government schools. South African, like Canadian, schools draw all classes of children, and bear little resemblance to the rough-and-tumble English Board Schools. So undesirable were some of the teachers sent out that the Department found it necessary to dismiss them.

The first, and probably one of the gravest mistakes made by the Department, was the refusal to re-engage any Dutch teacher suspected of pro-Boer tendencies. Looking back, it seems as if there could have been no doubt which was better, to keep such men in

---

4. Normal schools focused on training teachers; technical schools placed an emphasis on vocational training.

the government employ, thus muzzling them, so to speak, or to turn them adrift, poor, well-educated, with a definite grievance against the new order of things. Most of these men found employment in Cape Colony, where their grievances lost nothing in the telling, and did much to cause the increased bad feeling there. Still more unfortunately, the vacancies thus caused were frequently filled by objectionable people. In one town, for instance, there had been an excellent headmaster, a Hollander, respected by English and Dutch alike. After the war he had to take a small school in Cape Colony, until the Dutch Church engaged him as principal of an orphanage. In his place, after long delays, the Department sent a Scotchman, so broad in his accent that the children were constantly asking their teachers to please tell them what he was talking about; and so ferocious in his appearance that the townspeople nicknamed him "Mephistopheles."[5] The children in sheer fright would answer him "yes" or "no" at random, whereupon he used to cane them for telling lies. The School Committee complained of him several times to Bloemfontein, but only lately succeeded in having him removed. He left the town without saying farewell to a single inhabitant; surely a strange end to more than two years' work.

In another large town of the Orange River Colony, the Dutch headmaster was replaced by an Englishman, inefficient in his work, and so ignorant in other respects that the townspeople called him "The Beast." One met frequently with similar cases.

Another exceedingly unfortunate result of the weeding out process was that the Department was left without enough teachers capable of teaching high Dutch to meet the requirements of the school programme. In Fauresmith we agitated, in a vigorous Canadian way, for months before we were sent a Dutch teacher. In Jagersfontein they did not have one all that same year. In Kroonstad there was still none when I was sent there—Kroonstad, the second town in the

5. Mephistopheles is the demon in the legend of Faust

colony! The headmaster there, one of the best-educated and ablest in the country, an Oxford man, had studied Dutch himself, and was doing his utmost, unaided, to comply with the regulations. A short time after my arrival there the Dutch Church opened a separate school, whereupon the Department sought to clear itself by a piece of rank injustice. It sent a commission to investigate certain trumped-up charges against the headmaster, who was made the scapegoat and sent away to a little country school.

Mr. Sargent, who generalled this manoeuvre, next turned his attention to the Bloemfontein office, ousted the Assistant Director there, and then sailed for England, leaving the Orange River Colony with no head whatever, while the Transvaal was almost paralyzed under a tremendous legacy of debt. Mr. Gunn, who happened to be chief inspector in the Orange River Colony, did the office work as Acting-Director for some months, after which he was regularly appointed Director. In justice to Mr. Gunn it must be said that things have run much more smoothly under his management than ever before, in spite of the fact that he had to begin his duties with a great deficit in the treasury.

Of the wastefulness of the Department in keeping teachers constantly on the move, I have already written in the chapter on Fauresmith. This policy was not only harmful to the schools, continually upsetting them, but it was also peculiarly irritating to the school committees, whose recommendations were often unheeded. Some of the girls were sent on dreadful journeys. One Canadian started on a sixty-mile drive with a Kafir boy, the horses played out, and they were nearly three days making it; two English girls were sent a similar journey, were caught in a thunderstorm, and had to take shelter over night in a ruined block-house; another Canadian drove eighty miles over a shocking road in the rain, glad of any shelter that offered; and still another girl drove a like distance to a school where she was not expected, and where there was nothing for her to do. She went at once to Bloemfontein to investigate, where she learned that the Assistant Director knew nothing of the situation. He was profuse in his apologies, giving her then a better position than before. Similar instances might fill a chapter.

It is said that, "South Africa is a land of rivers without water, birds without song, and flowers without perfume."[6] It might be added, "and inspectors who do not inspect." During the twenty-five months of my stay in the country various inspectors came to see the schools, visited the townspeople, took their departure, and made scarcely any attempt to inspect the work, as we understand inspection in Canada. One wonders why some of them, young and inexperienced, were ever given such exceedingly responsible work.

At present everyone, English and Dutch alike, recognizes that the Education Department has failed for some reason or other. If, in days to come, it succeeds in cutting down expenses, doing with fewer officials and making them work; if it buys proper school furniture, so that the kindergartens are not forced to sit upon the floor; if it houses its pay schools in buildings at least as good as the Church schools; if it allows the school committees to be something more than an empty name, then, and not till then, can it hope to draw back to the government schools the children who, above all others, should be found there.

6. Naysayers employed a number of variations of this saying at the turn of the twentieth century to discourage prospective emigrants to South Africa, including "Flowers without scent/ Birds without song/ Rivers without water/ Women without beauty/ Men without honour."

CHAPTER XIV

The Farming Question

TOWNSPEOPLE THE WORLD OVER, and especially the wealthier classes, have a certain family resemblance. South Africans are no exception, but being, above all else, a pastoral people, it is on the farms that one finds the real South African life. Any Canadian who has not galloped over our great prairie lands will find it hard to understand the "monarch of all I survey" sort of feeling one experiences on the veldt, or the fascination it exercises. Imagine a great pasture field, five hundred miles long, fringed round with rugged, boulder-strewn kopjes, apparently the remains of a circle of extinct volcanoes; picture the only vegetation of these kopjes a few stunted sage bushes and thorn trees, and in the spring the most fragile and fleeting of wild-flowers, the veldt bare of trees except on the banks of the occasional watercourses, barc of grass except in the rainy season, brown, cracked by the sun's rays, repulsive to the newcomer. "What a desolation!" he cries; "it would drive anyone mad to live here." The old resident smiles and says, "Wait a year." One year in that clear crisp air, with ten months of dazzling blue sky and sparkling sunshine, with long free rides over the winding tracks or across the unbroken veldt, without seeing a house or sign of humanity for hours, is enough to conquer the most prejudiced outsider. Sometimes a man thinks he has escaped the spell, and goes merrily home, only to find that he cannot find room to breathe, and that his whole being cries out for the sunshine. Even Canadians do not escape. There were scores who turned home enthusiastically at the end of the war, but found they could not overcome the longing for "our Lady of the Sunshine," and sailed again to South Africa as soon as possible.

Olive Shreiner in "The Story of an African Farm," and Rider Haggard in "Jess," have pictured the old-fashioned farm life of Cape Colony and the Transvaal, a type which is gradually disappearing. In those earlier days a man's farm was as big as a county; and the farmhouse, with its outbuildings, "by-woners'" cottages, Kafir huts and cattle kraals looked at a little distance not unlike a small village. The man was practically supreme in his possessions, hiring a governess or tutor for his own and his overseer's children, dispensing justice to his Kafirs, keeping what firearms he chose, and shooting the game, then so abundant, whenever he pleased. Farming, as we understand the word, was unknown. There was a field of mealies—Indian corn—for the Kafirs, another of vegetables for the whites, and a fine fruit orchard; but these things were mere nothings. The real business of the farm was sheep. There were sheep in thousands, long-legged, fat-tailed sheep, well adapted to scrambling over the boulders, or racing over the plains; and provided by Nature with a supply of food against a time of drought, stored in their immense tails. It was a patriarchal mode of existence which harmonized beautifully with the primitive forms of religious belief held by the people, beliefs which permeated their whole life, but were crude at times to the verge of superstition.

With the large families common amongst the Boers, and the influx of new settlers, the huge farms became subdivided, and even before the late war men were beginning to realize that the old haphazard methods would no longer lead to fortune. In the early days one good year brought such enormous profits that a man could easily afford to make nothing, or even to lose, during a year or two of drought. But, as early as the nineties, experiments were being made with irrigation and other new systems. It was also generally recognized that certain localities were best adapted for special branches of farm industry; Cape Colony stood for ostrich farms and sheep, Natal for fruit, the Orange Free State for sheep, with grain on the Basuto border, the Transvaal for sheep, with hay in the north, and Rhodesia and Buluwayo for the heavier cattle.

In the Orange Free State—now the Orange River Colony—and the Transvaal many of the farms changed hands after the war, a change which marked a new era in South African farming. The Government bought up large tracts of land from old people who were delighted at the chance to sell and retire to town-life. This land was resold, or allotted to new settlers, or retained for experimental purposes. Poor settlers are not encouraged, as in Canada, for all unskilled labor is done by the Kafirs, and a white settler must have capital in order to succeed. The Government, therefore, requires a settler to have at least £500 capital before he is given a grant of land, varying in size according to its value; he may be given this capital as a loan, payable in twenty years without interest. The evident necessity for large capital has induced young men all over the country to engage in co-operative farming. I visited several of these co-operative farms during my stay in the country, and found the owners, in every case, enthusiastic over their prospects, in spite of the drought. One amusing feature of these farms was the invariable presence of a tennis court, regarded as a necessity for exercise. Imagine a Canadian farmer needing a tennis court for exercise! Here, again, the ubiquitous Kafir is the explanation—the white man is the head, and the Kafir the hands and feet of the South African farm.

On the farms granted to settlers holding twenty-year loans the Government retains a certain right of supervision, sending out inspectors at regular intervals to keep the farmers posted in the best of the new methods as shown by the experiments on the government farms.

These government farms, one of which, Strydfontein, has already been described in Chapter XII., were scattered throughout the Orange River Colony and the Transvaal. The Government of the Orange River Colony in particular, under Lieutenant-Governor Gould-Adams, showed the greatest enterprise in developing plans to help the farming community; delegations of Dutchmen were sent to America to visit various farming centres and study their methods, and an expert agriculturist was brought over from Canada to direct the agricultural department of the experimental farms. As it had always been recognized that the soil of the Orange River Colony was amazingly fertile, it was thought that an efficient system of irrigation should make an enormous production possible. Irrigation on a small scale had always been necessary for the fruit orchards and vegetable gardens of the old-fashioned farms; but only in isolated cases had it been tried on a large scale. The small irrigation systems had depended for their water on small dams, mere cisterns of rain water, liable to become dry in a season of drought. What was needed was a system of large dams capable of withstanding the severest drought. One farm with such a system was *Babienskranz* (Baboon Valley) on the Orange River south of Fauresmith. It had been a co-operative farm for years before the war, its owners making large profits, with a thoroughly up-to-date irrigation system from the river. Inland farms, however, by damming up dry watercourses, have almost equal chances, for in the rainy seasons the waterfall is enormous, amounting to several inches in a very short time. At present this water is almost all lost, partly because the surface of the earth is so hard that the first twenty-four hours' rain simply washes over it, and partly because the numberless rivulets and streams flow so swiftly to the coast that the country is soon drained dry again.

The Kroonstad dam on the Valsch River affords an excellent example of the possibilities of a very small stream. Six miles above the town the Valsch is a mere creek, easily crossed on foot; at Kroonstad, thanks to the enormous dam of solid masonry, there is a stretch of three miles of as charming river as one could wish to see. In places it is a hundred feet wide and thirty deep, shaded along the banks by tall blue-gums or graceful weeping willows. As it is used as a reservoir of drinking water, no bathing is allowed, but there is excellent fishing and boating, even sailing being possible. That stretch of river makes Kroonstad the most delightful spot from the Cape to Johannesburg, and the latter town uses it as a week-end resort. During the long drought the river lowered perceptibly, but, although water was drawn away by the car-load to Bloemfontein, and other points of famine, the greatest drop was only seven feet.

Besides the elusive water supply, the South African farmer has a dozen other difficulties to contend against. The breeder of cattle dreads the mange,[1] the tetse fly, or the more terrible horse sickness; so fatal is the last that in Rhodesia, where it is most prevalent, a thoroughbred, if green, will fetch only £15, while the sorriest

1. Mange is a contagious skin disease spread by mites.

old plug, safely recovered from the sickness, will be valued at £70. The sheep-raiser wages constant warfare against the tick and the burr, while the man with new ideas is helpless before the hen sickness, or the wire grass which ruins his hay. In the vicinity of the kopjes huge baboons come down and raid the orchards and the vegetable gardens. Near Fauresmith we used to see them in scores whenever we went out to the farms, but we never heard that they attacked anything except dogs. But the foe that is common to all and feared most is the locust. A flight of locusts means destruction of fruit, vegetables, hay, grass, everything that is green, both food for man and fodder for beast. It is encouraging to note that the organized efforts of the Government to fight this plague are proving successful. The Bacteriological Institute at Grahamstown supplies a poison fungus which is distributed to the Constabulary with instructions to use wherever needful, and it is also given to any farmers who wish it. The usual method of using the fungus is to kill some locusts and stir them into a mixture of warm water, sugar and fungus. After leaving them to soak for some time, the mixture is scattered amongst the live swarms in the early morning, when they eat it greedily and all die. This method applies both to the hopping locusts, or grasshoppers, and the flying locusts. The latter, however, need to be killed while still in the crawling stage, else the remedy comes too late to prevent damage. It is usually unnecessary to soak the fungus, if the swarm is discovered while too young to fly.

In spite of all these difficulties, however, no one can visit the farms of the Orange River Colony without feeling that they are full of hidden wealth. It promises well for the future of the country that the men at present on the land are so full of confidence in its resources, and so determined to overcome the present obstacles. One carries away the impression that the South African farmer is of the race of giants, a boy to-day, but realizing what his future is to be.

CHAPTER XV

Homewards

NATIONS, LIKE PERSONS, must have freedom in order to grow and to develop their individuality. Most South Africans, both Briton and Boer, maintain that their country cannot prosper until she has full self-government, as in Canada and in the Australian Confederacy. But whether the people are yet capable of governing themselves is the debated point. Some assert that no representative government can yet be strong enough to cope with the difficulties presented by such a mixture of antagonistic races and such widely divergent trade interests; that the better educated and more liberal Dutch will remain passive, or be influenced by their bigoted kinsmen, whose opinions find vent in the Transvaal in thrashing their children for daring to use English words at home, and in the Orange River Colony in singing an obscene Dutch parody to the tune of "God Save the King." Others claim that with the establishment of the promised self-government in the Transvaal and Orange River Colony, British and Dutch will unite in the endeavor to solve their own local problems, and the long-delayed commercial prosperity will begin. Still a third class predict that nothing will weld the two races together save the outbreak of the oft-threatened rising of the natives of Basutoland, thus creating a common peril.

As Miss De Wolfe and I lolled against the rail of R.M.S *Gascon*, in Cape Town harbor, July 7th, 1904, these and a thousand other uncertainties passed through our minds. Watching Table Mountain and the Twelve Apostles looming dimly through the rain and mist, a counterpart of the scene of two years before, we naturally began to contrast our first and last impressions of South Africa. In 1902 there had been curiosity mingled with hope; in 1904 there was hope mingled with anxiety, vague and formless, it is true, as the tablecloth of mist hanging over the mountains, but none the less depressing. It seemed as if those veiled mountains were typical of the hidden future of the vast, silent country to which they belonged.

Yet, at Easter, when we had completed our arrangements to go home to Canada together, a season of very heavy rains had raised everyone's spirits enormously; the partial payment of compensation claims had also tended to arouse a more hopeful spirit, making it easier for us to think of saying farewell to our South African friends. South Africans, like all plainsmen, are prodigal with their money when they have any, and Kroonstad showed the easier state of her finances by liberal donations to local charities, the hospital, and the young men's club-room of the Anglican Church. Out-of-door sports were entered into with a zest noticeably lacking during the preceding months, and the regular Wednesday half-holiday no longer failed to bring out an enthusiastic crowd to cricket, football, hockey, polo, or whatever happened to be the special attraction of the day.

This ready adaptability of the South African temperament was admirably shown in a most unique picnic which I attended on the Queen's Birthday. Luncheon had been spread at the foot of a long rocky bluff, at one side of the valley extending through Strydfontein, the government farm. Just as we had sampled the cold chicken we heard a loud "zip!" in the air above us, followed by the bursting of a shell at a distance of a mile or so down the valley. Startled investigation revealed the fact that the Bloemfontein artillery, who had come up to Strydfontein for practice, had chosen that particular time for firing off fifteen pounders from the rocks above us. We were really quite safe, and everyone settled down again with a fresh stock of jokes, but I found it most nerve-shattering to eat pie to an accompaniment of bursting shells, and no one, surely, could blame me for spilling coffee in my neighbor's lap.

Whether it was the exhilaration of the air, the influence of the irrepressible Kafirs, or that South Africa is a land of young people, the fact is that, whenever there was a chance to be hopeful, everyone had the knack of shaking off trouble with the facility of children. Some wiseacres shook their heads saying, "Such levity is the ruin of the country"; while others said, "Such buoyancy will be our salvation." Certainly to the average business-man, with his hours from eight A.M. to five P.M., and his Wednesday half holiday, life was vastly more worth the living than in America, where his type must slave daily from breakfast till bed-time.

Miss De Wolfe was to meet me in Cape Town, and on the journey there, broken by stop-overs with old friends, I found the same spirit of renewed hopefulness. Fortunately for their peace of mind, none could foresee the approach of another long drought. The farms, not yet disfigured by the annual winter grass-burning, had quite regained a homelike appearance. Houses and fences were neatly repaired and scarcely a trace of the war remained. Not a yard of barbed-wire entanglement was to be seen, nor a blockhouse, except the two large stone ones kept to guard the bridge at Norval's Pont. The big camps had vanished, leaving immaculate neatness behind them; and no landmarks remained save the occasional graves.

These solitary graves, marked with white wooden crosses, seemed inexpressibly lonely out there on the great bare veldt, especially when one remembered that those which happened to be in Kroonstad, or Bloemfontein, had been honored by handsome monuments.

South of the Hex Mountains, Cape Colony was enjoying her winter rains; but the Cape Town mud of painful memory had disappeared, and I spent two pleasant days there with up-country Dutch friends. On the third day the *Gascon*, of the Union-Castle line, arrived from East London[1] with Miss De Wolfe on board. It was good to see a jolly little Canadian girl once more, and to compare experiences in South Africa.

It was odd how we six girls who had been billeted together at the Johannesburg Convention in 1902 were continually crossing one another's track, although we seldom saw or heard anything of the other Canadians. When Miss Arbuckle went to Bethlehem she found Miss De Wolfe there; I followed the latter to Kroonstad; Miss Dutcher followed me to Fauresmith; and Miss Bremner, having married Major Castelli, of the Constabulary, came to live in Kroonstad during my

1. East London is located on South Africa's southeast coast.

year there. The sixth girl of the party, Miss Lee, died of enteric during our first year in Africa, the one death amongst the forty girls. A modest stone, erected by the other Canadians, marks her grave at Parys.[2]

As we steamed out of Table Bay the mood of the weather appeared to be in sympathy with the noisily tearful crowd on the docks behind us. The all-pervading moisture encouraged us in the hope that the quantities of ammunition stored in our hold might be sufficiently depressed to ensure our safety.

Two amusing encounters that evening made us feel quite at home on the *Gascon*. On being assigned to my cabin, the purser said to me:

"Pardon me, Miss Graham, but are you a Canadian teacher?"

On answering in the affirmative, he continued—

"My fiancée, Miss M——, another Canadian, was on the train with you last week, and told me that you might possibly be sailing this trip."

Of course I remembered the young lady, and congratulated him accordingly, and before the end of the trip we decided that she too was to be congratulated. At dinner that same evening the officer at our table turned to me with—

"Miss Graham, Miss De Wolfe tells me that you have just come from Kroonstad. Do you know Miss C——?"

"Oh yes!" I replied, "she's an English girl not out very long."

"Yes," said he, "she's my fiancée, and isn't she a ripping fine girl?"

We assured him she was, and wondered how many more congratulations we would have to give.

After dinner I found some old acquaintances in the "First," who soon put us on bowing terms with their deck. We were Second Class again, the Education Department having booked our passage to Southampton, and having given us in addition orders on Cook's, in London, for £8 each. We afterwards supplemented these orders ourselves, sailing to Canada first cabin.

The next day dawned bright and clear, typical of most of the days of that trip, and justifying the statement that the voyage from

2. Parys is located approximately one hundred kilometres southwest of Johannesburg.

Southampton to the Cape is the ideal one for invalids. Certainly we could easily believe it, with such delightful weather and such excellent service as we had on the *Gascon*. Life on a Cape liner is very pleasant, the long, wide, shady decks affording ample space for promenades, or games of various sorts. There is room even for ship-cricket, a long deck being easily converted into a cricket pitch, to the audible disgust of portly deck-cabin passengers who wish to doze all afternoon. For those of quieter tastes there is pleasure in watching the appearance, or disappearance, of the "Great Bear" and the "Southern Cross"; there is the excitement of watching a school of flying fish pursued by crowds of leaping porpoises, themselves in turn chased by swift sharks; and in the tropics there is the nightly wonder of the queer phosphorescent sea. There is always a third class, of goodly numbers, who apparently live to eat, while at sea; and woe betide them if a squall should come up. They begin before breakfast with hot coffee; they break the monotony until lunch time with hot bovril at eleven; they exist until dinner with the help of afternoon tea; and they gain strength to wander through the land of dreams by a hearty supper of sandwiches, or bread and cheese.

Our fellow-passengers were an interesting medley. In the "Second" was a large party of Rhodesians, with a plentiful supply of money and democratic ideas, going "Home" to advertise their country; in the "First" was a disbanded theatrical troupe, somewhat out-at-elbows, but trying to live up to "First" standards. With them were some moody Constabulary officers, on six-months' furlough, which would probably be extended into dismissal, as their force was being reduced by half. Their very natural dejection was shared by a group of ex-magistrates who talked feelingly about their grievances.

Some of the officers of the *Gascon*, in common with other ships of the Union-Castle line, were "Naval Reserve" men, and everything on board was managed with naval precision and immaculateness. Sundays, the crew was up for inspection, toeing the line on the main deck, then marching to service, read by the Captain; in the tropics, fresh ducks every day was the custom.

During the second week of the trip, there was a pleasant variation in the daily routine owing to the athletic sports open to competitors from all the decks. The programme occupied three days, and during the events the passengers of all classes were allowed on the top decks. There were races, serious and comic, jumping, tugs-of-war, etc., but the most popular event was the pillow-fight, in which we had the astounding spectacle of a military Captain, astride a greasy pole, facing a grimy opponent from the Third Class, who sent him flying with a well-aimed "biff."

Our mid-trip stop was at Las Palmas, a town on Gran Canaria, the largest of the Canary Islands. In many respects the visit there was a repetition of the day at Teneriffe—the same clamorous boatmen, the same Spanish wares, the same blue sea, the same pink and white buildings and volcanic peaks, and, on shore, the same filthy swarms of picturesque, assorted beggardom. But Las Palmas is a much more pretentious town, lying two miles from the quay, and containing a really fine cathedral, besides other points of interest to the tourist. Our shore party, seven in number, decided to hurry through the town and drive to the top of the central peak to the big hotel there, for lunch. We engaged a guide and two quaint, low-hung, basket carriages, each drawn by four ponies. The mountain road led up a gradual, winding incline, twelve miles in length, showing a more novel bit of scenery at every turn. To our right there were valleys terraced with rows upon rows of banana plantations; beyond them, on the slopes, were vineyards and date palms; to our left, between us and the rocky hill-side, rushed a little stream, confined in a stone ditch, along the side of which were squatted scores of Spanish washerwomen with gay bandanas on their heads. We decided unanimously that we would prefer to hire the lady who monopolized the clear water at the head of the line. Presently we halted in the street of a wee village perched on the hillside, with queer old houses, all tightly barred behind wooden shutters to keep out the sun; there we were so set upon by fruit girls, flower girls and beggars that we were thankful when the horses were sufficiently rested to start again. Above the village our road led through a charming avenue of shade-trees, with quantities of red geraniums growing wild by the wayside; and finally, after a hot, steep, dusty, winding climb, between slopes of bare volcanic deposits, we reached the summit and our hotel. It stood in the midst of a large garden, one blaze of tropical bloom, and from its balconies the panorama was magnificent. The great rugged, scored sides of the old volcanoes sloped far below us and revealed occasional fertile valleys, mere specks of green in the distance; miles below was the town, a blur of pink and green; and beyond the town, and all about, was the sea, one immense expanse of glittering blue silver, melting into the softer blue of the sky.

A few miles farther inland, the aborigines still live in caves hollowed out of the mountain sides, one row above another. Unfortunately, if one wishes to visit these people and see them working at their pottery and basket-weaving, a donkey ride is a painful necessity. These little donkeys are themselves a feature of the island. We met them in long strings, laden pack fashion with vegetables, fruit, wine bottles, beer kegs, and bundles of every sort; but one common sight, which never failed to make us wrathy,[3] was to see a man riding his beast, while his wife trudged alongside with a great bundle on her head.

After leaving Las Palmas our fine weather continued, and we reached Southampton Water at sunset, July 31st, just in time to witness an exciting speed trial of motor boats.

August 1st found us in old London again, where we did nothing for one whole day but wander up and down the streets in the rain, exclaiming over the fascinations of the shop windows.

The three weeks following were spent visiting in England and Scotland, and everywhere we were agreeably surprised at the increased interest shown in Canadian affairs. We supposed that after the excitement of the war had passed away the people of Great Britain would have paid less attention to Canada, but it was quite otherwise.

---

3. "Wrathy" is a colloquial term for angry.

The United Kingdom is aptly called the "Mother Country," for her attitude towards the colonies is distinctly maternal—the fondly proud manner of the elderly matron who expects her grown-up children to uphold the dignity of the family name.

August 20th we sailed from Glasgow on the *Sicilian* of the Allan Line. There were only twenty of us in the First, including a number of Scotch people, and, as we sailed down the Clyde, with its background of hills standing out majestically in the afternoon sun, they said to us:

"You can't possibly have anything finer than that in Canada."

We admitted that it was superb, but secretly hoped the weather would be kind to us in the St. Lawrence, a wish that was granted. Those two days in the Gulf and up the river were so ideal that the dourest Scotchman on board grew enthusiastic, while we Canadians became unbearable with conceit.

Monday afternoon, August 29th, we rounded Point Levi, and there lay Quebec, stately and beautiful in the bright sunshine. Without bias, that quaint old city, climbing above her walls to the fortress on Cape Diamond, surrounded on three sides by the St. Charles and the broader St. Lawrence, with the fir-clad Laurentians for background, presented the finest picture I had seen in all the long trip.[4]

Altogether that last voyage was the most enjoyable. We had the most interesting companions and the most genial of captains; the usual concert for the benefit of the sailors' widows and orphans was the most successful financially; and the sea showed us her biggest wonders, whales spouting, icebergs, and schools of white porpoises. It was with genuine regret that I said good-bye to Captain Fairfull and the *Sicilian* company at Quebec.

On shore there was a slightly revived interest in South African affairs, since the proposed statue to the South African heroes was

4. The Saint-Charles River flows south toward Quebec City from Saint-Charles Lake and into the St. Lawrence River.

almost an accomplished fact.[5] When I reached my own native town, Owen Sound, I found a similar feeling, owing to the proposal to erect a memorial tablet there to my three fellow-townsmen, Privates Ingram, Evans, and Day of the Strathcona's and the Second Canadian Mounted Rifles.

Thus to-day, in these and many another town throughout the Dominion, there are to be found these silent but potent links binding us to our sister colony across the sea.

5. Graham is referring here to the *Monument aux braves de la guerre des Boers* (Boer War Memorial) by Hamilton MacCarthy that was unveiled in 1905.

Bibliography

PRIMARY SOURCES

ARCHIVAL COLLECTIONS

Mary A. Meir Scrapbook, Grey Roots Museum and Archives, Owen Sound, Ontario

Secretary of State Correspondence, Library and Archives Canada, Ottawa, Ontario

BOOKS

De Wet, C. *Three Years' War*. New York: Charles Scribner's Sons, 1902.

Hobhouse, Emily. *The Brunt of the War and Where it Fell*. London: Methuen and Company, 1902.

———. *Emily Hobhouse: A Memoir*. Compiled by A. Ruth Fry. London: Jonathan Cape, 1929.

Reitz, Denys. *Commando: A Boer Journal of the Boer War*. London: Faber, 1933.

Theal, George McCall. *History of the Boers in South Africa, or, The Wanderings and Wars of the Emigrant Farmers: From Their Leaving the Cape Colony to the Acknowledgement of Their Independence by Great Britain*. London: S. Sonnenschein, Lowrey, 1887.

Wallace, Edgar. *Unofficial Dispatches*. London: Hutchinson, 1901.

Worsfold, William. *Lord Milner's Work in South Africa from its Commencement in 1897 to the Peace of Vereeniging in 1902*. New York: Dutton, 1906.

PERIODICALS

Annals of the American Academy of Political and Social Science

The Educational Review

The Globe/The Globe and Mail
Methodist Magazine and Review
Owen Sound Sun
The Varsity

PERSONAL COMMUNICATIONS AND REMINISCENCES

Becker, Helen Mary Millar. Recollections of Marianne Meir and the Meir family, January 2005. (Typescript copy in possession of the editors).

———. "Memoir of Maud." (Unpublished manuscript in possession of the editors).

Graham, Maud. Unpublished reminiscences, dated 1931, but with last chapter dated 1947. (Copy in possession of the editors).

———. Scrapbook. (Original in possession of the editors).

———. South Africa photo album. (Original in possession of the editors).

SECONDARY SOURCES

Allen, Richard. *The View from Murney Tower: Salem Bland, the Late Victorian Controversies, and the Search for a New Christianity*. Toronto: University of Toronto Press, 2008.

Apale, Alisha Nicole, and Valerie Stem, eds. *Generation NGO*. Toronto: Between the Lines, 2011.

Armitage, Andrew. *Owen Sound: Steamboat Days*. Erin, ON: Boston Mills Press, 1981.

Attridge, Steve. *Nationalism, Imperialism, and Identity in Late Victorian Culture: Civil and Military Worlds*. New York: Palgrave Macmillan, 2003.

Beinart, William. *Twentieth-Century South Africa*. Oxford: Oxford University Books, 2001.

Berger, Carl. *The Sense of Power: Studies in the Ideas of Canadian Imperialism, 1867–1914*. Toronto: University of Toronto Press, 1970.

Berton, Pierre. *Marching as to War: Canada's Turbulent Years, 1899–1953*. Toronto: Doubleday, 2001.

Black, Jeremy. "France and the Grand Tour in the Early Eighteenth Century." *Francia* 11 (1983): 407–16.

Blake, Susan L. "A Woman's Trek: What Difference Does Gender Make?" *Women's Studies International Forum* 13, no. 4 (1990): 347–55.

Boje, Johannes Gerhardus. "Winburg's War: An Appraisal of the Anglo-Boer War of 1899–1902 as It Was Experienced by the People of a Free State District." DPhil, University of Pretoria, 2010.

Bradford, Helen. "Gentlemen and Boers: Afrikaner Nationalism, Gender, and Colonial Warfare in the South African War." In *Writing a Wider War: Rethinking Gender, Race and Identity in the South African War, 1899–1902*, edited by Greg Cuthbertson, Albert Grundlingh, and Mary-Lynn Suttie, 37–66. Athens: Ohio University Press, 2002.

Brendon, Piers. *The Decline and Fall of the British Empire, 1781–1997*. London: Vintage Books, 2008.

Brink, Elsabe, and Sue Krige. "Remapping and Remembering the South African War in Johannesburg and Pretoria." *South African Historical Journal* 41, no. 1 (1999): 404–21.

Brouwer, Ruth Compton. *New Women for God: Canadian Presbyterian Women and Indian Missions, 1876–1914*. Toronto: University of Toronto Press, 1990.

———. "When Missions Became Development: Ironies of 'NGOization' in Mainstream Canadian Churches in the 1960s." *Canadian Historical Review* 91, no. 4 (2010): 661–93.

Brydon, Diana, and Jessica Schagerl. "Empire Girls and Global Girls: A Dialogue on Spaces of Community in the Twentieth Century." In *Moveable Margins: The Shifting Spaces of Canadian Literature*, edited by Chelva Kanaganayakam, 27–45. Toronto: TSAR Publications, 2005.

Buckner, Philip, and R. Douglas Francis, eds. *Canada and the British World: Culture, Migration, and Identity*. Vancouver: UBC Press, 2006.

———. *Rediscovering the British World*. Calgary: University of Calgary Press, 2005.

Burke, Sara Z. "New Women and Old Romans: Co-education at the University of Toronto, 1884–95." *Canadian Historical Review* 80, no. 2 (1999): 219–41.

Caine, Barbara. *English Feminism, 1780–1980*. Oxford: Oxford University Press, 1997.

Campbell, Gail. "New Brunswick Women Travellers and the British Connection, 1845–1905." In *Canada and the British World*, edited by Philip Buckner and R. Douglas Francis, 83–86. Calgary: University of Calgary Press, 2005.

Coetzer, Owen. *Fire in the Sky: The Destruction of the Orange Free State 1899–1902*. Weltevreden Park, South Africa: Covos-Day, 2000.

Coney, Sandra. Foreword to *Teachers for South Africa: New Zealand Women at the South African War Concentration Camps*, by Ellen Ellis. Paekakariki: Hanorah Books, 2010.

Cook, Sharon Anne. *"Through Sunshine and Shadow": The Women's Christian Temperance Union, Evangelism, and Reform in Ontario, 1874–1930*. Montreal and Kingston: McGill-Queen's University Press, 1995.

Dagg, Anne Innis. *The Feminine Gaze: A Canadian Compendium of Non-Fiction Women Authors and Their Books, 1836–1945*. Waterloo, ON: Wilfrid Laurier University Press, 2001.

Dampier, Helen. "'Everyday life' in Boer Women's Testimonies of the Concentration Camps of the South African War, 1899–1902." In *Crime and Empire 1840–1940: Criminal Justice in Local and Global Context*, edited by Graeme Dunstall and Barry Godfrey, 202–23. Cullompton, UK: Willan Publishing, 2005.

Darian-Smith, Kate, Patricia Grimshaw, and Stuart Macintyre, eds. *Britishness Abroad: Transnational Movements and Imperial Cultures*. Melbourne: Melbourne University Press, 2007.

Davey, Arthur. *The British Pro-Boers, 1877–1902*. Cape Town: Tafelberg, 1978.

Dawson, Michael. "'That Nice Red Coat Goes to My Head Like Champagne': Gender, Antimodernism and the Mountie Image: 1880–1960." *Journal of Canadian Studies* 32, no. 3 (1997): 119–39.

Denham, Robert D., ed. *The Correspondence of Northrop Frye and Helen Kemp, 1932–1939*. Vol 1. Toronto: University of Toronto Press, 1996.

de Reuck, Jenny. "Social Suffering and the Politics of Pain: Observations on the Concentration Camps in the Anglo-Boer War, 1899–1902." *English in Africa* 26, no. 2 (1999): 69–88.

Dubinsky, Karen. *The Second Greatest Disappointment: Honeymooning and Tourism at Niagara Falls*. Toronto: Between the Lines, 1999.

Dubow, Saul. "Afrikaner Nationalism, Apartheid and the Conceptualisation of 'Race.'" *Journal of African History* 33, no. 2 (1992): 209–37.

Duff, Sarah. "'Capture the Children': Writing Children into the South African War, 1899–1902." *Journal of the History of Childhood and Youth* 7 (2014): 355–76.

Eddy, John, and Deryk Schreuder, eds. *The Rise of Colonial Nationalism*. Sydney: Allen & Unwin, 1988.

Ellis, Ellen. *Teachers for South Africa: New Zealand Women at the South African War Concentration Camps*. Foreword by Sandra Coney. Paekakariki: Hanorah Books, 2010.

Etherington, Norman. *Preachers, Peasants, and Politics in Southeast Africa, 1835–1880*. London: Royal Historical Society, and Boyle and Brewer, 1978.

Fetter, Bruce, and Stowell Kessler. "Scars from a Childhood Disease: Measles in the Concentration Camps During the Boer War." *Social Science History* 20 (1996): 563–611.

Fisher, John. *That Miss Hobhouse*. London: Secker & Warburg, 1971.

Flake, L. Gordon, and Scott Snyder, eds. *Paved With Good Intentions: The NGO Experience in North Korea*. Westport, CT: Praeger, 2003.

Genge, Manelisi. "The Role of the EmaSwati in the South African War." In *Writing a Wider War: Rethinking Gender, Race, and Identity in the South African War, 1899–1902*, edited by Greg Cuthbertson, Albert Grundlingh, and Mary-Lynn Suttie, 136–58. Athens: Ohio University Press, 2002.

Gerson, Carole. *Canadian Women in Print, 1750–1918*. Waterloo, ON: Wilfrid Laurier University Press, 2010.

Gidney, R.D., and W.P.J. Millar. *Inventing Secondary Education: The Rise of the High School in Nineteenth-Century Ontario*. Montreal and Kingston: McGill-Queen's University Press, 1990.

Giliomee, Adam. *The Afrikaners: Biography of a People*. Rev. ed. Charlottesville: University of Virginia Press; Cape Town, South Africa: Tafelberg, 2009.

Giliomee, Hermann, and Andre du Toit. *Afrikaner Political Thought: Documents and Analysis*. Berkeley: University of California Press, 1983.

Glenelg. *Broken Shackles: Old Man Henson From Slavery to Freedom*. Edited by Peter Meyler. Toronto: Natural Heritage Books, 2001. First published 1889 by William Brigg (Toronto).

Green, E.H.H. *The Crisis in Conservatism: The Politics, Economics, and Ideology of the Conservative Party, 1880–1914*. London: Taylor & Francis e-Library, 2005.

Grundlingh, Albert. "The National Women's Monument: The Making and Mutation of Meaning in Afrikaner Memory of the South African War." In *Writing a Wider War: Rethinking Gender, Race, and Identity in the South African War, 1899–1902*, edited by Greg Cuthbertson, Albert Grundlingh, and Mary-Lynn Suttie, 18–36. Athens: Ohio University Press, 2002.

———. "Reframing Remembrance: The Politics of the Centenary Commemoration of the South African War of 1899–1902." *Journal of Southern African Studies* 30, no. 2 (June 2004): 359–75.

———. "The War in Twentieth-century Afrikaner Consciousness." In *The Impact of the South African War*, edited by David Omissi and Andrew Thompson, 23–37. Basingstoke, UK: Palgrave Publishers, 2002.

———. "War, Wordsmiths and the 'Volk': Afrikaans Historical Writing on the Anglo-Boer War of 1899–1902 and the War in Afrikaner Nationalist Consciousness, 1902–1990." In *Mfecane to Boer War: Versions of South African History*, edited by E. Lehmann and E. Reckwitz, 48–65. Essen, Germany: Die Blaue Eule, 1992.

———. "Why Concentration Camps?" In *The War at Home: Women and Families in the Anglo-Boer War*, edited by Bill Nasson and Albert Grundlingh, 22–43. Cape Town: Tafelberg, 2013.

Grundlingh, Louis. "Another Side to Warfare: Caring for White Destitutes during the Anglo-Boer War (October 1899–May 1900)." *New Contree* 45 (1999): 137–63.

Guildford, Janet. "'Separate Spheres': The Feminization of Public School Teaching in Nova Scotia, 1838–1900." *Acadiensis* 22, no. 1 (1992): 44–64.

Gwyn, Sandra. *The Private Capital: Ambition and Love in the Age of Macdonald and Laurier*. Toronto: McClelland and Stewart, 1984.

Hamilton, Carolyn, Bernard K. Mbenga, and Robert Ross, eds. *The Cambridge History of South Africa*. Cambridge: Cambridge University Press, 2010.

Heron, Barbara. *Desire for Development: Whiteness, Gender, and the Helping Imperative*. Waterloo, ON: Wilfrid Laurier University Press, 2007.

Hobhouse Balme, Jennifer, ed. *To Love One's Enemies: The Work and Life of Emily Hobhouse Compiled from Letters and Writings, Newspaper Cuttings and Official Documents*. Cobble Hill, BC: Hobhouse Trust, 1994.

Hundey, Ian. *Nine Habits for Success in Teaching History*. Toronto: Emond Montgomery Publications, 2007.

Jansen, Ena, and Wilfred Jonckheere, eds. *Boer en Brit: Afrikaanse en Nederlandse tekste uit en Om die Anglo-Boereoolog*. Pretoria: Protea Boekhuis, 2001.

Jebb, Richard. *Studies in Colonial Nationalism*. London: Edward Arnold, 1905.

Jeeves, Alan. *Migrant Labour in South Africa's Mining Economy: The Struggle for the Gold Mines' Labour Supply, 1890–1920*. Montreal and Kingston: McGill-Queen's University Press, 1985.

Judd, Denis, and Keith Surridge. *The Boer War*. New York: Palgrave Macmillan, 2003.

Kampkinders, 1900–1902: 'n Gedenkboek. Compiled by M.C.E. van School in collaboration with C.G. Coetzee. Bloemfontein: Oorlogsmuseum van die Boererepublieke, 1982.

Kessler, Stowell. "The Black Concentration Camps of the Anglo-Boer War, 1899–1902: Shifting the Paradigm from Sole Martyrdom to Mutual Suffering." *Historia* 44 (1999): 110–47.

———. "The Black Concentration Camps of the South African War, 1899–1902." PHD diss., University of Cape Town, 2003.

Keys, Barbara J. *Globalizing Sport: National Rivalry and International Community in the 1930s*. Cambridge, MA: Harvard University Press, 2006.

Klausen, Susanne M. *Race, Maternity, and the Politics of Birth Control in South Africa, 1910–1939*. Basingstoke, UK: Palgrave Macmillan, 2004.

Krebs, Paula. *Gender, Race, and the Writing of Empire: Public Discourse and the Boer War*. Cambridge: Cambridge University Press, 2004.

Krotz, Larry. *The Uncertain Business of Doing Good: Outsiders in Africa*. East Lansing: Michigan State University Press, 2009.

Laband, John. "Burying the Union Jack: British Loyalists in the Transvaal during the First Anglo-Boer War, 1880–1881." *History of Intellectual Culture* 4, no. 1 (2004): 1–19.

Laity, Paul. "The British Peace Movement and the War." In *The Impact of the South African War*, edited by David Omissi and Andrew Thompson, 138–56. Basingstoke, UK: Palgrave Publishers, 2002.

Lambert, John. "'Loyalty Its Own Reward': The South African War Experience of Natal's 'Loyal' Africans." In *Writing a Wider War: Rethinking Gender, Race, and Identity in the South African War, 1899–1902*, edited by Greg Cuthbertson, Albert Grundlingh, and Mary-Lynn Suttie, 115–35. Athens: Ohio University Press, 2002.

Limb, Peter, Norman Etherington, and Peter Midgley, eds. *Grappling With the Beast: Indigenous Southern African Responses to Colonialism, 1840–1930*. Boston: Brill, 2010.

Low-Beer, Daniel, Matthew Smallman-Raynor, and Andrew Cliff. "Disease and Death in the South African War: Changing Disease Patterns from Soldiers to Refugees." *Social History of Medicine* 17, no. 2 (2004): 223–45.

Lowry, Donal, ed. *The South African War Reappraised*. Manchester: Manchester University Press, 1985.

MacNaughton, Katherine F.C. *The Development of the Theory and Practice of Education in New Brunswick, 1784–1900: A Study in Historical Background*. University of New Brunswick Historical Studies, no. 1. Fredericton: University of New Brunswick, 1947.

Madeira, Ana Isabel. "Portuguese, French and British Discourses on Colonial Education: Church-State Relations, School Expansion and Missionary Competition in Africa, 1890–1930." *Paedagogica Historica* 41, no. 1/2 (2005): 31–60.

Malunga, Felix. "The Anglo-Boer South African War: Sekhukhune II goes on the offensive in the Eastern Transvaal, 1899–1902." *Joernaal vir Eietydse Geskiedenis/Journal of Contemporary History* 25, no. 2 (2000): 57–78.

Mangan, J.A. *The Games Ethic and Imperialism: Aspects of the Diffusion of an Ideal*. New York: Viking, 1986.

Marks, Shula. "British Nursing and the South African War." In *Writing a Wider War: Rethinking Gender, Race, and Identity in the South African War, 1899–1902*, edited by Greg Cuthbertson, Albert Grundlingh, and Mary-Lynn Suttie, 159–85. Athens: Ohio University Press, 2002.

———. *Reluctant Rebellion: The 1906–8 Disturbances in Natal*. London: Clarendon Press, 1970.

Marks, Shula, and Stanley Trapido. "Lord Milner and the South African State." *History Workshop Journal* 8 (Autumn 1979): 50–80.

McKay, Ian, and Jamie Swift. *Warrior Nation: Rebranding Canada in an Age of Anxiety*. Toronto: Between the Lines, 2012.

Merrill, Dennis. *Negotiating Paradise: U.S. Tourism and Empire in Twentieth-Century Latin America*. Chapel Hill: University of North Carolina Press, 2009.

Mgenga, Bernard. "The Role of the Bakgatla of the Pilanesberg in the South Africa War." In *Writing a Wider War: Rethinking Gender, Race, and Identity in the South African War, 1899–1902*, edited by Greg Cuthbertson, Albert Grundlingh, and Mary-Lynn Suttie, 85–114. Athens: Ohio University Press, 2002.

Miller, Carman. *Canada's Little War*. Toronto: Lorimer, 2003.

———. "Loyalty, Patriotism and Resistance: Canada's Response to the Anglo-Boer War, 1899–1902." *South African Historical Journal* 41, no. 1 (1999): 312–23.

———. *Painting the Map Red: Canada and the South African War, 1899–1902.* Montreal and Kingston: Canadian War Museum and McGill-Queen's University Press, 1993.

Mohlamme, J.S. "African Refugee Camps in the Boer Republics." In *Scorched Earth*, edited by Fransjohan Pretorius, 110–21. Cape Town: Human & Rousseau, 2001.

———. "Blacks in the Ex-Boer Republics of the Transvaal and Orange Free State in the Aftermath of the South African War of 1899–1902." *Joernaal vir Eietydse Geskiedenis/Journal of Contemporary History* 25, no. 2 (2000): 270–83.

Mongalo, B.E., and K.J. du Pisani. "Victims of a White Man's War: Blacks in Concentration Camps during the South African War (1899–1902)." *Historia* 44, no. 1 (1999): 148–82.

Moodie, T. Dunbar. *The Rise of Afrikanerdom: Power, Apartheid, and the Afrikaner Civil Religion.* Berkeley: University of California Press, 1975.

Morgan, Cecilia. *A Happy Holiday: English Canadians and Transatlantic Tourism, 1870–1930.* Toronto: University of Toronto Press, 2008.

Nasson, Bill. *Abraham Esau's War: A Black South African War in the Cape, 1899–1902.* Cape Town: David Philip, 1991.

———. *The South African War, 1899–1902.* London: Arnold, 1999.

———. "The South African War/Anglo-Boer War, 1899–1902 and Political Memory in South Africa." In *The Politics of War Memory and Commemoration*, edited by T.G. Ashplant, Graham Dawson, and Michael Roper, 111–27. London: Routledge, 2001.

———. *Uyadela wen'osulapho: Black Participation in the Anglo-Boer War.* Randburg, South Africa: Navan, 1999.

Nasson, Bill, and Albert Grundlingh, eds. *The War at Home: Women and Families in the Anglo-Boer War.* Cape Town: Tafelberg, 2013.

Nasson, W.R. "Tot Siens to All That? South Africa's Great War, 1899–1902." *South African Historical Journal* 32, no. 1 (1995): 191–205.

New, William H., ed. *Encyclopedia of Literature in Canada.* Toronto: University of Toronto Press, 2002.

O'Meara, Dan. *Volkskapitalisme: Class, Capital, and Ideology in the Development of Afrikaner Nationalism, 1934–1948*. Cambridge: Cambridge University Press, 1983.

Page, Robert. *The Boer War and Canadian Imperialism*. Canadian Historical Association Booklet no. 44. Ottawa: Canadian Historical Association, 1987.

———. "Canada and the Imperial Idea in the Boer War Years." *Journal of Canadian Studies* 5, no. 1 (1970): 33–49.

Pakenham, Thomas. *The Boer War*. London: Weidenfeld and Nicolson, 1979.

Phimister, Ian. "Unscrambling the Scramble for Southern Africa: The Jameson Raid and the South African War Revisited." *South African Historical Journal* 28, no. 1 (1993): 202–30.

Pickles, Katie. *Female Imperialism and National Identity: Imperial Order Daughters of the Empire*. Manchester: Manchester University Press, 2002.

Plaatje, Sol. *The Boer War Diary of Sol T. Plaatje; An African at Mafeking*. Edited by John L. Comaroff. Johannesburg: Macmillan, 1973.

Porter, Andrew. "The Origins of the South African War." *South African Historical Journal* 35, no. 1 (1996): 155–61.

———. "The South African War and Imperial Britain: A Question of Significance." In *Writing a Wider War: Rethinking Gender, Race, and Identity in the South African War, 1899–1902*, edited by Greg Cuthbertson, Albert Grundlingh, and Mary-Lynn Suttie, 287–302. Athens: Ohio University Press, 2002.

———. "The South African War and the Historians." *African Affairs* 99, no. 397 (2000): 633–48.

Potgieter, D.J. et al., eds. *Standard Encyclopaedia of Southern Africa*. Cape Town: Nasionale Opvoedkundige Uitgewery, 1970.

Pratt, Mary Louise. *Imperial Eyes: Studies in Travel Writing and Transculturation*. London: Routledge, 1992.

Randal, Florence Hamilton. "A Year in a Boer School." *The Canadian Magazine* 22, no. 5 (1904): 411–17.

Ranger, Terence. "African Attempts to Control Education in East and Central Africa 1900–1939." *Past and Present* 32, no. 1 (1965): 57–85.

Riedi, Eliza. "Teaching Empire: British and Dominions Women Teachers in the South African War Concentration Camps." *English Historical Review* 120, no. 489 (2005): 1316–47.

Roberts, Brian. *Those Bloody Women: Three Heroines of the Boer War*. London: J. Murray, 1991.

Schagerl, Jessica. "Global Imaginaries: Reading the International Interventions, Interactions and Imaginings of Women in English Canada, 1899–1919." PHD diss., University of Western Ontario, London, ON, 2006.

Shaw, Amy. "Dissent in Canada against the Anglo-Boer War, 1899–1902." In *Worth Fighting For: Canada's Tradition of War Resistance from 1812 to the War on Terror*. Edited by Lara Campbell, Michael Dawson, and Catherine Gidney. Toronto: Between the Lines, 2015.

Spies, S.B. *Methods of Barbarism? Roberts and Kitchener and Civilians in the Boer Republics January 1900–May 1902*. Cape Town: Human & Rousseau, 1977.

Stanley, Liz. "Black Labour and the Concentration Camp System of the South African War." *Journal for Contemporary History* 28, no. 2 (2003): 190–213.

———. *Mourning Becomes...Post/Memory and Commemoration of the Concentration Camps of the South African War 1899–1902*. Manchester: Manchester University Press, 2006.

———. "'A Strange Thing Is Memory': Emily Hobhouse, Memory Work, Moral Life and the 'Concentration System.'" *South African Historical Journal* 52, no. 1 (2005): 60–81.

Stoddart, Brian. "Sport, Cultural Imperialism and Colonial Response in the British Empire." In *Sport, Culture and History: Region, Nation and Globe*, edited by B. Stoddart, 114–40. London: Routledge, 2008.

Stoler, Ann Laura. *Carnal Knowledge and Imperial Power: Race and the Intimate in Colonial Rule*. Berkeley: University of California Press, 2002.

van Heyningen, Elizabeth. *The Concentration Camps of the Anglo-Boer War: A Social History*. Johannesburg and Cape Town: Jacana Media, 2013.

———. "The Concentration Camps of the South African (Anglo-Boer) War, 1900–1902." *History Compass* 7, no. 1 (2009): 22–43.

———. "'Fools Rush In': Writing a History of the Concentration Camps of the South African War." *Historia* 55, no. 2 (2010): 12–33.

———. "Medical History and Afrikaner Society in the Boer Republics at the End of the Nineteenth Century." *Kleio* 37 (2005): 5–25.

———. "Women and Disease: The Clash of Medical Cultures in the Concentration Camps of the South African War." In *Writing a Wider War:*

Rethinking Gender, Race, and Identity in the South African War, 1899–1902, edited by Greg Cuthbertson, Albert Grundlingh, and Mary-Lynn Suttie, 186–212. Athens: Ohio University Press, 2002.

———. "Women and Gender in the South African War, 1899–1902." In *Women in South African History*, edited by Nomboniso Gasa, 91–125. Cape Town: Human Sciences Research Council, 2007.

van Reenen, Rykie, ed. *Emily Hobhouse: Boer War Letters*. Cape Town: Human & Rousseau, 1984.

Vance, Jonathan. *Death So Noble: Memory Meaning and the First World War*. Vancouver: University of British Columbia Press, 1997.

Vipond, Mary. "Nationalism and Nativism: The Natives Sons of Canada in the 1920s." *Canadian Review of Studies in Nationalism* 9, no. 1 (1982): 81–95.

Warwick, Peter. *Black People and the South African War, 1899–1902*. Cambridge: Cambridge University Press, 1983.

Warwick, Peter, ed. *The South African War. The Anglo-Boer War 1899–1902*. London: Longman, 1980.

Wessels, Elria. "Die Rol van die Vrou Buite die Konsentrasiecamp Tydens en na die Orrlog." *Joernaal vir Eietydse Geskiedenis/Journal of Contemporary History* 27, no. 2 (2002): 22–30.

Whitehead, Clive. "The Concept of British Education Policy in the Colonies, 1850–1960." *Journal of Educational Administration and History* 39 (2007): 161–73.

———. "The Education of Women and Girls: An Aspect of British Colonial Policy." *Journal of Educational Administration and History* 16, no. 2 (1984): 24–34.

———. "The Historiography of British Imperial Education Policy, Part II: African and the Rest of the Colonial Empire." *History of Education* 34, no. 4 (2005): 441–54.

Wilcox, Craig. *Australia's Boer War: the War in South Africa, 1899–1902*. South Melbourne, Victoria: Oxford University Press, 2002.

Witz, Leslie, Gary Minkley, and Ciraj Rassool. "No End of a (History) Lesson: Preparations for the Anglo-Boer War Centenary Commemoration." *South African Historical Journal* 41, no. 1 (1999): 370–87.

Zietsman, Paul. "The Concentration Camp Schools: Beacons of Light in the Darkness." In *Scorched Earth*, edited by Fransjohan Pretorius, 86–109. Cape Town: Human & Rousseau, 2001.

Index

Page numbers in italics refer to photographs and maps.
MG refers to E. **Maud** *Graham, and SA refers to South Africa.*

203

Other Titles from The University of Alberta Press

This Wild Spirit

Women in the Rocky Mountains of Canada

COLLEEN SKIDMORE, *Editor*

508 pages | B&W photographs, colour section, bibliography, index

Mountain Cairns: A series on the history and culture of the Canadian Rocky Mountains

978-0-88864-466-4 | $34.95 (T) paper

978-0-88864-587-6 | $27.99 (T) EPUB

978-0-88864-848-8 | $27.99 (T) PDF

Women's Studies | Canadian History

Travels and Tales of Miriam Green Ellis

Pioneer Journalist of the Canadian West

MIRIAM GREEN ELLIS

Edited and with an Introduction by PATRICIA DEMERS

296 pages | 28 B&W photographs, map, notes, bibliography, index

978-0-88864-626-2 | $34.95 (T) paper

978-1-77212-694-1 | $27.99 (T) EPUB

978-1-77212-695-8 | $27.99 (T) Kindle

978-0-88864-801-3 | $27.99 (T) PDF

Journalism | Women's Studies | Feminism | Social History

Conrad Kain

Letters from a Wandering Mountain Guide, 1906–1933

CONRAD KAIN

Edited and with an Introduction by ZAC ROBINSON

512 pages | 30 B&W photographs, 3 maps, notes, bibliography, index

Mountain Cairns: A series on the history and culture of the Canadian Rocky Mountains

978-1-77212-004-2 | $34.95 (T) paper

978-1-77212-016-5 | $27.99 (T) EPUB

978-1-77212-017-2 | $27.99 (T) Kindle

978-1-77212-018-9 | $27.99 (T) PDF

Mountain Studies | Canadian History | Biography